YOUNG DOCTOR PUSEY

A Study in Development

by

DAVID FORRESTER

MOWBRAY

First published 1989
by Mowbray
A Cassell imprint,
Artillery House, Artillery Row,
London, SW1P 1RT

Typeset by Acorn Bookwork, Salisbury
Printed in Great Britain by Redwood Burn Ltd, Trowbridge

British Library Cataloguing in Publication Data
Forrester, David W. F.
Young Doctor Pusey.
1. Church of England. Pusey, E.B. (Edward Bouverie), 1800–1882
I. Title
283'.092'4

ISBN 0–264–67160–0

Illustrations are reproduced by permission of The Principal and Governors of Pusey House, Oxford.
Photographer: Norman Head, Banbury

In Memory
of
Archbishop Eugene Cardinale
Apostolic Delegate
to
Great Britain
1963–1969

CONTENTS

ACKNOWLEDGEMENTS

In writing this book I am indebted to the Principal and Governors of Pusey House, Oxford, for the use of their archives, for permitting me to quote extensively from these latter and for allowing the reproduction of pictures in their possession. I should also like to thank the following people for their help and encouragement in the preparation of this volume: the Revd Canon A.M. Allchin of Canterbury Cathedral; Dr J.D. Walsh of Jesus College, Oxford; Dr David Newsome, the Master of Wellington; the Revd Michael Hollings; Dr Eric Stone of Keble College, Oxford; the Revd Charles McCloskey; and the late Revd Henry Clarke. I am deeply grateful to Mrs Janet Lynch for having typed the manuscript of this book.

Chapter Three, 'Engagement and Marriage', was first published in *The Ampleforth Journal* (78), 1973, and is reprinted with permission.

DAVID FORRESTER

LIST OF ILLUSTRATIONS

PREFACE

As far as I am aware, no one has studied Pusey's life afresh in any real detail since the publication of Liddon's biography (1893–1897). Without exception, all authors subsequent to this, who have dealt with Pusey, have relied heavily on Liddon. In a sense this was inevitable; Liddon's four volumes were painstakingly detailed and his quotations extensive; there seemed little left to say. Liddon's *Life of E.B. Pusey* was indeed a remarkable achievement. Unfortunately, however, the deep respect which Liddon rightly earned for his labours has mesmerized later historians into an uncritical acceptance of his portrayal of Pusey and his times; the biography was and is too frequently approached with an emotion akin to awe. So great has been Liddon's success that, though some readers may not have liked what they found in the biography, they have largely considered it an accurate interpretation of Pusey and his era. Hitherto, it has seldom been appreciated that Liddon was too much an immediate disciple of Pusey, and too close to him in time, to see either his master objectively or the historical events of the period in perspective. Nevertheless, any analysis of the intellectual development of Pusey during the first fifty years of his life must of necessity take Liddon's picture into account; throughout this book therefore I have indicated where I differ from Liddon in my views.

Perhaps most important of all, I have discovered that Liddon's teleological assessment of Pusey's career is invalid. Liddon regarded Pusey's life chiefly in relation to the Oxford Movement; the editors who completed his work admitted this in the preface to the fourth volume of the biography and tell us that he had categorically partitioned Pusey's life into four phases to be entitled the Preparation, the Movement, the

Struggle, the Victory. I submit that this is a total misconception of events, at least up to 1844; it is the imposition of a theory and pattern on history which may only be true for the second half of Pusey's life. Up to the early 1830s there is almost no evidence to suggest that Pusey was ever likely to sympathize with the ideals which the Tractarians made their own, and much to the contrary. Hesitant about joining the Oxford Movement, even when ultimately a member of it, Pusey invariably occupied an extremely individual position within it.

Almost as significant as the demolition of Liddon's overall theory was the discovery that the prominence he gave to Tractarian concerns led him to underplay important events and information relating to Pusey's life, and to conceal or pass over in silence knowledge which he considered unsuitable for the reader. This inevitably led to a distortion of the truth. Nowhere in Liddon will one find, for example, a discussion of Pusey's extraordinary relations with his wife, or any appreciation of the importance and originality of Pusey's unpublished lectures on 'Types and Prophecy' of 1836; similarly he shows little awareness of the significance of Anglican expansion overseas, or of Pusey's deep-rooted affinities with the Evangelicals and no account is given of the evolution of Pusey's theology. Too much of Liddon's biography is devoted to Pusey's activities in Oxford and too little is said of his labours beyond the confines of the university.

Intensely devoted to the reputation of his leader, unduly concerned with Tractarian minutiae, and severely limited by his chronological treatment of Pusey's career, Liddon succeeded in concealing Pusey's greatness outside the Oxford Movement. Pusey's development was not one of steady progression, but was wrought out in two drastic intellectual revolutions; one in 1835 and the other in 1844. On the first of these occasions the effect on Pusey's outlook was little short of traumatic.

The major difficulty which probably confronted Liddon and which still faces the student of Pusey was the enormity of his task. Not only did Pusey's career more than touch on many aspects of national, ecclesiastical and university life, but the evidence might be considered overwhelming. At Pusey House the manuscript sources alone are intimidating. Amid the 138 volumes of bound letters, catalogued and inexpertly edited, the two chests of unbound, catalogued but unedited letters, and the two shelves of additional miscellaneous documents (all relating to Pusey), the problem of selection could be oppressive. In addition, from 1828 onwards, primary sources also come thick and fast; up to and including the year 1850, Pusey had published no less than seventy different works. These ranged from major treatises and volumes of sermons (approximately seventy nine sermons if considered individually), to tracts and devotional books, besides documents of a controversial nature and letters to the press.

Quite apart, however, from indicating the urgent need for a new approach to Pusey's place within church history in the 19th century, the major purpose of this book is to show the nature of Pusey's intellectual development from his birth in 1800 to about his fiftieth year. The term 'intellectual' is employed in its wide sense implying the whole man, emotional and rational; the word 'development' includes environmental, social and religious considerations.

After an exposition of Pusey's landed aristocratic background and his progression through Eton and Christ Church, Oxford, an attempt is made to indicate the characteristics he derived from his place in society and the qualities he shared with his contemporaries. Significant, however, is the knowledge that a large part of his personality and future outlook was conditioned by his relationship with his father. The elder Pusey was an autocratic and narrow-minded but benevolent martinet, who would brook no opposition to the smallest of his wishes. His all pervading dominance in the family was such that after his death Pusey remained excessively dependent on others for the remainder of his life. His father's Tory prejudices were a matter of notoriety and probably account for the young Pusey's ardent espousal of Liberalism; his harsh ban on his son's friendship with the girl, Maria Barker, undoubtedly intensified the seriousness and depressive side of Pusey's character; his death in 1828 fostered in Pusey the first signs of a latent obsession with sin and guilt.

Elected a fellow of Oriel, Pusey exhibited an outlook which was both remarkably confused and remarkably comprehensive. Participating in the general university renaissance of the 1820s, he nevertheless sought relief from his private sorrows in overwork. In politics he strenuously opposed the ultra-Tories and advocated the Repeal of the Test and Corporation Acts and Catholic Emancipation; sharing some of the features of his Noetic colleagues, he yet remained distinct from all parties; in religion it was impossible to align him totally with any of the traditional church groups, High Church, Evangelical or Latitudinarian. Pusey was however immensely concerned for Christianity in general, as was shown in his relentless but abortive attempts to convert the atheist and political revolutionary, Julian Hibbert.

A disciple of Charles Lloyd, the future Bishop of Oxford, Pusey was persuaded by his mentor to visit Germany in order to become acquainted with biblical criticism and Semitic languages. Resident in Germany in 1825 and 1826 to 1827, Pusey acquired not only a deep knowledge of German theology and proficiency in German, Hebrew, Arabic, Syriac and Chaldee, but was impressed first by such 'higher critics' as Eichhorn and then by such scholars as Schleiermacher; above all, he formed a warm friendship with Friedrich Tholuck. In the dispute over the rise of Rationalism in Germany which Pusey conducted with H.J. Rose in the years 1828 to 1830, it becomes clear how greatly Pusey was influenced by his contact with German thought, and how individual he was among Anglicans in his outlook on such questions as the need for revision of the Old Testament, the importance to be attached to Articles, the significance of the Reformation, the value of the episcopate and the place of inspiration in the Bible. Perhaps most important, it becomes apparent that Pusey's views had been lastingly affected by his study of German Pietism, particularly as found in the life and writings of Spener, and the new type of Pietism existent in Germany in the 1820s; from such as Tholuck, Neander and Lücke, Pusey received indelible impressions of the need for 'vitality' in religion as well as sympathizing with the aims of the *Vermittlungstheologie*.

In the early 1830s, however, Pusey experienced a profound intellectual revolution; this was due not only to the death of his father and Bishop Lloyd and the increasing influence over him of Keble and Newman, but also to political events, such as the demand for Parliamentary, Church and University reform. Pusey was especially concerned for the rights of property owners. Late in 1834, Pusey deliberately abandoned his former liberal opinions and broad churchmanship; he became disillusioned by events on the continent, regretted his previous adoption of German scholarship and imposed a strict regime of austerity in his domestic life; he now allied himself with the Tractarians. Thereafter, he steadily came under the tutelage of Keble and Newman; from them he probably acquired his ideas on Sacramentalism, his introduction to the Caroline divines and the Fathers, and his altered political views. His lectures on Types and Prophecy, however, show Pusey contributing a unique element to the Oxford Movement; his knowledge of German theology and the Old Testament (despite his firm refusal to assume the role of an innovator) enabled him to anticipate much modern thought on the question of prophecy. He also remained intensely individual in some of his opinions, such as on the status of Roman Catholics, the value of the Reformers and the role of Tradition, as well as in his sympathetic awareness of problems outside Oxford. Among the Tractarians as a whole, he was never identifiable exclusively with any of the differing groups, whether they were the Old High Church party, the sober Bisley School or Newman's followers. His interest and involvement in national affairs, his concern for church building in London, his attention to the enactments of the Church Commissioners and the state of the industrial towns of the north, and his regard for missionary activity and the erection of colonial bishoprics, rendered him unusual as a member of the Oxford Movement. His friendship with such politicians as his brother, Gladstone and Bunsen gave him an insight into politics. His knowledge of German universities made him an able advocate of the establishment of theological colleges in England. In his grasp of the affinities between Tractarianism and Evangelicalism, Pusey was the foremost member of the movement to exhibit eirenic tendencies towards the 'peculiars'. Until the early 1840s, indeed, Pusey regarded all his work as a means of reinvigorating the life of the Church of England as a whole; his membership of the Oxford Movement was simply one of his numerous multifarious concerns.

Following the death of his wife in 1839 and the rise of Romanism within the Oxford Movement, however, Pusey began to alter his outlook for a second time. This was most apparent in the evolution of his theological perspective and his changed views on the Sacrament of Penance and the idea of development of doctrine. In 1845 he was indicating to Henry Manning that he no longer valued the Reformers so highly, that he had changed his mind on such matters as Purgatory, the invocation of saints, the place of the Virgin Mary in devotion, and the decrees of the Council of Trent. He had advanced from the *via media* to full-blown Anglo-Catholicism; a position he was to hold for the remainder of his life and from which he led the Anglo-Catholic party in the 1850s and beyond.

INTRODUCTION: EARLY INFLUENCES

1. The family background

Edward Pusey's childhood and youth occurred at a critical time in his country's history. Not only was England then facing the problems caused by the development of the agrarian and industrial revolutions, but she was also actively engaged in war with Revolutionary and Napoleonic France. Pusey was born on 22 August 1800 at Pusey House, a stately home built in Georgian style, in the village of Pusey. This is situated in the historical Vale of the White Horse, four miles from the market town of Faringdon in Berkshire, with easy access to Oxford.

It was not until he was an adolescent, however, that Pusey was likely to have become aware that England was passing through a period of vast social and economic change. His first impressions at home were inculcated by his parents, both of whom were firm upholders of the traditions, privileges and responsibilities associated with the landed aristocracy of the eighteenth century. This tendency was reinforced by the fact that in 1800 Pusey's father was already advanced in age, having been born in 1746, the year of the collapse of the last Jacobite Rising at Culloden. He was the Hon. Philip Bouverie, the youngest son of the 1st Viscount Folkstone, and had changed his surname to Pusey as a condition of succession to the Pusey estate. His wife and Pusey's mother, twenty-four years younger than her husband, was Lady Lucy Pusey, daughter of Robert 4th Earl of Harborough and widow of a Sir Thomas Cave. Edward Pusey was the second of nine children, of whom only five survived to adulthood. His elder brother, Philip, had been born in 1799.

Like his cousin Lord Shaftesbury, the philanthropist and

champion of social reform, to whom he was also similar in temperament, Pusey was a long time maturing. At the age of twenty-eight he was still described by John Henry Newman as being 'like some definitely marked curve, meandering through all sorts and collections of opinions boldly yet it seems irregularly'.[1] Recently references have also been made to the diffuse and complex, if not confused, nature of the young Pusey's beliefs.[2] It was not only in his outlook, however, that Pusey gave evidence of slow development. His character too ripened belatedly; its roots lay in his heredity and the training he received as a child.

The assertion is sometimes made that Pusey inherited his intellectual gifts from his father's side and his emotional religious temperament from his mother's. Whatever the truth of this, Pusey's niece, Clara Fletcher, was to recall after his death that it was a marvel to all who knew the family that Pusey and his brother, Philip, were in the least academic. What is more than probable however is that Pusey's aristocratic background and inherited qualities deeply impressed him with notions of the existence of a permanent, immutable and gracious backcloth to human life. Very early on Pusey would appreciate that the landed classes governed the country and led society, not only because of their wealth and political power, but because they regarded themselves as an élite, educated and trained for responsibility.[3]

Pusey's father was an autocratic, though benevolent, martinet. The austere nature of life at Pusey House was dictated by this man, who had not married until he was fifty-two, by which age his habits had become firmly fixed. As Pusey once gently complained,

> From the early habit of ruling everyone, as he did first his own and my Mother, he seems to think it necessary that he should act for everyone; and it sometimes requires a little management to follow one's own plans, without seeming to set too little value on his advice.[4]

At Pusey House domestic arrangement and estate affairs were matters of strict routine, performed with an almost military exactness. Punctuality and formality were hall marks of the establishment. Meals, daily activities, calls on neighbouring gentry families and management of the property followed an ordered unchanging pattern, interrupted only by the family's visit to their residence in the capital for the London season.

Lady Pusey, controlling her strong emotions, either reinforced or adopted the precision required in everything by her husband, her manner being somewhat severe. Practical, outspoken and unsentimental, Pusey's mother was above all methodical. She was particularly assiduous in 'good works'. Just as it is easy to condemn Hannah More for emphasizing at this time the exercise of Christian benevolence, instead of concerning herself with social evils, so one might equally criticize Lady Pusey.

> Her time was laid out by rules: a certain portion was always given to reading the Bible; and another to some book of established literary merit – generally an historical author. She would read this book with a watch at her side; and as soon as the self prescribed time for such reading had elapsed, she eagerly turned to the more congenial task of needlework for charitable purposes. On Sundays, the time before, between, and after the Church services, was regularly spent in taking short walks or in reading sermons.[5]

Both Lady Pusey and Hannah More, however, like so many of their contemporaries such as Jane Austen were circumscribed in their outlook by birth, upbringing and the conventions of the period, especially as regards the place of women in the family and society. Because they did not express their feelings in the manner of a Mary Wollstonecraft, their lives were not necessarily effete. In Lady Pusey's case, her conscientiousness and self-effacing charity made a strong impression on her son Edward. Much of his later concern for the poorer classes was probably a reflection of his mother's teaching, narrow though it may have been.

The intellectual range of the home was also limited and the library contained little besides numerous sermons of the school of Barrow and Tillotson. It is likely that both of these divines were favoured by Pusey's father. Barrow's theology is characterized by its mathematical precision and Tillotson – one of the dominant influences in the Anglican Church of the eighteenth century – appealed deliberately to sober common sense, stressed reason rather than revelation and taught 'the Gospel of Moral Rectitude'.[6] Tillotson would have fostered the Pusey family's sense of duty.

By the time Pusey was born the Bouveries already had a long record of parliamentary and public service. Pusey's grandfather, who married the daughter of Baron Romney, a Governor of Dover Castle, had been an associate of Walpole and Recorder and M.P. for Salisbury before his elevation to the Peerage. His second son succeeded him in the Commons. The family's firm support for the Hanoverians had also been rewarded in 1765 when George III created Pusey's eldest uncle the Earl of Radnor. It was not surprising, therefore, that the political views of Pusey's father were deeply ingrained and that his sons evinced an interest in affairs of state early in life. Clara Fletcher coyly recalled years later, however, that Pusey's father was 'a Tory of the bluest school with an equal horror of Whigs and Atheists, though I am afraid he used the conjunction *and* instead of or'.[7] Because his outlook was so prejudiced, social contacts between the Pusey family and others were deliberately restricted, even when the Puseys resided in their London home during the season. This bias also accounted for the opposition he later made to the marriage of Pusey's brother, Philip. For four years Philip was forbidden by his father to marry because the lady's father, Lord Carnavon, was a Whig who had spoken publicly on behalf of Queen Caroline.

Both Pusey and his brother indeed stood in awe of their father. In view of his strong will, reserved habits and authoritative character, there was invariably a sense of constraint between the father and his children. In addition he did not care for the company of young people and left their early training in the hands of his wife. It was primarily for this reason that his two daughters, as well as his sons, were later sent to boarding school. The thought of opposing the wishes of his father was foreign to Pusey's nature however and even more so to that sense of obedience and respect which he had inbibed from his mother's teaching.[8] On the occasions when Pusey might have considered his father's will to have been harsh, he invariably felt obliged to interpret it as well meaning, though he feared his contemporaries might sometimes 'extract much pleasantry on the fancied rigidness of my father or my apparent constraint'.[9]

Severe and inflexible though Pusey's father may have been, he was dedicated to philanthropy on a national scale and the number of societies which were either served or supported by him was surprisingly large.[10] There is little doubt, indeed, that Pusey was inculcated very early in life with a strong sense of the importance of such institutions; he later contributed to forty-nine societies and held office in twenty-one. This activity nevertheless was not the product of Evangelicalism in the family, for Pusey's father acutely disliked the Evangelical School, fearing that in their teaching emotion was more highly regarded than conscience. Such a view even so did not prevent the Puseys from joining in the vanguard of a much wider movement, begun as early as the 1770s and 1780s, and aimed at developing in England an awareness of social ills and a notion of the need to improve the state of society.[11] Thoughts of solemn duty and of responsibility were therefore of the very ethos that Pusey first encountered in life.

The accumulated strain of twenty-eight years of his father's heavy influence, however, ultimately had tragic results for Pusey. In the end he no longer understood what it was to exercise a sense of independence, and he came to rely enormously on friends when he was making the smallest of decisions. At the time of his father's death, Pusey confessed,

> What indeed the natural character was, I scarcely myself know, yet I feel myself now, as a branch which has been so long bowed down, that even when the weight which depressed it, has been removed, though it can partly, cannot wholly recover its original direction.[12]

In addition, having previously sometimes dared to think of

his father's will as like a 'citadel' which needed to be 'shaken', 'snapped' and forced to 'yield' if only indirectly, Pusey was tormented with guilt. Shutting himself away for days, refusing to attend the funeral, and unwilling to receive visitors, Pusey described his feelings at the time as 'more an involuntary undefined depression, an internal burning, than actual grief'.[13] Thereafter, his encounters with death in his family circle were associated with feelings of personal guilt.

It is not surprising that the total effect on Pusey of his early environment and upbringing was the acquisition of that 'sombre, ungenial and unjoyous gravity'[14] by which he was later so frequently characterized. Isaac Williams, the Tractarian, for example, remarked that Pusey's presence always silenced him and held Newman in check.[15] It is also very likely that his parents' reserve compelled Pusey to repress many of his natural instincts. When these emotions, denied expression for so long, eventually fastened on an object during his last year as a schoolboy, one should not wonder that they were intense, if not violent. Experience of school, however, tended to reinforce the lessons Pusey had learnt at home.

2. Training for leadership

Before going to Eton at the age of eleven, Pusey spent four years at a Preparatory School at Mitcham in Surrey, where two of his contemporaries were the Stanleys – the future Earl of Derby and his brother, Lord Carlisle. He thereby began very early in life to associate with future leaders of nineteenth century society. Even so and despite receiving here his first grounding in the classics, the chief impression which the school left on his weakly, shy, and delicate temperament was a firm belief in the efficacy of corporal punishment. Discipline at Mitcham was harsh and excessive. Unlike his cousin Ashley who, as a result of severe home training, was driven in manhood by a resolve to minimize the sufferings of children, Pusey was later to rear his own children according to the grim methods he had learnt at his first school.

From Mitcham Pusey proceeded to Eton, a school steadily

rising in prestige[16] and then under the Headship of Dr Keate. As a result of the patronage bestowed on the school by George III, the number of boys at the turn of the century had reached five hundred, and there was keen competition among Tory aristocrats to secure places for their sons.

Although pupils had increased, however, the staff and their teaching methods had remained unchanged and, in consequence, they had little control over their pupils. Rebellions in the school were not infrequent and the most serious occurred a few months after Pusey left. On the whole indeed, even though Keate may have been a strong headmaster, in general a state of war was assumed and life among the boys was largely untouched by his influence. When one considers this, together with the fact that Eton resisted for a long time the tendency to develop a close-knit group life based on the prefect system, esprit de corps and organized games, it is possible to understand, whatever one's views on the value then and now of public schools, the little effect that the school had in altering Pusey's character. At both Mitcham and Eton even religion played no great part in his development; the Anglican services were in most schools of the period regarded as matters of convention rather than formation.[17] As one of Pusey's school friends was later to ask him, 'What was there that required concealment, in the fact that a man whose religious education had of course been neglected at Eton, had become an infidel?'[18]

Nevertheless, Pusey could not help acquiring some of the accepted and important opinions of his associates at Eton. He would not have been able, for example, to resist the tendency to regard himself and his school-mates as springing from a select stratum of society, for which the school especially catered. In his own form his colleagues numbered a future Prime Minister, a Lord Lieutenant of Ireland, a Colonial Minister and First Lord of the Admiralty, a Chancellor of the Duchy of Lancaster, a Treasurer of the Household, a Speaker of the House of Commons and three Ambassadors.[19] Coming from the ranks of the landed aristocracy, it would have been natural for them at this time to consider themselves equipped by birth and tradition for leadership in the world outside school. Newman at least grasped the significance of this when, on the occasion of Pusey's accession to the Oxford Movement, he thought of him as being able 'to give a name, a form, and a personality to what was without him a sort of mob'.[20]

Pusey was not only of a privileged social group, however, but linked by similar home training and outlook with the sons of the rising middle classes and especially with that select group who ultimately became the intellectual élite of the Victorian age.[21] Like the offspring of William Wilberforce for instance Pusey had been brought up to 'godliness and good learning';[22] he too was a child of that age of anxious optimism which succeeded the Napoleonic wars and he also was to spend his life in endeavouring to make the world a morally better place. His aristocratic background might account for the interest he and his contemporaries at university were to show in politics, but it was probably his rigid upbringing at home, together with his classical education, which gave him affinities also with those who were encouraged as children to read seriously, talk earnestly and strive so desperately to increase their knowledge.[23]

Before going up to Oxford, however, where he was to continue associating on equal terms with many destined for future leadership, Pusey spent his final fifteen months as a schoolboy under the private tuition of Dr Edward Maltby, Vicar of Buckden near Huntingdon, afterwards Bishop of Chichester (1831–1836) and then Bishop of Durham (1836–1859).

It is possible, since Maltby was well known for his liberal views and indeed was appointed to a bishopric in the first place on account of them,[24] that he may have been partly responsible for Pusey's political and theological opinions in young manhood. Pusey himself however largely remembered his time at Buckden for the hard work he was made to do in preparation for Classical Honours at Oxford and, above all, for the occasion in 1818 when he first met his future wife, Maria Barker. As Pusey later wrote to her, 'I was no free agent (unless principle bade me stop) after I had seen you . . . Everything has been the necessary consequence of that'.[25]

Maria was then seventeen, beautiful, vivacious, undisciplined and a complete Tom Boy. Pusey fell deeply in love with her. It is probable that he had never previously encountered a female – or anyone for that matter – so free in the expression of her opinions and so uninhibited in her behaviour. Pusey had always been compelled to repress his feelings, but now he was literally distracted.

When Pusey's father inevitably issued an ultimatum and forbade him to communicate any further and in any way with Maria, the effect on Pusey's outlook was disastrous. An undergraduate at the time, Pusey considered leaving Oxford without taking his degree. Naturally timid, he now and ever after became a depressive, genuinely fearing he would go mad. His closest friend, Richard Jelf, a future Principal of King's College, London, was outraged by the attitude of Pusey's father and the ban imposed on Pusey's relations with Maria.

> Can I believe [wrote Jelf] that any human being can form a determination [relative to the happiness of a child] which is to yield in no circumstances, which is to take its course though it break the heart or poisons the future existence of the wretched victim and that victim too a child? No, No. . . .[26]

Jelf, however, was reckoning without intractability such as was to be found in Pusey's father who remained inflexible for six more years. In the meantime, Maria's father let it be known that he too was opposed to the relationship. It is not surprising that during these years Pusey surrendered himself to grief and that, when the ban was finally lifted, his health had deteriorated to such an extent that he suffered a nervous breakdown which lasted four months.

3. 'Byronism'

No account of the early years of Pusey would be satisfactory which did not mention, at least briefly, the early influence on his outlook of his youthful addiction to the poetry of Byron. It is likely that had he never experienced an apparently ill-fated passion for Maria Barker, Pusey would still have been affected by the Romantic Movement in general, since its impact in England occurred precisely and most strongly during his impressionable years.

Towards the end of the 18th century this movement had already succeeded in challenging, if not destroying the widely held beliefs and assumptions concerning human destiny of two millennia.[27] With its emphasis on subjectivity and its revolt against hitherto widely accepted values, it might have been a movement tailored for the young Pusey, hamstrung by the outmoded 18th century dictates of his parents. Even though he was temperamentally incapable of open defiance of his father, Pusey showed how much he was nevertheless a child of his age by seeking relief for his sorrow in introspection and indulging in a cult of 'the prophet of the disappointed'.[28]

It is probable that Byron's personal dilemmas woke subconscious echoes in Pusey. Byron's physical deformity, which the poet himself described as a 'discouraging weight upon me like a mountain'[29] and 'the bane of my life',[30] remind one of Pusey's thoughts concerning the oppressive nature of his father. Much more, however, and in addition simply to the extreme force and beauty of Byron's poetry, Pusey was attracted by its mingling of 'remorse without repentance' and the aspect of the poet as his own self destroyer.[31] Coining the word 'Byronism' to depict his feelings at this time, Pusey described the Byronist

> as being the god of Epicurus, it becomes in imagination the being of another world, and looks down upon the miseries and struggles of this, and leaves the unhappy wretches to their fate while it philosophizes upon them, or at best it comments with almost a contemptuous pity on the ills it sees.[32]

Though Pusey was later to eschew 'Byronism' on the grounds that it rendered 'the mind unpractical, undisposed to apply the relief of Christianity to the ills it dwells upon',[33] it is possible that Byron's almost pathological concern with his own self and his frequent sense of guilt left a lasting impression on Pusey's outlook.[34]

As an undergraduate at Christ Church (1819–1822), Pusey led a singularly uneventful life, deliberately overworking himself in semi-seclusion in order to take his mind off his misfortune and until this way of life became a habit with him.

> I have lived so retired [he wrote later] that of me is known less than the little which it [the world] ordinarily knows of any one; it has only known that I have been at times, intensely employed: it has given me the credit for being so always, and not knowing any of the mixed motives, anything of the distress of mind, which this study was partly intended to cure or at least to stupify . . .[35]

Until 1821 Pusey's father would not permit him to travel abroad, and then he was allowed to journey to Paris only to meet his brother returning from a trip to Spain. In 1822 however Pusey was finally able to spend three months in Switzerland as a reward for having achieved a First in Greats. Even this visit did little to relieve Pusey's depression. His journal recording the event[36], though evidence of the degree to which like so many of his contemporaries Pusey was also influenced by the Romantic cult of nature, contains many Byronic overtones of despair.

By the time Pusey was twenty-two, many of his basic character traits, which were thereafter to condition his outlook, had already become part of his nature. The austerity of Pusey House, the autocratic rule of his father, his place in society and disappointment in love had all played a vital part towards shaping his future development.

1
A FELLOW OF ORIEL

1. The Seed-time

In the Oxford of the early 1820s, the highest academic distinction that could be achieved in open and rigorous competition was the winning of a Fellowship to Oriel College. This Edward Pusey succeeded in doing in April 1823.

Since the turn of the century, Oriel had been steadily rising in reputation. First Eveleigh and then Copleston, successive Provosts, had endeavoured to make it known as a place which provided a liberal and fashionable education, and conscientious tuition over the years had consistently reaped rewards for the college in the Examination Schools, first introduced in 1800. Discipline and regard for religion at Oriel were also of a high standard; so much so, that even William Wilberforce preferred to send three of his sons there rather than to Cambridge – his old university, the seat of Simeon and the accepted breeding ground for Evangelicals.

In addition, Oriel's fame was enhanced by the presence among its Fellows of such men as Richard Whately, Edward Hawkins, Thomas Arnold and John Keble. Except for the latter, these dons were members of a new school, sect or clique, known as Noetic; their distinguishing feature being an ability to criticize ruthlessly all received traditions and institutions in the Socratic manner.[1] Whately in particular, the future archbishop of Dublin, was notorious for his clinical analysis of religious doctrines,[2] and closely associated with him was Blanco White, at least a precursor of the modern latitudinarian school in the Church of England. White was then midway on his journey from Roman Catholicism to Unitarianism, and was soon to exercise an influence on the ill-fated R.D. Hampden.

As Newman recalled, the Oriel Common Room 'stank of

logic'[3] and for this reason as well as out of envy, the Noetics were not without enemies. These latter chiefly comprised the 'old unspiritual high-and-dry' occupying the chief posts of influence in the university, and dons of the smaller and less distinguished colleges – 'the representatives . . . of the country party'[4]. To these Noetic was synonymous with free-thinking and their disparagement of the term fore-shadowed a bitter attack on the Oriel school made in *John Bull* in 1830.

Though Pusey was never to come under the influence of his colleagues to the same extent as Newman, choosing instead Charles Lloyd a future Bishop of Oxford as his mentor, the liberal tone of his political and religious outlook during the 1820s suggests that he was not altogether unaffected by the questioning ethos of Oriel.

This atmosphere, however, was merely one symptom of a wider and more general renaissance taking place throughout the greater part of the university in this decade. Not only was the whole of Oxford being transformed by an academic revolution, culminating in a new respect for learning, but almost all the many existent memoirs of the period depict it as a time of exuberance, buoyancy, and optimism.[5] When viewing Oxford within the context of the 1820s, it is difficult to resist the conclusion that Pusey's broad ideas and portentous industry owed something to the ethos of the place. He would have been aware at least that the university was peculiarly rich in talent and, possibly, that it was acquiring for the first time in its history a distinct corporate unity.

Pusey's election to Oriel also followed swiftly on a significant turning point in the nation's history. The suicide of Castlereagh in 1822 had heralded not only a reshuffle of cabinet ministers, but a further stage in the gradual change in government policy from the repression, typified by Peterloo and the Gag Acts, to moderate reform. Improvers, if not reformers, the Tory Ministry, headed by Liverpool and backed by Canning, Peel and Huskisson, sought gradually to alleviate the evils of industrial and agrarian depression, pauperism, a harsh penal code, and restrictions on trade. The hopes raised by the liberal-Tories were such, that the later ministry of Wellington found itself compelled to acquiesce also to a new principle and take a long step towards the complete civil equality of all Christian denominations. Until the Whigs under Grey began tampering with Church property, Pusey was an avowed supporter of reform; Blanco White declaring him to be 'one of the most liberal members of the university'.[6]

2. Political outlook

Initially Pusey's vigorous liberalism may have begun as an indirect protest against his father's inexorable views and only quickened in the stirring climate of university life. Whatever the cause, however, when he was not either preoccupied with study or downcast by his misfortune in regard to Maria Barker, his thoughts most frequently turned to politics. The marriage of his elder brother, Philip, to Lady Emily Herbert, the daughter of a notable Whig family in 1822, would have encouraged this tendency. Relations between Pusey and his sister-in-law were close from the start, and being a woman who showed a keen interest in current political events, she may have subtly influenced the direction of Pusey's views. It was during Pusey's years at Oriel that his brother was also laying the foundations of his close friendship with the Chevalier Bunsen and preparing himself for a career in the Commons. Both he and Pusey kept themselves particularly informed about the successive ministries formed in the late 1820s and invariably they were in agreement in disparaging the ultra-Tories.

The complexion of Pusey's outlook was certainly no secret from his contemporaries even before he went to Oriel. As early as 1821, his friend Jelf, who was inclined to Tory sympathies, had mocked Pusey on the death of Queen Caroline.

> How you Whigs will lament, not for her death, [he wrote to Pusey] but for the destruction of those hopes which through her would have offered the seals of office to Lord Grey for the third time![7]

Another friend, travelling in Italy and writing to congratulate Pusey on his election to Oriel, probably anticipated agreement when he suggested that,

> Nothing can exceed the beggarly state of Italy in general. The Arch-Duke of Tuscany is a . . . worthy prince . . . and under him that part of Italy is prospering and happy. But in Sardinia and Naples all is beggarly and roguery and in the Roman States what can one expect when petticoated Dotards pretend to guide with their feeble hands the reins of government . . . I am now quite Carbonaro and pray devoutly for the downfall of tyranny in this ill-fated country. That abominable wretch, now wearing the crown of Naples will probably end his vile existence . . . at Vienna.[8]

It would not have surprised his colleagues to know, therefore, that in 1827 Pusey regarded Navarino as a 'memorable battle, the most useful to Greece since Salamis'[9] and that he welcomed it as a decisive step in a hitherto temporizing policy of the allies. Similarly, Pusey's friends in the following year could have anticipated that he would say in relation to civic equality for dissenters –

> I am very anxious about the Test and Corporation Acts. I think them both in their means and end a disgrace and detriment to religion. They more than anything else keep alive the bitterness of party spirit among Christians agreeing in the same essentials of faith in England.[10]

Pusey's political outlook in the 1820s, however, is shown most vividly on the subject of Catholic Emancipation. From the beginning of the century Oxford was peculiarly sensitive to the constitutional issues raised by the emancipation question, and parliamentary candidates for the university invariably found their elections bedevilled by this controversy.[11] Annual petitions against concessions to Catholics were also a regular feature of university life. By 1829, however, the whole question had become a national issue; brought to a head by the activities of Daniel O'Connell and the Catholic Association. By then the Noetics were making no attempt to conceal their opinions on the matter. In 1828 both Hawkins and Whately opposed the annual petition sent up by the university and favoured emancipation. The following year Arnold published a booklet entitled, *The Christian Duty of Conceding the Roman Catholic Claims*, in which he maintained that every Englishman ought to support the claims of Irish Catholics on grounds of natural justice.

How much Pusey was influenced in his attitude by the Noetics, or how much by his old Christ Church tutor, Thomas Vowler Short, later Bishop of St Asaph, and by Professor Lloyd (both of whom were fervent Peelites) is debatable. What is not open to question is the strength of Pusey's conviction on the side of emancipation. As early as 1825, when a motion in favour of granting Catholics civic rights was before Parliament, Pusey was declaring –

> My conviction is very strong that on the passing of that Bill depends much the civilization, prosperity, and enlightening of Ireland, our political safety, the hope of increase of Protestantism in that country, and the extinction of Catholicism in this; the enlargement of toleration abroad, and a consequent removal of a stigma which is most prejudicial to religion in general. With these opinions, which discussion has (as usual) more and more fixed, I cannot but much deplore the late decision in the House of Lords, while from having seen the unfavourable effect which the Clerical petitions on the question had on public opinion, and the ill impression with regard both to religion and its most effectual support in this country ... our church, that subject pains me more than I can express.[12]

In the Oxford election of 1829, which revolved around Peel's change of mind concerning emancipation and which foreshadowed the collapse of Tory hegemony in the country, Pusey's politics caused him to be viewed as an opponent of Keble, Newman, H. Froude and R. Wilberforce. Unlike these future Tractarians, Pusey had no hesitation in giving Peel his vote, but it was probably fortunate that by then he had ceased being a Fellow of Oriel. The election caused great

E B Pusey, engraving, circa 1826

E B Pusey, drawn by his niece, Clara Pusey, Summer 1853

E B Pusey, engraving, Oxford, circa 1834

bitterness in Oxford and left an unpleasant backwash of acrimony. In no college were the divisions so acute, however, as in the Oriel Common Room, with the young resident dons ranged against the Noetics; a state of affairs which was to continue into the 1830s.

Liberal though Pusey may have been in the 1820s, there was nevertheless a definite note of moderation in his espousal of the cause of reform. He was in no sense a Radical, and when in the next decade he considered that innovations had gone too far, and the rights of property owners seemed endangered, he was not slow to call a halt. Convinced as he was that the English constitution was a model for the whole civilized world and open to improvement only in minor details, he was not as headstrong as some of his contemporaries. It is doubtful whether in 1824, for example, he fully applauded the action of his friend Stanley, who, having made a name for himself in the Commons, was soon to visit America where there was 'the ideal perfection . . . of government and the blessings of Republican liberty'.[13] Indeed, in the 1830s, when Pusey came under the influence of Keble, the appeal for restraint became the dominant theme in his writings.

An element of moderation had nevertheless always been there. Having sprung from the ranks of the upper classes and having been influenced by the writings of Edmund Burke, Pusey valued keenly the hierarchical and traditional frame of society even in his liberal days. Such latent 'Conservative' features in his make-up, coupled with his awareness of the evils of industrialism and the importance of the landed interest, gave him in time a kinship with much of the political thought of Disraeli[14] and the Young England party.

It is possible, indeed, that Pusey's liberal stand as a young don may simply have been a passing, but genuine and pragmatic means of opposing the stagnant policy of the ultra-Tories. In this, he would have resembled the majority of his intellectual contemporaries, in as much as none of them were real apologists (if one discounts Eldon, Croker and those found in the *Quarterly Review*) for things as they were in the 1820s. Even such figures as Coleridge, by temperament naturally 'Conservative', were not on the side of the government of the day, and all the ablest ministers in the Tory administrations from 1822 onwards were advocates of some degree of reform. The development from liberalism to moderate conservatism in Pusey's political views in the next decade was therefore explicable. This was not the case to quite the same extent, however, in respect to his religious opinions.

3. Questions of churchmanship

Ecclesiastical history in the early nineteenth century abounds in contradiction, and not least when it comes to questions concerning the state of the Church of England at that time.

On the surface, the Anglican Church might have been soundly asleep, not yet having shaken off the forces of conservatism, which had overtaken it at the advent of the French Revolution and the publication of Tom Paine's *The Rights of Man*. Despite growing criticism, the general acceptance of pluralism, sinecures, absenteeism, and the anomalies of the quasi-medieval structure of the Church, together with the glaring disparities in clerical income, all suggest that torpidity still prevailed. People in general were described as being utterly indifferent to theology except in those spheres in which it impinged on personal conduct.[15]

At a deeper level, however, and among certain groups of Anglicans, this was a period of immense vitality and fermentation. For the heirs of the eighteenth century Evangelical Revival, this was the hey-day of the Clapham Sect and the spring-time of the many religious societies. To the Hackney Phalanx, a relatively small collection of High Churchmen, versed in the Caroline divines and active ever since Joshua Watson retired from business in 1814[16], it was a time of energetic church building and concern for the affairs of the National Society for Promoting the Education of the Poor. Among the liberal churchmen, or those open to new ideals and proposals for reform, the extent to which they were very much awake, could be judged either from the writings of

Sydney Smith in *The Edinburgh Review*, or from the interests of the Noetics.

The complexity of the religious scene in the 1820s is vividly illustrated when one endeavours to determine the nature of the churchmanship of such an individual as Pusey. On the one hand, one cannot doubt the seriousness with which he regarded religion at that time. In 1823, for example, Pusey made a strong impression on Newman, who was then a most earnest Evangelical.

> That Pusey is Thine, O Lord, how can I doubt? [Newman wrote] His deep views of the Pastoral Office, his high ideas of the scriptural rest of the Sabbath, his devotional spirit, his love of the Scriptures, his firmness and zeal, all testify to the operation of the Holy Ghost . . .[17]

On the other hand, however, and like the majority of Anglicans of the period[18], Pusey cannot be fitted, in an exclusive sense, into any of the three existing and most characteristic parties; the High Church, Liberal or Evangelical.

A churchman frequently cited as typifying the High Church point of view is Hurrell Froude's father, the Archdeacon of Totnes.[19] To such people, religion consisted of rigid orthodoxy in doctrine, energetic assertion of the rights of the Church of England as the National Church, a fierce dislike of dissenters and an unbending opposition to every kind of reform in Church or State. One only has to consider Pusey's political liberalism in the 1820s, to appreciate that that alone would render his high-churchmanship at least suspect; his view of dissenters made it even more so. As far as Nonconformity was concerned, Pusey might have been a latitudinarian. He was of the opinion, for example, that differences of outlook among the principal bodies of dissenters, (excluding the Socinians), were akin simply to the varying degrees of emphasis placed on certain doctrines by the high church and evangelical parties, in the Church of England; and as such, were neither of vital importance nor to be confused with the truth itself.[20] Independents and Presbyterians might disagree on questions of church government, and Baptists might hold different views concerning the timing of baptism, but 'the main principle that persons should be baptised is admitted by both'.[21] Pusey, indeed, adhered strongly to the liberal point of view that there were certain 'essentials' common to all denominations; the most vehement disputes among different Christian groups, recorded down the ages, being over matters, intrinsically of the least importance. To one seeking information on the evils of party spirit, Pusey recommended the reading of the Noetic Whately's essays on party feeling in religion.

In view of this, it is not difficult to appreciate Thomas Arnold's misgivings when he saw Pusey allying himself with the Tractarians in the 1830s. Many of Pusey's ideas on dissenters had hitherto borne a resemblance to those that Arnold was to propound in his *The Principles of Church Reform*. Pusey at Oriel, however, wore his liberalism in religious matters with a difference.

Unlike the liberal Sydney Smith, who, famed for his advocacy of social justice and interest in reform, nevertheless harboured a cynical contempt for missionary activity, Pusey was passionately concerned to see the bounds of Christendom extended. By the 1840s indeed he became perhaps the leading Tractarian in this field. Already in the 1820s, however, one of Newman's earliest memories was of a conversation he had with Pusey on the subject of Henry Martyn the missionary; Pusey having spoken 'beautifully on the question, "who are to go?"'.[22] Not long afterwards, Newman was so impressed by Pusey's 'active devoted spirit' that he prayed that Pusey would not 'like Martyn, "burn as phosphorous"'.[23] In 1824 Pusey and his brother discussed between themselves how funds might be raised for schools in Ceylon and India, and three years later, Pusey was engaged in correspondence with the High Churchman W.F. Hook on the role of missionaries in India. Shortly afterwards, Pusey wrote admiringly of the labours of German Pietists in printing and distributing copies of the bible and in propagating the Gospel among the Jews and Mohammedans. Even when a mature Tractarian, Pusey acknowledged the debt that Anglicanism owed to eighteenth century German Protestant missionaries in India.

Though neither a typical high churchman nor a thorough-going liberal, the young Pusey was also not an Evangelical. Much as the ardent Evangelical Newman, in the early 1820s, wrote approvingly of Pusey's zeal and dedication, he felt obliged to record his fear that Pusey was 'prejudiced against thy children (the Evangelicals)'.[24] Together they argued over baptismal regeneration; Newman inclining to separate regeneration from baptism, Pusey doubting its separation.[25] The chief criticism, however, that Pusey had against the Evangelicals was centred on his inherited dislike of emotional display. In 1827, when Maria Barker was troubled over the preaching of the Evangelical Francis Close, later Dean of Carlisle, Pusey went out of his way to warn her of the dangers of sermons 'which would make people cherish grief as an end ... and use it as a measure of sincerity'.[26] He thought 'the employing the feelings as a criterion of religion is mischievous because delusive'.[27] Nevertheless, Pusey allowed none of this fear to deter him from witnessing to the many positive features in Evangelicalism, and, throughout his life, he expressed affection for the Evangelical party. His friendly disputes with the young Newman never prevented him from acquiring for Newman the curacy of St Clement's in Oxford. Pusey indeed followed his colleague's pastoral activities in the parish with the greatest of interest, even to the extent of hoping to work alongside him there.

Nothing illustrates, however, to quite the same extent how much Pusey stood at Oriel outside the bounds of any of the usual party positions as his attitude towards Roman Catholicism.

In England in the early nineteenth century, there was a strong and widespread feeling that the Roman Catholic religion was antagonistic to almost every English virtue. Whether they were High Church, Liberal or Evangelical, and whether they expressed their sentiments temperately or immoderately, Anglicans in general were united in a common detestation of Popery. They were convinced that Protestantism had originated in a revolt against Rome, and, in consequence, they held firmly to the idea that it was as good as Popery was bad.[28] Pusey, however, held a different point of view; possibly as a result of the strong social links which his family enjoyed with their Catholic Throckmorton neighbours at Buckland. In 1828 Pusey was of the opinion that –

> The Roman Catholics, though they have mingled up superstitions with and adulterated the Faith, have yet retained the foundations. I do not mean to deny the practical idolatry into which they have fallen, or that the "good works" of self-emaciation, hairshirts, flagellations etc., have not had a merit ascribed to them which interfered with the merits of Christ: yet still, whatever they may have added, they did hold that acceptance was through Christ; and as to the mediation of the saints, it was, in *theory*, only the same as one asking a good man to pray for us. The danger was that it might be *practically* more, yet so as rather to lead to *idolatry*, than to an interference with the Atonement. Yet I ... doubt not that there have been hundreds of thousands of sincere men among the Roman Catholics, and that every sincere man has been led into that degree of truth which was necessary to salvation; and that there are many ... at whose feet it would be happiness to think that we might sit in the kingdom of heaven.[29]

Such remarks, when viewed in conjunction with his attitude towards dissenters, not only illustrate the comprehensiveness of his outlook in the 1820s and the extent to which he stood outside party boundaries, but they also explain his admiration of the German theologian, Georg Calixtus (1586–1665). At about the same time as Pusey was emphasizing the positive features to be found in Roman Catholicism, he was also praising the eirenic tendencies shown by Calixtus during his life-time, and inveighing against the opponents of Syncretism.[30] It is possible, indeed, that much of Pusey's breadth of outlook and preference for stressing the beliefs held in common by Christians of all denominations, resulted from an enthusiastic study of Calixtus' works. There is no mistaking, at least, how much Pusey went out of his way to commend Calixtus' notion that 'all a Christian need believe ... to (obtain) salvation was contained in the ancient creeds and decisions of the councils; that whoever agreed with these doctrines of the ancient Church, he was in heart united with him.[31]

This idea of unity on the basis of creeds and the ancient Church perhaps also supplies the clue as to why Pusey, so individual in his thinking in the 1820s, nevertheless considered himself to be of the High Church. Wider in his sympathies and different in other respects as he was from so many of his High Church contemporaries, he would have found among them a measure of respect for antiquity. It was probably for this reason that in 1828 Pusey could make the otherwise inexplicable claim that, while he knew of no subject of controversy between the High Church and the Evangelicals, in which he did not agree with the former, he had no intention of preaching on the issues in dispute.[32] When it came to matters of doctrine, Pusey ever feared to be considered unorthodox. It is clear, however, that Pusey preferred not to ally himself with any party unless it was absolutely necessary; a factor which partially explains his delay in joining the Oxford Movement. Until then, he was pious in the sense of practising his religion as laid down in The Book of Common Prayer, but without examining its deeper implications. In later years he admitted this when writing to W.F. Hook and refuting the suggestion that Hook was a disciple of the Tractarians.

> As for your being our disciple, the thing is absurd; Newman said in *The Christian Observer* that you had formed or received your views long before many of the writers in the Tracts (long before myself upon many points, tho' many, as Baptism and the Succession, I held as far as I understood them) ... You have held them earlier than Newman probably and for longer and more consistently than ourselves.[33]

The essentially undogmatic character of Pusey's religious

outlook in the 1820s was partly, therefore, a reflection of the lack of vitality and cohesion in the theology of High Churchmen outside the Hackney Phalanx[34]; the confusion of ecclesiastical party lines was the result of inadequate theological training. Only in 1833 did Pusey himself fully awake to the absence of theological colleges for ordinands of the Church of England, and then he became one of the foremost advocates of their establishment. During his years at Oriel, he tended merely to accept current opinions concerning the role of the clergy and their place in society.

In the early nineteenth century, a career in the Church of England was looked upon as a profession particularly suited to the younger sons of the upper classes. With government, war, law, and medicine, divinity was indeed one of the few occupations that a young gentleman could adopt without committing a social solecism.[35] Many of the clergy were scholars, but intellectual pretensions and more than a general acceptance of the Thirty-Nine Articles were not the immediate requirements for the priesthood; still less any need to possess a sense of vocation. The Anglican clergy were frequently regarded more as officials of the Establishment, akin to judges and army officers, than as ministers of Christ, and this aspect of their occupation gave them an equivalent social standing.[36].

As a younger son of a landed family, it was natural that Pusey should share these views. Besides himself, many of his closest friends at Oxford eventually sought ordination almost as a matter of course; viewing holy orders as an agreeable prospect. When Pusey learnt in 1824 that his friend R. Salwey was to be ordained, it was precisely in this tone that he wrote to congratulate him; as yet attaching no sacramental significance to the office of a priest.[37] Often Pusey's friends informed him of their parochial activities and especially of their efforts to increase the numbers attending their churches, but their sense of values invariably betrays their social origins. His future brother-in-law, for example, the Revd J. Luxmoore, a son of the Bishop of St Asaph, asked the farm labourers in his parish to attend church in order to gain greater respect from their richer neighbours.[38]

Clerical careers were also dependent more than most on patronage: this led to some professional attitudes which appear shocking to later generations more accustomed to regard the Church as a career open to talent.

Whilst younger sons of the landed aristocracy and gentry could expect financial backing from their families, in the form of an allowance at the start of their careers, it was understood that sooner or later they would seek patronage and secure access to revenues within the Church. Thus it was that R.L. Edgeworth could confidently state that 'Church benefices may . . . be considered a fund for the provision of the younger sons of our gentry and nobles.'[39] In his turn, when offering a post, a patron was expected not only to take into account a candidate's character and abilities, but also his antecedents.

The extent to which in the 1820s, at least, Pusey was very much influenced by these current mores, is illustrated by his behaviour in 1828. Aware that he had been suggested for the vacant Regius Professorship of Hebrew in the university, Pusey saw no harm in asking Robert Wilberforce to exert influence and have his name brought to the notice of the Prime Minister, the Duke of Wellington.[40] (Certainly it seems that Robert's father, William, keenly favoured Pusey's candidature.)[41] Even so, by that time Pusey was also alive to the opportunities that such a position would give him for deepening his knowledge of theology; his interest in this field having been first aroused by Dr Charles Lloyd.

4. A disciple of Lloyd

Charles Lloyd, student and tutor of Christ Church, who became Regius Professor of Divinity in 1822 and Bishop of Oxford in 1827, has been described 'as a fat, ambitious and unpleasant man, determined to extract the last ounce of advantage from his connection with Peel'.[42] Whatever his character, however, there is no doubting his energy and talent and determination to raise the standard of teaching within the theology faculty. One of his first actions on attaining the professorship was to institute a course of lectures for a handful of graduates, and it was at these, accompanied by three Oriel colleagues – R. Jelf, J.H. Newman and W. Churton – that Pusey began his theological education.

The lectures were catechetical in form; Lloyd taking little part in them, beyond asking questions of those attending, directing their discussions and requiring exact and accurate answers to the problems he posed. Those which Pusey attended were primarily devoted to a study of Sumner's *Records of the Creation*, Graves on the Pentateuch, Carpzov on the Septuagint, and Prideaux's *Old and New Testament Connected*. It seems clear from Pusey's correspondence at the time, that Lloyd was bent on giving his pupils a thorough grounding in such matters as the historical accuracy, authenticity, and linguistic interpretation of the bible. He also impressed Pusey by the conscientiousness of his methods; as late as 1878 Pusey recalled how Lloyd 'gave himself altogether to us. His work was indefatigable and his pains individual'.[43] In one hour Lloyd never explained more than three or four verses of the text under discussion; preferring to exhaust the background of doubtful interpretations, to debate the significance of every word, every construction, each clause and argument. After that, he sought to decide the history of the passage in theology, its bearings on doctrine, the disputes it had caused or settled and its importance for the Church.

How much Pusey was aware of the contents of Lloyd's later lectures on the origins of the Prayer Book and its connection with primitive and medieval liturgies is unknown, but it was perhaps to these that he referred in later life, when he remarked that 'the Oxford Movement did come from the Professor's chair. I think that Bishop Lloyd gave us the great impulse'.[44] At a time when there were few in Oxford with any understanding of Roman theology and liturgy, Lloyd possessed a greater grasp of thought than was usual; having acquired this through friendship with French emigré clergy, as he related to Parliament at the time of Catholic Emancipation.[45] In addition to imparting this knowledge to his pupils, he also taught them to value authority in the Church, episcopacy and the apostolic succession; all of which were to be reproduced later in the writings of the Tractarians.[46]

Unlike Pusey, Newman in later life went to some trouble to deny that Lloyd has ever exercised any influence over his own intellectual development. He recalled Lloyd's mocking manner and kindly ways, but gave him no credit for having taught him anything original.[47] When Newman contrasted Lloyd with Whately on this score, however, he described almost all the features in the professor's make-up which would have attracted the young and earnest Pusey.

> Lloyd was a scholar, and Whately was not. Whately had the reputation specially of being an original thinker, of which Lloyd was not at all ambitious. Lloyd was one of the high-and-dry school, though with far larger views than were then common; while Whately looked down on both High and Low Church, calling the two parties respectively Sadducees and Pharisees. Lloyd professed to hold to theology, and laid great stress on a doctrinal standard, on authoritative and traditional teaching, and on ecclesiastical history; Whately called the Fathers 'certain old divines', and, after Swift or some other wit, called orthodoxy 'one's own doxy', and heterodoxy 'another's doxy'. Lloyd made much of books and reading, and, when preacher at Lincoln's Inn, considered he was to his lawyers, the official expounder of the Christian religion and the Protestant faith, just as it was the office of his Majesty's Courts to lay down for him peremptorily the law of the land; whereas Whately's great satisfaction was to find a layman who had made a creed for himself.[48]

The relationship that developed between Lloyd and Pusey in the 1820s was particularly close. By 1826 Pusey was telling him that, 'I am understood (and indeed rightly) to value your opinion and advice more than that of any one else'.[49] It was

Lloyd who initially persuaded Pusey to visit Germany, encouraged him to undertake the immense task of revising the authorized translation of the Old Testament, acted as a go-between in Pusey's difficulties with his father, and eventually first suggested him for the Professorship of Hebrew and the Canonry of Christ Church in 1828. When Lloyd died in the following year, Pusey experienced a great emotional loss; he apparently could not bring himself to believe that Lloyd would die, and only later on with Keble was Pusey to enjoy a similar relationship and of the kind for which he felt a great need. Shortly after Lloyd's death, Pusey wrote:

> one there was – the counsellor, friend and guide of all who had the happiness to come within his influence, to whom I owe a debt of gratitude which could never have been repaid, who had for six years shewn me the kindness of a second father, and in the enjoyment of whose theological instruction my opinion had been principally formed. With his counsels and his countenance I should not have dreaded any reproach. But a mysterious Providence has withdrawn to his rest and reward, him whom I, in common with others, venerated as one of the ablest supports of our Church; and I have lost the guardian friend, with whose guidance I had hoped to steer securely amid all the difficult shoals, through which the course of a theologian must in these days probably be held.[50]

5. Encounter with Atheism

Six months after becoming a Fellow of Oriel, Pusey renewed his acquaintance with a former Eton colleague, Julian Hibbert; an event which was fraught with consequences as far as Pusey's outlook was concerned.[51] Hibbert was the son of a wealthy Whig, Thomas Hibbert (1761–1807), who named his two sons Julian and Washington to indicate his sympathy with radical principles.[52] Whilst a schoolboy, Hibbert had already begun to question the tenets of Christianity and by 1823, after studying at Cambridge and visiting France, he became enamoured of the writings of the French

Enlightenment. From his correspondence with Pusey, it is clear that he thought highly of the works of Voltaire, Freret, Dumarsais, Boulanger, Helvetius, Diderot, Rousseau, d'Holbach and Volney, but was most influenced by Charles Dupuis, the author of *Origines de tous les cultes en religion universelle* (1795). Subsequent to joining a sect called the 'Physitheists', Hibbert became one of the first followers of the Reverend Robert Taylor, a heterodox Anglican clergyman whom he called 'the Deistical Priest' and who was later to be active in disseminating anti-Christian ideas at The Rotunda in Blackfriars Road, Southwark.[53]

Simultaneously with his renunciation of Christianity, Hibbert became an associate of Richard Carlisle and an intimate and benefactor of James Watson, the radical publisher and later Chartist and friend of Mazzini.[54] Together with Watson, Hibbert became a convert to the schemes of Robert Owen, served on the committee of The London Co-operative Trading Association, and in 1829 joined forces with The National Union of the Working Classes, which also held weekly meetings at The Rotunda. These 'Rotundanists' were so doctinaire and revolutionary in their political outlook as to evoke fierce criticism from Francis Place and trepidation in the government.[55]

Not knowing the extent to which Hibbert had abandoned his faith since leaving Eton, Pusey initially wrote to him asking his advice as to how translations of certain English religious works might be circulated among French Protestants. Naturally enough, Hibbert replied that such a task was diametrically opposed to all his thoughts and labours. 'Before you rechristianise France', he wrote to Pusey, 'look to your own country and you had better put down Richard Carlisle, who is the greatest philosopher that ever existed'.[56] When he learnt the truth regarding Hibbert's outlook, Pusey received a shock so great as to leave an impression of horror with him for the rest of his life. As late as 1882, he spoke of his encounter with Hibbert as 'my first real experience of the deadly breath of infidel thought upon my soul. I never forget how utterly I shrank from it'.[57]

Even so, for at least three years Pusey made persistent and dogged efforts to change Hibbert's mind going to the lengths of studying the French writers who had influenced Hibbert and attempting to write a refutation of Dupuis. He also enlisted the aid of his friend R. Salwey to prove to Hibbert that 'all ill-will, uncharitableness and . . . persecution is not only not permitted by, but is directly in opposition to the fundamental principles of Christianity'.[58] Pusey even persuaded his own brother to write an explanation of how he had recovered his faith, but Hibbert remained unconvinced and wrote:

> I should imagine that your brother had been a Theist. I am an Atheist. The same arguments therefore will not hold good. I firmly believe in the Prophecies, as well as in the Divinity of Christ, the fall of man and the greater part of the Apostolic and Nicene Creeds. According to Dupuis' system all these things become intelligible. He proves (in my opinion) that Jesus is the Sun and the Constellation Virgo his mother. Till I see a refutation of this system, all Christianity will appear to me only a perversion of natural Religion. But I will not argue with thee about Christianity. Thou wouldest be shocked at my blasphemy and I should be amused at thy credulity. Suffice it to say, that I consider the Bible as by no means superior to the Koran, either in common sense or morality. Reasoning upon Trinitarian theology I have long thought useless. Shall I reason on a science that sets reason at defiance? As to the morality of the Bible, I think it too bad, even to be refuted.[59]

Nevertheless, Hibbert was prepared to argue with Pusey over 'the being of a Deity' or the existence of 'a spiritual creator'. As a materialist, however, he claimed to reject the idea of spirit. He was ready to allow a great appearance of design in the universe, but he considered the manifest existence of evil a sufficient apology for atheism. If Manicheism were not then 'a very unfashionable doctrine' he would be inclined in that direction, though good and evil seemed to him to be equally divided. He also professed to believe in a theory of evolution, suggesting that nature first created plants, next shell fish, then quadrupeds and 'a very short time ago, man'. It was possible, he argued, that 'a great convulsion' of the globe might end in the replacement of man by another race of beings far superior to man. In the meantime, Hibbert declared that the Christian persecutions of Richard Carlisle filled him with 'hatred for all religions'.[60]

The patience and zeal with which Pusey entered into debate with Hibbert were remarkable and often won the admiration of his opponent. Frequently Hibbert regretted that Pusey should be throwing away his learning on such an ignorant individual as himself, and at one stage he endeavoured to point out that 'it is mere ploughing in the sand attempting to convert me'.[61] Only after almost a year of proselytizing did Pusey admit defeat, (though he continued to maintain correspondence with Hibbert for at least another two) and come to the conclusion that for the moment he was engaged on a hopeless task.

> Not that he [Hibbert] seems to be in practice a debauched man, though his principles of morality are lax; but he appears to be the victim of the most deplorable vanity I ever witnessed. It is distressing to apply harsh terms to the character of one who was an early friend, but so much obstinacy, such unconscious want of candour, such self-sufficiency, and such a cold-blooded sneer, as he now invests himself with, I never met with.[62]

It was these early encounters with unbelief that strongly influenced Pusey in his resolve to study the subject at universities where conflicts between faith and rationalism had long existed. Charles Lloyd initially encouraged Pusey to visit Germany, but his experience with Julian Hibbert assisted him to welcome the idea. 'If any country more than another acted the part of an intellectual battery, administering through the works of its foremost thinkers a series of shocks to mere traditional convictions and stagnant methods of ratiocination, that country was Germany'.[63] The effect on Pusey's intellectual development of his decision to visit Germany was, therefore, likely to be great.

2
PUSEY IN GERMANY

1. A pioneer

Edward Pusey's first visit to Germany lasted from June to October 1825. When questioned as to his motives for such a journey, he declared that he was neither in search of a particular book, nor bent on studying a certain aspect of theology. He wrote

> I hope to derive great assistance from the German Literature in all the critical and scientific parts of Divinity; and particularly, if I am ever enabled to write anything on the Evidences, there are some of their works, such as the untranslated part of Less[1], etc. which I should wish first to study.[2]

In this Pusey was encouraged by Charles Lloyd, who was especially keen for him to become acquainted with German Biblical Criticism. In Oxford at this time a profound ignorance, indeed, existed about the German language; Dr Cardwell, the principal of St Alban Hall and Mr Mill of Magdalen being reputed to be the only two persons familiar with it. An even deeper want of knowledge existed in the Church of England concerning the state of theology on the continent; a dearth caused partly by the manner in which Anglicanism had developed from the time of the Reformation onwards.

Whilst the Elizabethan settlement allowed more room in the Church of England for the traditionally minded than was usual among Protestant bodies, apart from the Lutheran Church, so the growth of scholarship in patristics and the history of the Early Church in the late sixteenth century fostered a conservative and distinctly Anglican element, unknown on the continent. From 1640 onwards, political circumstances increased this tendency to such an extent that the High Church tradition, at least, was conceived as one that did not include Calvinism.[3] (To such as Pusey, who claimed to be High Church, Anglicanism as eventually taught him by Newman meant the teaching handed down through Hooker, Laud, Thorndike, Bull and Jeremy Taylor, rather than through Whittaker, Davenant, Hall and Baxter.) At the same time, differences between Anglican and continental thought were further increased over the questions of justification and the value of episcopacy; Anglican writers were less keen to employ the old decisive language of *sola fide*, and their regard for the episcopate was stronger than that felt by all reformed bodies, including those Lutherans prepared to consider the adoption of episcopal orders as a means of promoting reunion.[4] The advent of the Enlightenment widened the gap between Anglican and continental thinkers still more. By 1800, certainly High Churchmen saw little in common between their Protestantism and that of Geneva or Wittenberg, but isolation from the continent was a general feature throughout the Church of England between 1650 and 1850.[5] In 1831 this state of affairs was bitterly commented on by a contributor to the *Edinburgh Review*.

> It is, we think, high time for the well-paid champions of Orthodoxy in this country, to awake from the dignified slumbers in which it is their delight to indulge, and to take some notice of those incursions into their sacred territory, which the theologians of Germany have been so long permitted, without any repulse to make.[6]

He also contrasted 'the poor, active, studious and inquisitive theologians of Germany' with 'the sleek, somnolent, and satisfied divines of the Church of England'.[7] In these opinions he was not alone, for H.P. Liddon also considered at least the 1820s as a time when Englishmen, conversant with German politics and literature, were painfully ignorant of the state of German Protestant theology.[8]

Only a handful of scholars before Pusey ever attempted to explain what was happening in Germany, and their work was either ignored or viewed suspiciously in England. As early as 1793, Herbert Marsh, Fellow of St John's College, Cambridge and later Bishop of Peterborough, had translated from the German J.D. Michaelis' *Introduction to the New Testament*. Marsh seems to have recognized that Michaelis (1717–1791) was a pioneer in critical biblical studies, and in his Preface Marsh claimed Germany to be the most distinguished in Europe for theological learning.[9] He nevertheless laboured largely in vain to point out to his countrymen the value of Michaelis' examination of the title, authenticity, inspiration and language of the New Testament; the *Edinburgh Review* remarking acidly how his efforts brought forth no response from orthodox Anglican theologians.[10]

Hand in hand with ignorance went suspicion. In 1825, in an attempt to familiarize English theologians with German methods of biblical exegesis, Connop Thirlwall published his translation of F.E.D. Schleiermacher's *Essay on the Gospels of St Luke*. For this however, he was marked down as 'unsound'; Lord Melbourne referring the work in 1837 to the Bishops of Ely and Chichester who 'expressed a want of confidence in its orthodoxy'.[11] In his Introduction to Schleiermacher's *Essay*, Thirlwall had spoken strongly of the prevailing atmosphere at Oxford in regard to German theology.

> It would almost seem as if at Oxford the knowledge of German subjected a divine to the same suspicion of heterodoxy which we know was attached some centuries back to the knowledge of Greek; as if it was thought there that a German theologian is dangerous enough when he writes in Latin, but that when he argues in his own language there can be no escaping his venom.[12]

Apart from Marsh and Thirlwall, English divines were not inclined to study German theology and only warnings against it had been heard. Bishop Jebb of Limerick (appointed 1822) had mentioned it in his Primary Charge, and Dr Pye Smith, a Nonconformist, had counselled Englishmen against it in his *Scripture Testimony to the Messiah*. In 1827 Dr D.G. Wait was to translate and write a Preface to J.L. Hug's *Introduction to Writings of the New Testament*, but largely because he considered Hug to be a conservative thinker. By 1830 Dr S. Lee, Professor of Arabic at Cambridge, had also written a dissertation on *The Reasonableness of the Orthodox Views of Christianity, as opposed to the Rationalism of Germany.* The *Edinburgh Review*, however, whilst praising Lee's learning, suggested that he would have made a sorry figure in the hands of the theologians of Halle.[13]

Until the 1850s, indeed, such matters as inevitably came to light with the rise of higher criticism were left largely in the hands of German theologians. In visiting Germany in 1825 in order to study the language and theology, Pusey was therefore very much a pioneer, and, as was the case with Julius Hare and S.T. Coleridge, his outlook underwent profound modifications as a result.

2. The impact of the 'higher critics'

Perhaps the first impression that Pusey received of German university life was one of astonishment. Whereas at Oxford in the early nineteenth century there were only two Professors of Divinity with their deputies, by comparison the sheer quantity of professional theologians in Germany was remarkable. As late as 1877 Pusey was endeavouring to bring this state of affairs to the notice of his contemporaries and pointing out that, after he had carefully studied the figures, he had discovered that among the German universities one had fourteen teachers in Divinity, another thirteen, another twelve, two had ten, five had nine, three had eight and only two had six.[14]

Even as early as 1820 the contrast in the constitutions of German and English universities had been brought to public notice by Thomas Hodgskin. Questioning the long considered superiority of Oxford and Cambridge, he attacked them as corporate bodies, regulated by laws of their own, and for possessing chartered privileges and endowments. He also compared them unfavourably with Göttingen, whose corporate revenue was the equivalent of the income of four heads of houses in England, and where 'there is no warm and well-lined stall of orthodoxy, and no means are taken to influence the students' conscience through their stomach'.[15]

The English system nevertheless had its defenders. The *Quarterly Review* was of the opinion that the German universities failed precisely because they lacked the college system, were poor in endowments and were reliant upon professorial instruction.[16] Fear of scepticism led certain individuals, such as Samuel Parr, William Wilberforce and Reginald Heber, to oppose the introduction of foreign methods of teaching.[17] It was only in later life, however, that Pusey fully shared these opinions. In 1825 he was more concerned to benefit from his studies under the 'higher critics'.

On his arrival at Göttingen Pusey first began attending the lectures of D.J. Pott on the Synoptic Gospels and the content of Jewish ideas found in the New Testament. Pott was then sixty-five and had been a Professor of theology since 1810. The feature of his teaching which most impressed itself on Pusey and which in a similar way he had encountered in the writings of Gottfried Less, was the naturalistic explanation given to the early miracles of Christ. Much of Pusey's concern for miracles at this stage was due to Newman's preoccupation with the subject;[18] in conducting research into various German theologians' ideas on the question of post-apostolic miracles on behalf of his friend, Pusey's own views began to alter. Now able to read Gottfried Less in the original German, Pusey reported to Newman how Less supposed miracles to have ceased with the immediate successors of the Apostles, because they alone were able to communicate the necessary power, and because 'not one of the one thousand of miracles seems to have an adequate end'.[19] Pusey at least was almost convinced from his reading of Less and Michaelis that the fire at the Temple of Jerusalem was a natural occurrence.[20] He was also eager to relate to Newman how these same authors, when dealing with the resurrection, 'both deplore the use of the word "appearance" applied to our Saviour shewing

Himself to His disciples, as giving a faulty idea of His then body, of the length of His stay with them ... giving an unnatural air to the narration and contrary in many places to the Greek'.[21] How much then Newman's *Essay on Miracles* (1826), with its sharp divisions into scriptural miracles, which were to be received, and the so-called ecclesiastical miracles, which were to be rejected[22], was indebted to Pusey's discoveries in Germany is open to conjecture.

The Göttingen professor who did most to stimulate Pusey's outlook, however, was undoubtedly J.G. Eichhorn. At the time of Pusey's visit Eichhorn was seventy-three, having been a professor since 1788 and one of the first commentators to compare biblical books with other Semitic writings. He had also been among the earliest of the higher critics to appreciate the separation of Genesis into 'Jehovist' and 'Elohist' elements and the importance of distinguishing the priestly law in Exodus, Leviticus and Numbers from the popular code in Deuteronomy.

Whilst being impressed by Eichhorn's zest, insight and the vast quantity and range of his literary output, Pusey was shocked by the professor's profanity and preference for reducing religious questions to problems of literary and critical analysis; a common and weak point in much of subsequent German scholarship. A few years later Pusey was of the opinion that

> The persuit of novelty, to the comparative disregard of truth ... was the besetting temptation of this (Eichhorn's) original and elegant but ill-regulated mind.[23]

His immediate reaction to the impact of the higher critics as a whole was one of fear for England, once German ideas had begun to cross the channel.

> I can remember the room in Göttingen in which I was sitting when the real condition of religious thought in Germany flashed upon me. 'This will all come upon us in England; and how utterly unprepared for it we are!' From

> that time I determined to devote myself more earnestly to the Old Testament, as the field in which Rationalism seemed to be most successful.[24]

What in fact Pusey had awoken to was that for many Christian thinkers in Germany, dogmatic attachment to the Bible or to the letter of old confessions had become increasingly difficult. Eichhorn and Pott were part of a process which sprang most immediately from the earlier investigations of Lessing and Semler; the leading influences in German Protestantism in the second half of the eighteenth century, who opened the gates to Rationalism on a scale unthought of in England.[25] Not all German critics, as Pusey struggled later to point out, had been destructive. Many of them, including Eichhorn's teachers, J.A. Ernesti and J.D. Michaelis, either genuinely considered they were doing Christianity a service by openly facing philological and historical contradictions in the Bible, or were unaware that they were setting fuses in the form of daring ideas, which only later generations would ignite.[26] Such men were not in the same category as J.S. Semler, who denied the equality in value of the Old and New Testament, rejected the Divine authority of the accepted Canon, questioned the accuracy of the text and revived doubts concerning the authorship of the various books[27], or G.E. Lessing, who published passages from Samuel Reimarus' posthumous and controversial *Fragmente eines Ungenannten*.[28] Nevertheless, theologically radical notions were widespread.

Much of the confusion for any observer of the German scene, such as Pusey, was due to the lack of distinction or division in the field of scholarship between the different disciplines. German professors were often not specialists in one or two subjects only, such as biblical theology, dogmatic theology, church history or philosophy, but authorities in several. As early as 1787, J.P. Gabler had called for the confinement of scholarship into separate departments, but theologians like W.M.L. de Wette in the nineteenth century continued to produce such multifarious works as an outline of Protestant theology and Christian ethics, an edition of the letters and papers of Luther, and a critical portrayal of the religious teaching of Hebraism, Judaism and early Christianity. Others, such as Ewald, Eichhorn's pupil and Pusey's friend, wrote a full scale history of Israel, a Hebrew Grammar and seven books on the New Testament. It was, therefore, inevitable, that such diversity of approach to theological issues would lead to a variety of conclusions being drawn from the same evidence; a state of affairs which only increased English suspicion. The penetration of theology by and its subjection to different individuals' philosophies were matters which Germans themselves found particularly difficult to deny.

Despite this confusion, Pusey was of the opinion that German enquiry into different subjects was 'much more solid than usually among us'.[29] He gave a tentative welcome to the new methods of biblical analysis and appreciated the value of investigating the human element in the composition of the Bible. Understanding the importance of studying the complexities of authorship and of observing the Bible's patchwork of legend, myth, sacred history and poetry, he also learnt the significance of investigating its style, vocabulary and content in comparison with other Semitic writings. Above all, Pusey hoped that he might interpret and mediate to his fellow countrymen ideas which were alarmingly new to them.

In seeking to achieve this aim, however, many of Pusey's own ideas in the 1820s, and particularly on such matters as the meaning of revelation and inspiration, were influenced by what he had discovered in Germany. At times, and although he invariably expressed himself cautiously, there is evidence that he appreciated that the work of the higher critics was not simply destructive. He seems to have been aware, as Lessing believed, that there was some value in regarding revelation not as a static and complete body of dogma, but as a means whereby God progressively educates the human race. By widening the terms of revelation and inspiration, the German theologians had been enabled to distinguish between what they considered was God's teaching and the texts that simply recorded it.[30] Certainly Pusey shared early on the critics' opinion that inconsistencies in Scripture did not destroy the validity of the message it contained:

> Revelation was and must be *progressive*; there were many things Christ told his disciples, which they *then* could not bear; it was when the Spirit of Truth came that they were to be guided into *all* truth; Christ, as if to show that His teaching was not the main object of His coming into the world, that He came to be the *Object* of a Revelation, not merely to make one, condescended, as a Teacher, to be Himself only a preparatory Instructor.[31]

Similarly and as to contradictions in Scripture, Pusey considered that 'in *essentials* there are none. By essentials I mean doctrine.' None that he was aware of affected, in the sense of diminishing the sacredness, inspiration, authority or credibility of Scripture. He stoutly maintained that 'the object of the Holy Spirit' was 'to preserve us such a record as might serve as a foundation for our faith and means of edification, not to inform us of all the incidental minutiae of our Saviour's life'. As to the different doctrines found in each of the Gospels, Pusey asserted that this was intentional on the part of the Holy Spirit, 'in order that as no one human mind could comprehend all in their full extent, we might by the union of all, in each of which something was comparatively omitted, possess all in a fuller extent'.[32]

Acutely aware, however, that his outlook had been affected by his studies in Germany, Pusey also took pains later to reconcile his newly acquired ideas with those most current in England. This was by no means easy for him and, in his exposition of certain texts, he frankly admitted that some would regard him as heterodox.[33] In particular, he confessed:

> I cannot then think that while our Saviour was upon earth, it could have been by any believed that He was 'God manifest in the Flesh'; it seems to me too tremendous to

> have been known, nor then useful: all the passages which bear upon this point, while He was upon earth, I consider as containing nothing more than the germ of the truth, not the truth itself, as preparation for the discovery, not the discovery.[34]

Anxious not to be considered unsound, Pusey endeavoured to minimize his difficulties, suggesting that mistakes in the Gospels were only incidental and related to minute matters of fact. He was especially critical of people who 'choose to meddle with other points, not immediately practical, such as Election, Predestination etc. and support their system with regard to them by Scripture, I see no reason why they should expect satisfaction; and yet it is on abstract points, that most difficulties have arisen'.[35] In less than a year Pusey himself was experiencing trouble in relation to one of these 'abstract points' and endeavouring to clarify his thoughts for Bishop Lloyd's benefit:

> With regard to the procession of the Holy Spirit, I receive the words as they stand in Scripture, but I cannot but think that the speculations even in the Ante-Nicene Church, made a higher mystery of this expression than is in Scripture, in that they considered it as describing some relation (so to speak) of God to Himself, whereas it seemed to me in Scripture only to relate to the Spirit coming, as the common gift to man. I do not think I have in Scripture any ground for defining the nature of the relation of the Holy Spirit to the others of the Blessed Trinity.[36]

Eleven years later Pusey had changed his mind completely, but as yet he was preoccupied with the knowledge he was gaining from higher critics.

3. Schleiermacher and his followers

From Göttingen in 1825 Pusey proceeded to Berlin, the home of F.E.D. Schleiermacher, whose work at the close of the eighteenth century had opened a new era in theology and in the scientific interpretation of religion. His classic works were *Religion, Speeches to its Cultured Despisers* (1799) and *The Christian Faith, systematically set forth according to the principles of the Evangelical Church* (1821).

In his *Speeches* Schleiermacher had shown that he felt that men should be led back to the idea that religion is an experience, not an intellectual process to be analysed; more a matter for living and enjoying than for investigating. He also considered that religion, especially during the Enlightenment, had been misunderstood. For him it was not science, or morality, or the seat of reason or essentially a function of the conscience and will, but the direct touch of the soul with the Divine, and this was centred in 'feeling'.[37]

Schleiermacher's *The Christian Faith* has been reckoned by H.R. Mackintosh as 'Next to the *Institutes* of Calvin . . . the most influential dogmatic work to which evangelical Protestantism can point'.[38] Without it, Mackintosh maintains, modern systematic thought can no more be understood than could biology without Darwin.[39] Certainly Schleiermacher, intent on realizing his aim of discovering the contents of the Christianly pious soul, brought to his study all that was then available in philosophy and psychology, besides traditional theology. Continuing to emphasize the role of 'immediate self-consciousness', he was especially concerned with the feeling of absolute dependence. Other religious feelings have their place, he thought, but this feeling of unconditional or absolute dependence on God is 'the self-identical essence of piety' – the core of religion. Schleiermacher had arrived at this conclusion by considering that man perceives in his experience the antithesis of the multifarious and fluctuating over against a principle of unity and permanency; such contrasts being equivalent to the Absolute and eternal – God – without whom all would be chaos, and the world, without which all would be void. Whilst God, being absolute, is immanent in His world, man is in himself a microcosm, a reflection of the universe. Comparing himself with that which is universal, absolute and eternal, man feels himself finite, limited, temporary and fundamentally dependent. It was for this reason that Schleiermacher could proclaim dependence as the basic feeling of all religion.[40]

Pusey's initial reaction to Schleiermacher's teaching was one of reserve. Whilst he respected Schleiermacher's scholarship and breadth of culture, he found his system difficult to understand, feared that Schleiermacher had a tendency to pantheism, and considered that his view of the Atonement and the Divinity of Christ smacked of Socinianism.[41] Nevertheless, Pusey's overall impression was of a 'great man, who, whatever be the errors of his system, had done more than (some very few perhaps excepted) any other, to the restoration of religious belief in Germany'.[42] At Berlin Pusey attended Schleiermacher's lectures, was received by him in private and corresponded with him on his return to England. In terms of direct influences, however, Pusey was much more affected by the presence of Schleiermacher's disciple, Friedrich Tholuck. Almost of the same age, Pusey and Tholuck had first become aquainted during a visit of the latter to Oxford in the previous year; a relationship which blossomed into deep friendship and which elicited from Pusey the remark that 'with no one were my best hopes for Protestant Germany so bound up as with Tholuck'.[43]

Friedrich Tholuck (1799–1877) is reputed to have been weaned as a young man on pantheism, Islam and scepticism by Baron Ernst von Kottwitz, a Moravian, and in later life to have been powerfully influenced by Johann Neander, a follower of Schleiermacher. Pusey was certainly impressed by Tholuck, and the notes which he made of Tholuck's lectures in 1825 subsequently formed the basis for much of his later *Theology of Germany*. It was possible, therefore, that Pusey derived his fervent admiration of the Pietist Jacob Spener from Tholuck. What Pusey probably did not appreciate, during his visit to Germany, however, was that Tholuck was at that time undergoing a severe trial of his faith.[44] There is no hint of this in any of the letters which Tholuck sent to Pusey well into the 1860s.

Pusey's admiration of both Tholuck and Neander may

have been partly respect for their position as chief representatives of the *Vermittlungs-theologie* – a school of theologians endeavouring to combine traditional Protestantism with modern science, philosophy, and theological scholarship. Pusey's first impression of Neander, indeed, was of 'a divine of very deep piety, comprehensive views, and genuine orthodoxy, one possessed of a thorough knowledge of human nature and of a very extensive and judicious reading'.[45] Much more, however, Pusey was probably taken with the warmth contained in the devotional outlook of these two eminent theologians, which contrasted vividly with the formal and sober religious practices in which he himself had been reared.

Before returning to Oxford, Pusey also met on this first trip Ernst Hengstenberg, the future founder of the *Evangelische Kirchenzeitung* – an organ in which he was to attack the theology of Schleiermacher. At this stage, Hengstenberg was still Pietist in his tendencies, but it came as no surprise to Pusey that he would later attempt to reforge the fetters of verbal inspiration to biblical studies, particularly in regard to prophecy in the Old Testament. As early as 1829 Pusey had feared this was the direction of Hengstenberg's theology and he likened this 'returning to the Theology of the seventeenth century' to the act of 'wilfully throwing away our experiences'.[46]

On arriving back in England in October 1825, Pusey was convinced that he had merely scratched the surface of German language and theology and that he should, therefore, prepare himself for a second visit; a decision which entailed postponing his ordination and the prospect of becoming Newman's assistant at St Clement's. Almost immediately, he set about examining the evidence for the books of the Old Testament, and decided to acquaint himself with as many of the cognate dialects of Hebrew as was possible. It was with these aims in view that he returned to Germany the following year.

4. Studies in theology and Oriental languages

Reaching Berlin in 1826 with the dual purpose of continuing his investigations into higher criticism and mastering not only Hebrew, but also Syriac, Chaldee and Arabic, Pusey was under no illusion as to the immensity of his task. He told Newman:

> In England we have no idea of the time which is usually employed, and which ought to be employed on these languages; Hebrew is here universally commenced at school; probably at fourteen; Arabic frequently a year or two later, at all events at the university; we think twenty two or twenty three a proper time for entering on the study of the language of one portion of our Scriptures and if the rest are learnt at all, they necessarily follow at a still later period.[47]

Nevertheless, the labour which Pusey employed in learning these Oriental languages was enormous even by German standards. In June he studied Syriac and Chaldee under Hengstenberg. Throughout the summer he read Arabic for an average of fourteen to sixteen hours a day under Salomon Munk. From September to November he gave his attention to learning Syriac and Arabic works under the tuition of Kosegarten, especially the writings of the Syriac historian Bar-Hebraeus and the *Life of Saladin* in Arabic. For the remainder of his visit, Pusey worked under Freytag and read the *Life of Timur* and the *Hamasa* in their original languages. Thus, by studying under some of the most distinguished Orientalists of the time, and by pursuing a relentless routine of work, Pusey returned from Germany a year later a Semitic scholar of a very high order; his innate conscientiousness and admiration of German thoroughness having enabled him to fulfil tasks which would have daunted an average person. He was quite certain, however, as to his motive. 'It was worthwhile', he maintained, 'to be an Arabist that perchance something more might be known about the Sacred language, than would otherwise have been possible'.[48] In spite of an illness in February 1827, occasioned by overwork and aggravated by the death of his younger brother, Henry, Pusey persisted in his efforts; his absence from England also relieved him to some extent from the depressions he experienced, when reflecting on his misfortune with relation to Maria Barker.[49] The most that Pusey ever complained of was his distaste for non-Christian literature and the intricate effort involved in his work.

At the same time, Pusey had not forgotten his interest in German theology, and he found time to attend the lectures of Neander on early ecclesiastical history and the later Epistles of St Paul, and those of Schleiermacher on the principles of practical theology and the Epistles to the Thessalonians and Galatians. Pusey seems to have been particularly impressed by his reading of Schleiermacher's *Kurz Darstellung des theologischen Studiums*, which deprecated the introduction of philosophical systems into theology, and which Pusey later described as,

> a work which, with a few great defects is full of important principles and comprehensive views, and which will form a new era in theology whenever the principles which it furnishes for the cultivation of the several theological sciences shall be acted upon.[50]

In addition, Pusey had also been requested by Charles Lloyd to send him information on the *Catechism of Justus Jonas* and the text of the Augsburg Confession, together with opinions of the German Commentators on St Paul. The first two of these tasks Pusey found reasonably easy to perform, but he was at a loss to describe the outlook of German professors; 'Schleiermacher being too independent, and Marheineke too devoted to a modern school of philosophy to enquire about the opinions of others, and the orthodox going back almost exclusively to the Fathers or the Reformers'.[51]

It was clearly useful to Lloyd to have Pusey acting the role of an observer of the German scene. He learnt from Pusey, for example, that 'the state of criticism ... has been turned among the moderns almost exclusively to the Old Testament or the historical books of the New',[52] and he received information from him concerning the authors that German theologians chiefly prized.

Just as important from the point of view of Pusey's own development, however, was his increasing personal contact with the German theologians themselves. Whilst studying under Freytag at Bonn for instance, Pusey formed a deep friendship with the professor's 'famulus', Heinrich Ewald; a relationship which in later life was to become strained. At the time of Pusey's visit, Ewald was preparing to publish his *Hebrew Grammar*, which was to be a landmark in the history of Old Testament philology, and later he was to produce his even more influential *Geschichte des Volkes Israel*, which revealed in the Old Testament a line of historic development hitherto unappreciated. It is rather ironic, therefore, that, during this visit to Germany, Pusey was especially anxious to resolve certain doubts he had in regard to the genuineness of the whole of the Book of Daniel. It was precisely on this matter that in 1864 Pusey and Ewald were to disagree for, by then, Pusey had become thoroughly conservative in his theological outlook.

Equally as significant as his friendship with Ewald, however, was Pusey's encounter with other leading theologians in Bonn, most of whom were disciples and exponents of the theology of Schleiermacher. It is remarkable how Pusey in Germany almost invariably gravitated towards the followers of Schleiermacher. In Bonn, for example, he became acquainted with Augusti, the future authority on liturgical antiquities and Gieseler, the Church historian, but he was most intimate with Nitzsch, Sack and Lücke – the chief propagators at the university of Schleiermacher's views.

5. Revision of the Old Testament

Pusey arrived back in England from his second visit to Germany in July 1827, and, as though anxious to prove how much his mind had been stimulated by intercourse with German theologians and linguists, he announced almost immediately his intention to embark on a revision of the Authorized Version of the Old Testament. In this task he was encouraged by Charles Lloyd, cheered on by his friend Jelf and found a willing helper in Maria Barker. Pusey stated his aims:

> My object is not a new translation but, retaining the old as far as possible, to correct it, wherever it appears to me to have mistaken the original, or wherever . . . it has left the meaning obscure. I purpose . . . using . . . all the aids which I can find for the better understanding of the Old Testament, and contributing what I can myself from my knowledge of the Eastern languages allied to Hebrew.[53]

At the end of four months from his return, Pusey had progressed to the extent of having corrected Job, the Psalms, the Minor Prophets (with the exception of certain parts of Hosea), and the first forty-two chapters of Isaiah. By that time, however, he had also awoken to the need for caution and was showing an awareness that 'There are many who dread all change, many who idolize our present translation, many who think a new translation will unsettle men's minds, many who in their principles of translation differ from mine'.[54] Two months later Pusey was confident of being within five months of the completion of his revision; a time when he said he would be willing to commit his 'bark to the winds and the waves . . . Of the more difficult books of the Bible, Ezekiel and Zechariah will alone remain untouched'.[55] It was at this point, however, that he laid aside his revision for the more urgent purpose of writing his *Theology of Germany*, and within a few years Pusey was bitterly regretting ever having considered correcting the Bible.[56]

Whatever the intrinsic value of Pusey's revision of the Old Testament, his refusal to resume his labours in this field ever again was symptomatic of the intellectual revolution he was to undergo in the early 1830s. Above all, Pusey was acutely aware how easily his views might be misinterpreted in England. 'No one', he was shortly to write, 'would willingly remain an object of suspicion; nor, especially in a period of some anxiety for the temporal welfare of our Church, be unduly supposed to hold opinions injurious to her well-being'.[57] Before the publication of his *Theology of Germany*,

John Keble, engraving by Samuel Cousins from the painting by George Richmond, 1845

J H Newman, engraving by R Woodman, circa 1843

Maria Pusey 1828,
wife of E B Pusey

Philip Edward Pusey 1840,
only son of E B Pusey

Lucy and Mary Pusey 1841,
two of Pusey's daughters

he was especially afraid that he would be misunderstood by the English critics.

> I have in fact been 'unlike other people' in my language as in everything else . . . I do not expect very merciful handling from Reviews. The sentiments scattered up and down will fare still worse than the style; and I expect to be thought one third mystic, one third sceptic and one third (which will be thought the worst imputation of all) a Methodist, though I am none of the three.[58]

In the event, the generally hostile reception accorded to Pusey's first publication confirmed all his worst suspicions; he expressed the fear that he entertained little hope of ever wholly effacing the charges made against him.[59]

The distrust that surrounded Pusey in 1828 coincided with a series of significant events in his personal life and, very soon after, in the life of the nation as a whole; none of which would have served as an incentive to continue blazing a trail in biblical scholarship, and, indeed, would rather have deterred Pusey. In April 1828 Pusey suffered a severe shock by the death of his father and just over a year later Pusey's mentor, Charles Lloyd, also died. By now Pusey had assumed the responsible position of Professor of Hebrew in the University and Canon of Christ Church. All of these happenings, together with his own marriage, would only have further deepened Pusey's innate seriousness and prevented him from assuming the role of an innovator in theology. The political situation and widespread talk of Church reform at least led Pusey to modify his former politically liberal outlook, and the subsequent influence on his intellectual development of Keble and Newman, who laid particular stress in biblical studies on typology and allegorical exegesis, probably further arrested the tendencies to which Pusey had been prone on his return from Germany.

Pusey's general change in outlook rendered him a 'painful enigma' to Connop Thirlwall.[60] The *Quarterly Review* suggested that Pusey's adherence to the Oxford Movement was part of his plan for combating the forces of biblical criticism which he knew one day would reach England. He was reported to have described his later work as an attempt to construct 'an impregnable fortress, which the desultory assaults of criticism could neither shake nor scale'.[61] Nevertheless, whatever the immense service Pusey performed by bringing to public notice the teaching of the Fathers and Anglican Divines, and valuable to the Church of England as was Tractarian emphasis on Authority, the *Quarterly Review* also appreciated that the questions posed by German scholarship had to be answered. In the event, and in spite of his early knowledge of German theology, it was not Pusey that responded to the German challenge in a positive manner, but the Cambridge school of Lightfoot, Westcott and Hort.[62] By 1864 Pusey had so altered his views that his only answer to *Essays and Reviews* was to publish his monumentally conservative *Lectures on Daniel the Prophet.* His fears also communicated themselves to H.P. Liddon, who was particularly upset in 1889 when he considered that Charles Gore's contribution to *Lux Mundi* accepted some of the views of biblical higher critics.[63] Shortly before his death, Pusey had come to adopt precisely the views on biblical scholarship which he had feared would greet his own Revision in 1828. Concerning the proposed publication of the Revised Version of the Bible in 1881, Pusey termed it a 'product of vanity'. He thought the changes in the New Testament would promote a general unsettlement of English religion, and alterations to the Old Testament would be equally productive of evil.

These were not his thoughts in the years immediately following his return from Germany. Until he actually joined the Oxford Movement in 1834, Pusey did not publicly deny his indebtedness in early years to German theology. Initially he was merely concerned to maintain the orthodox nature of his views and at the same time applaud certain of the efforts of his German friends. It was the combined pressure of personal events, and gradual disillusionment with the direction that national affairs were taking, that eventually compelled Pusey to eschew much of what he had learnt on the continent.

3
ENGAGEMENT AND MARRIAGE

1. H.P. Liddon's silence concerning Maria Barker

In September 1827, two months after Pusey had returned from his second visit to Germany, his parents finally agreed to his engagement to Maria Barker. Pusey was then aged twenty-seven and Maria was a year younger. He described his first visit to Maria as 'the melting of the ice after a Northern Winter'[1], but his pleasure was slightly marred soon after, when his health broke down, and he was compelled to spend the next four months recuperating at Brighton. It was there that Pusey began his Revision of the Old Testament and wrote the first part of his *Enquiry* into the theology of Germany.

For posterity's sake at least, Pusey's illness was a fortunate occurrence; it was then that he and Maria indulged in a lengthy correspondence, and these letters of 1827 to 1828 reveal the young Pusey's mind more than any other documents of the period. Such is the importance of these manuscripts, indeed, that H.P. Liddon based almost the whole of Chapter VI of his *Life of E.B. Pusey* on them. Remarkable, however, was the bias with which Liddon selected the excerpts he quotes and the fact that, of those he chose, none are from Maria's letters. All Liddon's quotations from this particular correspondence are from Pusey's letters, and we are thus prevented from seeing any inter-change and cross-fertilization of ideas, and from determining the nature of the influence that Maria exercised on Pusey. Liddon's methods here are in striking contrast with his usual procedure of quoting copiously from Pusey's correspondents.

Not until Liddon is referring to events which occurred late in 1835 and when he has reached page 86 of his second volume, does he venture to include an excerpt from any letter of Maria's. In view of the depth of Pusey's love for Maria, the effect on his character of the previous six years' ban on their attachment, and the grief into which he was thrown by her death in 1839, Liddon tells us very little indeed of Maria – the one human being who entered into Pusey's life and thoughts the most. Liddon's veil of silence was probably deliberate; had he not been so reticent, he would doubtless have inflicted pain on various of Pusey's relatives still living, such as his brother, William, and his daughter, Mary. Much more, however, it is likely that Maria's character and behaviour either did not accord with those that Liddon considered were expected of a wife of a Canon of Christ Church and Professor of Hebrew, or else he was puzzled by her. The only direct intimations we have of Liddon's uneasiness concerning Maria, are found in the qualified remarks he inserts in his one description of her in her early years.

> Besides the attraction of her good looks, she was undoubtedly accomplished; while her character, although as yet very unformed, combined, with elements of impulsiveness and self-will, qualities of very rare beauty, which Pusey believed himself to have discerned from the first and instinctively.[2]

Unfortunately, as a result of Liddon's almost total silence or verbal dexterity when compelled to mention Maria, we have been led to receive a distorted picture of Pusey in the years 1827 to 1839. Liddon was clearly happier when dealing with Maria in later life, but even then he was not objective. He tells us that 'the growth of her character during the eleven years of her married life was a remarkable testimony to the strength and nature of her husband's influence'.[3] He lists some of the results of her 'growth' in character[4], but he does not explain the methods whereby Pusey wrought such a change. Even from the correspondence of Pusey and Maria in the years 1835–1839, Liddon chose for quotation only excerpts from Maria's letters which dealt with specifically religious subjects.

There is little doubt that Maria did experience a change, if not growth, in her personality during the years of her marriage, and for this Pusey was largely responsible. A difference in her outlook was particularly apparent in her letters of the last four years of her life, and some of it was probably due to the increasing ill-health of herself and of her three children. It is equally certain from Pusey's letters to Maria of this time, that, from 1835 onwards, Pusey employed questionable means of fostering the change in Maria. Liddon, however, says nothing of these and we are thus prevented from knowing that, in a sense, the alteration in Maria was only an intimation of a revolution which was taking place in Pusey himself. Pusey's gloom and austerities did not commence, but only increased in 1839 on Maria's death; they had begun in 1835. In that year a second 'Northern winter' set in for Pusey, but this time it was of his own making. The tragedy was that he inflicted it not only on himself, but on Maria and the children. Had Liddon so chosen, he could have shown from Pusey's correspondence with Maria, how Pusey developed into what R.W. Church has described as 'a venerated and rather awful person, from his position not mixing in the easy intercourse of common-room life, but to be consulted on emergencies'.[5]

When beginning Pusey's biography, however, Liddon had made extensive use of the unpublished 'Narrative' of Pusey's niece, Mrs Clara Fletcher. In this he would have learned that Mrs Fletcher was reluctant to discuss Maria. She confessed:

> I cannot touch on so sacred a subject as the peculiarities of his [Pusey's] wife on paper – though I feel you ought to know them (if indeed you do not already) because they illustrate some phases of his perfect character and some otherwise rather inexplicable events connected with the past.[6]

From a conversation he had with Cardinal Newman in 1883, Liddon also learned that Newman too remembered Maria's eccentricities:

> She was a tall, handsome person. Before her marriage she had no interest in religion, but she must always have had

> qualities of goodness . . . which only required to be drawn out by Grace. She was however at first, after their marriage, very odd, and I did not like to go to the house. Her oddities were the talk of Oxford. Whately, who was a rough, noisy talker, was open-mouthed about it. She underwent a great change, and I loved her exceedingly in her later life.[7]

Whereas Newman was perhaps unaware of the methods by which Pusey had brought about the change in Maria, Liddon was not. To have written of Maria's 'peculiarities' and 'oddities', however, would have involved Liddon in revealing similar or connected failings in Pusey, and this he could not do. Liddon's suppression of these features in Pusey's relationship with Maria, which are crucial to an understanding of his intellectual development, render Owen Chadwick's comment on Liddon's work only too true. 'It was tragic that his [Pusey's] biography should have been entrusted to the obvious author, the most intimate of his immediate disciples, H.P. Liddon.'[8] If one turns to the letters of Pusey and Maria in the years 1827 to 1839, the picture of Pusey that emerges is different from that which Liddon gave us, though it loses none of its stature.

2. Pusey and Maria in private

Maria Catherine Barker was the youngest child of John Raymond Barker of Fairford Park in Gloucestershire, and only after he had died was she free to accept Pusey's offer of marriage. Very little is known concerning the physical appearance of Maria, but her forceful and uninhibited letters to Pusey reveal that she possessed a particularly strong personality. A friend of hers once remarked that, had she been blind, she would have pictured Maria as 'a large, strong masculine looking, ruddy, athletic person'[9] and a cousin spoke of her as 'better fitted to attack the oppressor than comfort the oppressed'.[10] By contrast, and as reported by Pusey's niece, her uncle possessed in his make-up 'the gentleness of a woman'. Inevitably, therefore, such a variance in temperament sometimes led to strong differences of outlook between Pusey and Maria in their early years together, but Pusey was utterly convinced that 'we agreed in principles, though we appeared in stating our opinions to differ'.[11] R.W. Jelf, Pusey's closest friend in the 1820s, at least rejoiced in what he termed Maria's 'despotism' and dominance over Pusey at this stage, since he thought of Pusey as 'a child, quite unfit to be trusted with the management of his own health'; he nevertheless begged Maria to 'let the rod, with which you rule him, be invisible or clad in velvet'.[12]

It is quite clear, however, that during their courtship Pusey revelled in Maria's passionate enthusiasms and ungovernable emotions. He compared her to Kate in *The Taming of the Shrew* and his efforts to withstand her demands as a 'Falstaff-like shrew of resistance'.[13] Very quickly he became accustomed to her outbursts of rage and such occasions as, when she remarked that, her fingers had a strong tendency to turn into 'tiger's claws'.[14] Relations between Maria and her mother were frequently strained, owing to what Maria described as her mother's plausible nature and her knowledge of how to 'administer small doses of flattery where they will be acceptable'.[15] Pusey spilt a great deal of ink reminding Maria of the need to honour parents, but it is doubtful whether his words had much effect. Certainly Maria's behaviour in society remained unchecked; she continued to be remarkably outspoken, critical of her mother's friends, and indifferent to the impression she gave, 'not being . . . at all solicitous', she said, 'for the favourable opinions of persons I never care to see again, can always talk nonsense to anyone, and moreover can always lead people to talk of that most interesting person *themselves*'.[16]

Happily, Pusey and Maria Barker shared a common political outlook, both despising the ultra-Tories, applauding the Greek war of independence, favouring the Repeal of the Test and Corporations Act and following the efforts to introduce Catholic Emancipation. On the one hand, Maria declared her detestation of the Duke of Wellington, 'so accustomed as he is to the arbitrariness of military discipline his every feeling and idea must be in favour of despotism'[17], and on the other, Pusey poured scorn on the party he led:

> The country is except in a time of excitation or distress naturally Tory, and it is perhaps as well that persons who cannot think for themselves should acquiesce in others thinking for them, if our Tories did but think! or rather if one were but not quite certain beforehand that the result at which they arrive by thinking, is the very same with which they set out.[18]

Allied to Maria's robust opinions was her Romantic interest in heroes. After reading J.F. Cooper's three volumed novel, *Red Rover*, she developed an infatuation for all things to do with the navy, describing it as a profession, 'which as an English woman I have a right to glory in', and delighting in 'the coolness in the hour of danger which is so beautiful and so general among our naval heroes'.[19] Skill in fighting won Maria's particular admiration; she was keenly interested in the activities of George Washington, Körner, Joan of Arc, Edward the First and Robert Bruce.

Pusey tried desperately hard to show a similar enthusiasm for Maria's hobbies. He made the gallant effort of reading *Red Rover*, insisted that he shared her preference for the naval way of life over all others save his own, reported that he had enjoyed Southey's life of Nelson, and sent her descriptions of ships to be seen off Brighton, but clearly his thoughts were not always in tune with those of his fiancée and he began making the first attempt to re-direct her outlook to more serious concerns. Until they were actually married, however, Maria was able to resist Pusey's tendency to moralize and to chide him with being 'formidable', 'gloomy', 'grave' and 'stuffy'.[20] Only when she was eventually convinced that Pusey indeed understood her, or as she told him, 'You were the first person I ever knew, to whom I fancied myself not incomprehensible'[21], did Pusey's efforts to eradicate, what he called, each 'deficiency' in her nature succeed. Ultimately Maria was to become a sad parody of Pusey himself, especially as she lacked his natural intellectual and devotional bent, but at least she could not have doubted his emotional dependence on her.

It is perfectly clear that Pusey was fascinated by Maria, especially when he recalled how for many years he had been merely 'a reading automaton'[22], and how he had previously been so depressed that, 'from the autumn of 1822, till September 1827, I never ventured to open a book of poetry or to enter any scenery in which there was any chance of excitement'.[23] At times he found it difficult to express the depth of his feelings and felt obliged to tell Maria that, if only he had 'a window' in his breast, she might read 'what else you can never know, how deeply, fervently grateful and obliged is your Edward'.[24] After seeing her briefly in London he was similarly overcome:

> My visit to London has been to me . . . one long, or rather short day; you were the centre round which every part of it (as indeed of so much of my existence) turned, and every interval was but as the divisions of a many sided figure in rapid motion, in which all the distinctions of the several parts are lost in the whirl. Now that the motion has somewhat relaxed . . . It leaves me convinced that whatever defects one so softly, beautifully, gently kind may discover in me, she will still look as favourably upon them, and that we shall go on hand in hand, alternately perhaps assisting, reminding, comforting each other until the time come, when both shall be translated to the presence of a pure and holy God. Everything shews me more and more how great a treasure God has given me in you . . .[25]

Not only were there occasions when 'everything appears so inadequate, and one's heart often swells so much as to choke utterance'[26], but Pusey also had a premonition of what would be his reaction should he lose Maria.

> I cannot picture to myself what would be my condition without you: it seems as if it would be a long, long time

> before I could then so sanctify memory as to dwell solely, as I do generally in the present case – I will not go on, for you will think it, as it indeed is, horrible; but kind as you are, beyond all human kindness to me, and deeply as I love you, we must not become so necessary to each other, as to 'sorrow without hope' were the other taken . . . I fear I shall be plunging deeper and deeper, if I continue.[27]

It is not surprising, therefore, that though high-spirited and strong willed, Maria eventually became submissive to Pusey, her emotional anchor; the vacuum in her religious outlook he also succeeded in filling, though it cost her much through the repression of some of her more endearing characteristics. Because Maria needed and enjoyed Pusey's tremendous love, she permitted him in time to indoctrinate her with his views on religion, including his more obsessional ones.

3. Maria's conversion

Until comparatively recently, it has frequently been suggested that the loss of faith in Christianity, so evident in the lives of such eminent Victorians as Francis Newman and James A. Froude, owed its origins to the discoveries in geology and biology and to the advent in England of 'higher criticism' in biblical studies. It is now evident, however, that the decline in orthodoxy was produced in the first instance more by a fundamental conflict between such cherished beliefs as Original Sin, Reprobation, Baptismal Regeneration, Vicarious Atonement and Eternal Punishment (all of which might be considered 'salvationist' ideas) and the increasing tendency of the age to regard the life of man on earth as capable of steady improvement.[28] The events which followed the publication of Darwin's *Origin of Species* were, in this context, merely the climax to a trend already under way; the scientific theories and facts simply became the weapons used by the growing number of people, who had become dissatisfied with Christianity. In what was probably her first letter to Pusey, Maria Barker made it clear that she was of those who, in the early nineteenth century, were experiencing difficulties in religion; in her case the problem centred on contradictions in Scripture, but did not cease there. She told Pusey:

> Religion has certainly never been to me the source of comfort and serenity which it has to others. I could not but admire the beauty of its precepts and the sublimity of its views, and as far as a trust in a Supreme Being in temporal concerns goes, so far, I have felt its use in calming my mind; but there does appear to me so much uncertainty, if not of contradiciton in Scripture itself, so much more of that contradiction in the opinions of men . . . that I could frequently only find peace of mind, in banishing the subject from my thoughts . . .[29]

She was particularly puzzled why revelation was not 'a clear and distinct annunciation' of God's will, and why, if the Holy Spirit enlightened and directed the minds of everyone who applied for his aid, 'some are apparently misled, and many, unable to obtain fixed opinions, are in danger of running on, in endless mazes'.[30] Having previously encountered unbelief in his brother and in Julian Hibbert, Pusey clearly regarded Maria's outlook on religion as a challenge; his efforts to convert her acutely reveal the nature of his own intellectual outlook at this time.

Pusey was convinced that Maria's doubt had arisen from her 'over-looking the real nature of evidence, and its necessary variations according to the subjects to which it relates'. Basing himself on Butler, he informed her that as soon as one went beyond the bounds of 'pure abstract science', 'one enters upon a different province, and one requires a different guide adapted to the country'.[31]

> this is called *moral evidence*, which differs from mathematical in that it never mounts beyond a very high degree of probability . . . Yet this evidence being founded on *probabilities* alone, it lies in its nature that there would be other . . . against it . . . [but] according to a valuable distinction

of Butler's, an objection against *the thing proved* is very different from an objection against *the mode* of proof.[32]

Pusey then hinted that Maria's mind was of the kind which was habituated 'to dwell on objections rather than on the positive evidence', especially when she may have been in particular moods or have read certain authors who placed too much emphasis on objections to Christianity. (Pusey frequently advised Maria against the dangers of 'Byronism'.) Such was Pusey's concern that he sent Maria a copy of Butler's *Analogy*, telling her that, 'It has done more towards satisfying doubt, and relieving anxiety, than any other human book since the world began. There passes not a year in which some one has not occasion to bless God for it'.[33]

It is fearful to think how near you were to the borders of entire unbelief: your heart (which is the main thing) was a better believer than your intellect, but there is probably scarcely any male mind, which had got as far as you did, and to some of the principles in which you seem to have almost acquiesced, which would have stopped short of abandoning Christianity. Do not distress yourself about this; I mention it as proof of God's mercy to you, and in part to shew the danger of the principles, not to blame; I should not *necessarily* by any means think any man the worse for having been not only on the verge, but within the prison of unbelief . . . The unbeliever is to me the object of deep compassion not of censure.[34]

For some time, however, Maria was able to withstand Pusey's relentless pressure on her to conform and was not averse to challenging his opinions. After reading a few verses of the Epistle to the Romans, she informed Pusey that 'had that Epistle been given to me to read as a mere human production, I should have thought its author was . . . either a fool or an hypocrite, either ignorant of what he was about, or willing to deceive with a shew of understanding what no one else could'.[35]

It is equally clear from Maria's correspondence with Pusey,

that her frequent mention of the Evangelical Close's preaching at Cheltenham was not chiefly out of an interest in religion, much more Maria was angry at the ill-effect of Close's views on a friend of hers. 'How comes it', she asked, 'that he is permitted to disseminate doctrines capable of doing so much harm?'[36] She lamented the fact that her friend ate nothing but the coarsest food, described herself as a great sinner, spent hours on her knees in apparent distress and preferred not to speak to anyone. Describing Close as perhaps 'a useful awakener of the careless, but a *very bad guide* and discomforter of those who are humbly seeking after better things',[37] Pusey struggled hard to inform Maria of the proper role of feelings in religion and said that he would be glad when she would be out of the vicinity of Close. It is ironical that, in later years, both Pusey and Maria at least changed their minds on the value of rigid fasting.

On the whole, indeed, Pusey's religious outlook in years 1827 and 1828 was buoyant and optimistic, even in his didactic letters to Maria and on the subject of sin:

> Sorrow indeed must accompany us until we are finally freed from its parent, sin; yet the 'godly sorrow' which a Christian must daily feel, if he thinks daily upon himself need be no harrassing feeling . . . his sorrow . . . quickens his diligence, his anxiety, and petitions for assistance, but does not make him despond.[38]

Not long afterwards Pusey was informing Maria of the entire absolution which came to the sinner completely penitent.

> . . . the past must be to every Christian a source of sorrow; yet one knows that on repentance the past is forgiven us, that our sins are blotted out in the blood of Christ, that in the sight of God they are pardoned, as though they had never been . . . the sting of the sorrow is removed, its fruits are not or need not be 'uneasiness'.[39]

These views are utterly different from those he was later to enunciate in his 1835 *Tract on Baptism*, with its emphasis on the gravity of post-baptismal sin and rigorous language concerning the 'hard and toilsome way of Repentance', which some critics thought smacked of Novatianism. Until then, Pusey remained largely the character, Edgar Belmore, described in his sister-in-law's novel *Waldegrave* published anonymously in 1829 and which spoke of him as one who 'in the constant search of palliatives for human frailty . . . saw the faults of mankind through a glass which dimmed them, whilst their virtues appeared magnified by the same medium'.

It was also during his courtship of Maria that Pusey first gave expression of his feelings for John Keble, telling Maria that 'I always loved J.K. for his connection with Fairford, but all he has said and done and written makes me esteem him more. There is a moral elevation in his character which I know in no other'.[40] When Pusey stressed the place of reticence in religion he perhaps recalled a similar teaching in *The Christian Year* – a work which he frequently quoted in his letters to Maria. In a similar way, Pusey informed Maria of his fondness for Newman; he wrote to her at length of his friend's composure on the death of his favourite sister, Mary Newman, as evidence of his 'pure Christian faith which thanks God (as N. does thank Him) for whatever He may send'.[41]

Thus it was that in 1828 Pusey was able to write so eloquently of his religion to his fiancée:

> Christianity is not intended to go contrary to, to annihilate our natural feelings but to sanctify them. It is the same spirit working differently in each mind, according to the natural gifts, which have been bestowed on them. As the same life-giving sap in different members of the vegetable world produces different fruits . . . The leaven which was to leaven the whole mass of mankind, recovers all from the corruption and mouldiness to which they were otherwise prone; yet the bread, which is formed, may vary indefinitely, according to the original character of the grain, yet all correspond in the one essential point. It seems to me that it is from the neglect of this observation, that much of the want of charity in judging others, much misconception in

> judging ourselves, (depressing or exalting us unreasonably according to the natural tendency of our minds) much perversion of the Gospel and its preachers has arisen. The view is to me a cheering gladdening view; it makes the prospect around me more comfortable, the greatness of the compass of the Christian scheme for our improvement more immeasurable.[42]

The almost halcyon quality, indeed, which was so much a feature of Pusey's early correspondence and outlook, remained with him throughout the first few years of his married life. Though heavily engaged with his teaching of Hebrew, the writing of part two of his *Enquiry*, and the beginning of his five years' task of completing the catalogue of Arabic Manuscripts in the Bodleian library, Pusey joined Maria in maintaining an arduous social routine of entertaining and exchanging hospitality; they were very much a part of what H.P. Liddon termed 'the old Hebdomadal Oxford'.[43] By 1834, however, and in spite of his marital happiness, Pusey had already given several indications that he was losing some of his earlier optimistic outlook.

4. The years of change

Apart from his personal distress in the late 1820s, chiefly caused by the loss of his father and Bishop Lloyd and the bleak reception afforded to his *Enquiry*, Pusey was soon to be intensely worried about the 1830 Revolutions in Europe. He told his brother:

> Spain and Portugal must very soon follow the example of France: in Italy, even if the S. States remain quiet, which they might do, were there any to overawe them (for they are perfect cowards) there is much seed for future disturbance in Piedmont and the Milanese, who are of a different stamp, are very discontented and have little of religion to control them. Holland seems already divided. Of Germany I should have better hopes, but that I dread something from the natural excitability of their character, and their tendency to act too much upon impulse: . . . A new order of

> things, (whether we or our children shall see the development of it, or whether we, as is more probable, shall only witness its fearful preludes) but a new state of things must, I imagine come . . .[44]

Shortly after this letter Pusey suffered a serious illness, which lasted for five months. Liddon suggests that, from this 'dates . . . a deepened earnestness of character and purpose. It was the moral lever which raised him [Pusey] from the atmosphere of Bonn and Berlin to that of the Oxford of late years'.[45] It is certainly the case that, whilst as late as 1833 Pusey was insisting in his *Cathedral Institutions* that the Church should adapt itself to changing conditions, he had increasingly come to distrust government motives regarding the rights of property owners, and he feared that the whigs under Grey were guilty of ignoring moral issues in their legislation. This was the basic cause of Pusey's change of heart concerning liberalism.

In Pusey's mind the University and the Church were also inextricably bound up together. Thus it was that, when the issue of Subscription (the admittance to the university of dissenters) erupted in Oxford in 1834, he could regard it as a matter of principle. 'We must not be afraid of names', he told Maria. 'The country . . . might justly blame us, if, convinced as we are of the peril of these measures, we did not tell them.'[46] His apparent volte-face in political outlook is not surprising, when one appreciates that his fear of an impending crisis was echoed in the writings and sermons of churchmen in all parties during this time.[47] Six years earlier, Pusey was able to write in jest to Maria 'the love of liberty, whether displayed in Whiggism, Radicalism, Liberalism etc. you *know* means for the most part nothing more, than the love of being one's self free, perhaps with the additional privilege of tyrannizing others'[48], but by 1835 he had come seriously to believe it. At about the same time, Pusey also had the first of several disagreements with his elder brother Philip, to whom he had hitherto given loyal and strenuous political support; their differences at root being occasioned, not by questions concerning the need for Church reform, but whether politicians had the moral right to interfere in ecclesiastical affairs.

Until Pusey, therefore, awoke to the Liberal threat to the Church, he retained his earlier sympathies, his optimism, and even an interest in things not technically religious. In 1835, however, he deliberately narrowed his outlook and, with the appearance of his *Tract on Baptism*, publicly threw in his lot with the Tractarians, particularly with Keble and Newman. Thereafter, Pusey was of the number who openly set themselves to oppose the Liberalism of the 1830s, which bore the aspect of a philosophy of rational enlightenment; its adherents believing firmly in material progress and abhorring the other-worldly aspects of Christian teaching.[49] To such as Pusey, Liberalism became the enemy, not because it favoured improving the condition of England, but because it tended to ignore or denigrate spiritual concerns.

5. Austerity in the family

The tragedy in Pusey's opposition to Liberalism and in the general change which came over his mental attitudes, lies in the effect that it had on Maria and his children; in a sense, they became victims of his personal revolution. It was from 1835 onwards that one can trace the beginnings of Pusey's insistence on seeing everything from a religious standpoint, and which ultimately led him to be viewed as someone who 'was incapable or had made himself incapable, of taking interest in anything that was not directly technically religious, or that was not explicitly connected with religion'.[50] To the same period, one can track down Pusey's almost excessive concern for moralism, which, though initially present in his character, had not previously taken such a rigorous form.[51]

The earliest evidences of Pusey's change in outlook coincided with his urge to contribute money for the building of churches in London. In a letter to his wife, which was redolent not only of religious overtones, benevolence and humility, but also of stern conviction and veiled determination, Pusey was particularly concerned to stress the importance of their similar outlook.

> I trust we shall continue to pray to be more completely like-minded, i.e. 'if in anything we be otherwise minded, God may reveal even this unto us'. I do not mean in this to allude to any special thing; only I should wish that we should be like-minded in all – nor as if you were to come over to me in all things, but that we may be like-minded.[52]

Much as Pusey claimed that he was not thinking epecially in this letter of his wish that they should forgo the bulk of their income on behalf of London churches, it is very clear that this was what he desired. Maria was under no illusion that this was not so, and she informed him that 'I prayed God to lead me aright respecting *your* money wish, and if I am not deceiving myself I prayed about it in Oxford more than once'.[53] In the event Pusey donated £5,000 and persuaded Maria to sell her jewellery for the same purpose; this compelled him to reduce the number of their household servants, to sell their carriage, and to live more stringently.

It was in 1835 that Pusey began expressing real antipathy to frequenting society; once exasperatedly exclaiming 'Eheu! fugaces labuntur anni in dinnering'.[54] In November of the same year he also began fasting seriously for the first time. Whereas for Pusey these increasing austerities were introduced either through inclination or with the highest of motives, they reaped havoc for Maria, who felt impelled to follow his example and force the children to do likewise. As Dr E.R. Williams so rightly said, 'Pusey's moral theology suffers from the drastic limitation that it was developed by a man who believed he had tested it empirically upon himself, without realizing how singular was his anomalous temperament'.[55] It was at this time that Maria developed the first symptoms of the tuberculosis which was to cause her death; the four years from 1835 to 1839 became for her an increasingly arduous battle with disease. Besides this the care and education of the three children, Lucy, Philip and Mary, rested chiefly in her hands, and they too suffered from a wide variety of illnesses and physical disabilities. Nevertheless they all adhered to the strict regime initiated and approved of by Pusey. At first Maria was able to regard this with amusement, but her letters of the last three years of her life are totally devoid of humour. On one occasion at least, when the oldest of the children was only nine, and when Lucy was suffering from an inflammation of the eyes, Philip was thought to be dying and able to move only on crutches, and Mary was having leeches applied to a swollen foot, their restriction in diet to 'plain food' caused a heated argument between Maria (now a firm believer in the value of fasting) and the doctor attending them. A few years previously, and when austerity was first introduced into the family circle, Maria had attempted to explain to a friend the motives behind such action:

> I told her that in these days (you will recognise dear, holy, John [Newman]) of Christian profession, especially in circles where Christian excitement was admired, there was a fearful, a horrible possibility that we might only be Christians in name, that when tried in the hour of active, all endeavouring exertion, we might be found nerveless: that if we would be ready for the hour of fight our armour must be always buckled on: had the subjugation of the body even in indifferent, in innocent matters been useless, the early Christians never would have practised it ... The subjugation of the body was necessary, that I believed it so, as firmly as I believed anything: that the 'soft and silken profession' of the present days are what the devil himself might rejoice in; that religion without habitual self-denial was a mockery – a contradiction in terms.[56]

It is clear that Maria herself had partaken of the revolution which overtook her husband in the early 1830s.

For his part, Pusey also began to regret his former views on the subject of sin and repentance; an attitude which only increased the solemn and depressing side of his own outlook, and the grim atmosphere of the home. He now told Maria:

> One way in which persons commonly and sadly injure

> their repentance is – not of course by referring lightly to the sin itself, but by taking pleasure in some circumstances more or less connected with it . . . as supposing a period of life to have been one of comparative forgetfulness of God, but to have been one of great emotion, or pleasurable feeling or even of human happiness, the forgetfulness of God ought to sadden the whole memory of it, and if a man refers to it, after some time, with regard only to that pleasurableness, he will probably find himself reproved by his conscience, 'Thou shouldest not speak of this so, there was sin mixed up with it'. Thus, with regard to myself, had the ten years during which I loved you before we were one, been years in which I had patiently waited God's will, then I might have had a right to refer to them with joy: as it is, shame ought to mix itself with the joy and thankfulness that God did, notwithstanding, bestowe you on me; and so though one may refer to it with gratitude . . . yet I could not, without doing harm to myself, refer to it without the solemn memory of past sinfulness . . . I think this should be extended further: and that we should never speak buoyantly of anything wherewith sin was more or less connected though distantly, and hence one great danger of speaking of self or one's past life. It violates conscience.[57]

It is probable that these sentiments were at the root of his later thoughts concerning his own utter depravity. It was at this time that Pusey became convinced that the death of his daughter, Katherine, in 1832 was a chastisement for his sins, just as in 1839 he regarded Maria's death in the same light; a sentiment that Keble and Newman did their best to warn Pusey against.

The deliberate narrowing in Pusey's outlook – a policy which was slavishly imitated by Maria – had the unfortunate side-effect of making them censorious of persons and things outside their ardent but restricted field. Whilst Maria, for example, criticized her brother-in-law, William Pusey, for his reluctance to discuss religious and intellectual topics, her husband decided that his 'high-churchism has no root and it is too outward . . . it is in the style of the day, "the Kingdom of God is without you" instead of "within you"'.[58]

Pusey's attitude to things worldly would have been amusing if he had not been in deadly earnest; his disapproval ranged over a variety of things, some frankly absurd, such as his detestation of dress-making as 'being concerned with folly and vanity'[59], and his serious wonder whether railroads were harbingers of evil.[60] The ultimate result, however, of his insistence on, or at least strong encouragement of Maria to follow his highly idealistic path from 1835 onwards, was her reduction to a state of intolerable suffering from religious scruples. Convinced of the extreme gravity of even venial sins, Pusey succeeded not only in troubling his wife, but in making the life of his children a veritable night-mare. He was later to preach:

> The sins of childhood are the images and shadows of the deeper sins of the full-grown being. Some deceit to cover a childish fault, some wrong curiosity, some unchecked feeling of envy or jealousy, some indulged anger, or wrong desire of human praise, or vanity, some preference of self or emulation of others, have been, alas! too often the forerunners of years of deadly sin, or of a wrong aim in all life, of direct evil, or the eating out and cankering of that which was good.[61]

6. Corporal punishment

The manner in which Pusey and his wife brought up their three children, provides us with perhaps the clearest evidence of the serious steps which certain early Victorian families were prepared to take to eradicate 'sinful' tendencies in their young. Compared, however, with the earnest but joyful atmosphere so frequent in such staunch Evangelical circles as those of the Wilberforces and Thorntons, the grim and harsh spirit of the Pusey household further illustrates the harm that can be wrought on others, when religious principles are pursued to fanatical lengths. Even when strongly criticized by his elder brother, Philip, for the excessive discipline which he meted out to his off-spring (in his will Philip forbade his own children to be entrusted to the care of Pusey), Pusey remained adamant. 'Our system', he told Maria, 'if it is worth anything must be contrary to the world's system, and so must cost us something.'[62] What he probably did not appreciate was the effect his 'system' had on the outlook of himself, as well as the psychological ill to his family as a whole.

Besides conducting daily inquisitions with his children as to their behaviour, Pusey pursued an unrelenting campaign of religious instruction and the removal of their childish habits; even at the age of two and a half, Mary was taught to make the most commonplace naughtiness the subject of prayer. The penalties for disobedience in Mary's case as a baby, ranged from being denied food to being tied in a chair for several hours. As a boy of five and a half, Pusey's son, Philip, was not regarded with much favour by his father. 'One thing to be guarded against in him', Pusey told his wife, 'is display and other forms of self'. Mrs W (the housekeeper) however said that she thought his 'truth' increased . . . 'so there is, one may hope, the beginning of order in the chaos of the poor child's mind'.[63] As a remedy for Philip's lack of progress, Pusey was in the habit of beating him with bundles of rods; when he was considered to have improved, an equivalent amount of birches was destroyed by way of reward.

Perhaps the saddest result of Pusey's and Maria's methods of education was the heartless indifference it bred in them towards the physical suffering of children. When Pusey informed his wife on one occasion of the death of a friend's son by drowning at the age of seventeen, he thought this 'how much better far than to have lived in sin'.[64] A year later, when their own son, Philip, was believed to be dying, Maria uttered a similar remark.

> He [Philip] has been very strange and *un-nice* in his conduct lately in one or two respects: his improved strength gives me little pleasure; far, far rather would I see him gradually sinking in body, if he were but more in heart and conduct what I would wish . . .[65]

Nothing quite illustrates, however, the brutality which could go side by side with deep spirituality in Pusey's nature, ever since the revolution in his outlook of 1835, as his neglect to intervene in a family crisis enacted in the last summer before his wife died. At that time Maria and the three children, all of them in a desperately poor state of health, were at Weymouth for the sake of the sea air, whilst Pusey, in spite of his wife's entreaties, (she was now displaying all the symptoms of advanced tuberculosis) obstinately refused to leave Oxford for fear of giving his critics grounds for accusing him of neglecting his university duties.

From 6–16 June, 1838, and afterwards on a minor scale, Maria became obsessional about the behaviour of her daughter, Mary, then aged five and a half and suffering from a distended foot. For her husband's benefit, Maria wrote a detailed account of the trouble, but at no time did he express concern about the treatment being accorded to Mary.

Because Mary obstinately refused to pronounce a certain word during a reading lesson, her mother not only described her as selfish, impatient, extremely passionate, proud and disobedient, but, by way of punishment, had her almost permanently tied to a bed post and resorted to 'whipping' her, sometimes as much as four times a day. On the eleventh day 'Mary yielded about midnight', her mother having caused her hands to be tied together in bed and having spoken to her 'about bad spirits being about her bed when she was naughty'. After this, Maria was of the opinion that Mary's pride 'has, I think, had a thorough humbling'. Ironically, Mary was the only child of Pusey's to survive him.

As far as Pusey's domestic life was concerned, it is a pity that Keble did not become Pusey's spiritual director officially until 1846; he might have been able to prevent Pusey making such heavy demands on Maria and the children. The tragedy of Pusey's marriage lies not in his willingness to foster in himself a new way of life, begining in 1835, but in his reckless encouragement of Maria to follow his example, and in the almost macabre relationship he enjoyed with his children.[66]

Dr Owen Chadwick has repeated the idea that it was the

death of Maria in 1839 which left Pusey a changed man,[67] and this is the natural conclusion one draws from reading H.P. Liddon's official biography, but Maria's death in fact only speeded up a process already established. Pusey himself was very probably one of those persons described by Mohler, upon whom 'God has conferred a spiritual eccentricity', and in whom 'the urge towards the divine, the holy and the eternal is so strong and vital that only a very weak thread ties them to the finite and the temporal'.[68] Because of this, Pusey's austerities and abstinence from earthly pleasures would have occurred to him as a consequence of his chosen way of life. By contrast, however, Maria was simply a devoted, obedient and imitative wife.

4
PUSEY AND THE OXFORD MOVEMENT

1. Relations with Keble and Newman

It cannot be disputed that Pusey's fear for the safety of the Church and University at the hands of the politicians encouraged him to join the Oxford Movement. This apprehension alone, however, is not sufficient to explain his becoming a Tractarian. It came as a shock to some of Pusey's friends when he took his place alongside Keble and Newman. Thomas Arnold, for example, in acknowledging his receipt of Pusey's first tract, entitled *Thoughts on the Benefits of the System of Fasting, enjoined by our Church*, expressed the idea that Pusey was co-operating with a party 'second to none in the tendency of their principles to overthrow the truth of the Gospel'. He admitted that Pusey's tract was free of intolerance, but said that it grieved him to see Pusey connecting himself with the Tractarians. 'The system pursued in Oxford', he suggested, 'seems to be leading to a revival of the Nonjurors, a party far too mischievous and too foolish to be revived with success', but capable of doing harm and of obstructing 'the progress of the Church of Christ'.[1] These sentiments of Arnold foreshadowed the even stronger views he was to exhibit later in *The Edinburgh Review*, when he wrote his article on 'The Oxford Malignants'. Arnold was not, however, the only one to voice concern. Pusey's German friends were also amazed at his adhesion to the Oxford Movement; the Pusey they knew had, they believed, been a man 'stark evangelisch, ganz protestantisch'.[2] Even as late as 1836 Whately endeavoured to separate the outlook of Pusey from that of Newman: Newman he considered 'a real enthusiast' but not Pusey, whom he would be sorry to consider a hypocrite'.[3]

What were the causes, other than mere fright, which emboldened Pusey to ally himself with the writers of the Tracts? Broadly speaking, there were two. On the level of personal, emotional attachment, in the years after 1829 Pusey became more amenable to the friendly influence of Keble and Newman; meanwhile, on the level of intellectual conviction, he became persuaded that the ideas which the Tractarians were propagating were valid. Both of these tendencies, inseparably connected, are indicated in his letters, particularly from 1835 onwards. The qualities which Pusey saw in Newman, and deeply admired, are revealed in a letter which Pusey wrote to his wife.

> He (Newman) has held a steady course, I have not: I studied evidences, when I should have been studying the Bible: I was dazzled with the then rare acquaintance with German theology and over-excited by it: I thought to do great things, and concealed self under the mask of activity: I read; he thought also, and contemplated: I was busy; he tranquil: I, self-indulgent; he, self-denying: I exalted myself: he humbled himself . . .[4]

Pusey's words are not only important as evidence that like so many others he tended to idealize Newman; they also imply that he was not well acquainted with Newman's development up to 1835, which had been neither steady nor in the least tranquil. They are indeed the expressions of a neophyte, for 1835 represents in the life of Pusey a parting from his former ways. Whereas he may have disliked certain Tractarian tendencies, such as the pouring of scorn on the Evangelicals, and therefore requested that his initials be attached to his Tract on fasting to distinguish him from the anonymous majority, the crisis over Subscription forced him to work closely with Newman and to overcome his initial hesitations. By 1835, Pusey was willing to publish a second tract, much more uncompromising in tone than the first, and this change in outlook was also reflected in the more austere nature of his domestic life. The Hampden struggle of the following year, only wedded him more strongly to the Oxford Movement, personified for Pusey in the shapes of Keble and Newman.

The story of the Oxford Movement has been often told. But no one has yet shown or explained the precise manner in which Pusey was influenced by Keble and Newman, nor described the ideas he absorbed after 1835. When Newman remarked that Pusey was to the Oxford Movement all that Rose might have been, he also mentioned significantly, the indispensable addition which Pusey had and Rose (resident elsewhere) lacked; 'the intimate friendship and the familiar daily society of the persons who had commenced it'.[5] Before Pusey the Tractarian can be adequately understood, we must consider his intellectual debt to Keble and Newman.

Pusey began his acquaintance with Keble from his earliest years as a Fellow of Oriel, though Liddon probably exaggerates when he suggests that a strong wish to know Keble had prompted Pusey's candidature in the Oriel election in the first place: at that time Pusey was more concerned to join his friend Jelf. In 1827 though, there is no doubt that Pusey greatly admired Keble's highly moral character and this had encouraged Pusey's devoted reading of *The Christian Year*. Pusey was not alone in being moved by the publication of Keble's poems: Newman suggests that they 'woke up in the hearts of thousands a new music'.[6] Not many works, it has been claimed, influenced more deeply early Victorian intellectuals.[7] Until 1829, however, Keble exerted little or no direct personal influence on Pusey, because Keble had gone out of residence from the college a few months after Pusey's arrival in 1823. Until Bishop Lloyd died in 1829, it was to him that Pusey looked for guidance.

It was in 1823 also, that Pusey had first come to know Newman. But although they became friends they were acutely different in outlook. When Pusey was away in Germany they exchanged letters, and Pusey went to some trouble to procure for Newman volumes of the Fathers unobtainable in England. When it seemed possible that Pusey might become a tutor at Oriel in 1826, it probably pleased Newman to hear that, if appointed, Pusey hoped to interest himself in the moral aspects of the office, for it was by holding such opinions that Keble earlier and Newman later incurred much displeasure.[8] Hawkins, the future Provost, was of the view that a tutor's concern with his pupils did not extend to such lengths. Pusey did not become a tutor, however, and three years elapsed until he drew any closer to Newman.

It was then that there occurred not only the death of Pusey's father, but also that of Bishop Lloyd; events which weighed extremely heavy on the young Pusey and probably caused him, in spite of his political differences from Keble and Newman, to lean more on them for advice. On the publication of his *Enquiry* into the theology of Germany, Pusey had included Keble and Newman among those to whom he sent copies; when it became necessary for him to issue a second part the following year, he was requesting their advice and criticism; from this time onwards, one can witness a steady progression in Pusey's friendship with Keble and Newman. By 1835 Pusey was describing Keble, Newman, and himself as a 'triple cord'.[9] In certain respects, however, Pusey remained utterly distinct in outlook from Keble and Newman, though this has long been obscured by Pusey's disinclination to give voice to differences within the Oxford Movement, and by his frequent, optimistic refusal to accept that such disagreements could not be resolved. Pusey was probably encouraged to conceal divisions within the Oxford Movement by the polemical, faction-ridden ethos of Oxford at that time. Not only did this favour the development of such a movement as Tractarianism, with its emphasis on academic and spiritual values, so utterly opposed to the England of the Reform Bill and the Industrial Revolution[10], but it also fostered all the worst features of small closed communities. It was no accident that R.W. Church recognized similarities between Tractarian Oxford and late medieval Florence.[11] Amid all the jealousies and contests of the years 1834 to 1845 in Oxford, Pusey preferred to remain silent when he differed from his partners in the triumvirate.

One can see how Keble exerted such an influence over Pusey. For him the Oxford Movement represented 'a holy warfare' against three foes – Erastianism, Rationalism and

Nominalism. Throughout his whole life (1792–1866) Keble never departed from the cavalier and non-juring tradition of his home background. His intellectual life was one of calm consistency; impressive continuity. From his earliest years he learnt to conceive of the universe, including its spiritual and intellectual elements, as a whole with God at its centre. Unlike most of his contemporaries, he saw the world not so much as a field of activity as a sphere of relationships. He did not consider it man's mission to transform and act upon the material world, but to be influenced by it. Religion for Keble was the essence of life and the determining factor in all fields of man's life. He detested the separation between religion and philosophy, considering the latter no longer adjusted to the reality of human existence since, with science, it aimed only at attaining useful knowledge as a means to obtain material prosperity. It was for this reason that Keble so strongly opposed what he termed 'the irreverent use of reason' – the tendency

> to treat as profane what may be sacred, though not as yet proved to be so ... To slight Divine mysteries, because we cannot comprehend or explain them ... To forfeit divine grace, because, being unable to trace its workings, we will not be at the trouble to seek it.[12]

As Keble's biographer, Lock, remarked of Keble's outlook –

> Truth was a master to be served, not to be criticized and patronized; it was like the ark which he dreaded to touch with unconsecrated hands.[13]

Keble was not content to advocate what he considered as a return to the original Christian spirit, based on the Bible and Tradition: in company with his brother Tom, he also endeavoured to put his ideas into practice. In time, indeed, there arose within the Oxford Movement a group known as the Bisley Tractarians, who made it their duty to put into pastoral practice the doctrines being disseminated from the university. The key figures in this school were Tom Keble, Isaac Williams and Sir George Prevost, all of whom were conservative theologians however, preferring the Caroline divines to the more radical non-jurors, maintaining their distrust of Rome and attempting to steady the Oxford Movement by the publication of such works as the *Plain Sermons*. To the Bisley Tractarians, the traditions of Bishop Wilson and Bishop Butler were the means of keeping the movement safe, especially when they feared that John Keble was perhaps becoming as radical as Newman in his thinking. Keble's essential contribution to the movement, however, was one of complete contrast to the questing intellectualism of Newman. For the latter, Keble's devotion to Butler's doctrine of probability 'did not go to the root of the difficulty'. It was beautiful and religious, but it did not even profess to be logical.[14] While Newman thought there was an intellectual cowardice in not finding a basis in reason for his beliefs, Keble distrusted any high estimate of the powers of human reason. Keble regarded Truth as a gift obtainable less from ratiocination than from the practice of religion.

The closer that Pusey advanced towards Keble in the years after 1829, the more he became aware of the main-springs of Keble's outlook on life. After receiving his copy of the first part of Pusey's *Enquiry*, Keble centred his main criticism on Pusey's language concerning the inspiration of the historical books of the Bible, and it is clear that Pusey was anxious to placate his friend. A year later he was perhaps equally troubled and influenced by Keble's words –

> I much question the wisdom and practical kindness of 'collecting doubts as strongly as they can be put' in a published work. The persons *first* to be considered in all religious publications, I should say, are the unlearned good sort of people: and if the learned have doubts, why should they not correspond among themselves till they find answers, instead of disturbing the devotions as well as the opinions of their quiet neighbours?[15]

When the need to answer Rose's *Letter to the Bishop of London* occurred, and Pusey felt obliged to prepare a second part to his own book, he was keen to obtain Keble's advice:

> I should be much obliged to you if you would say whether there is anything in them [Pusey's views] as now stated which you think would give pain or offence to good Christians. I would gladly modify them as far as I could, without compromising what I believe to be true.[16]

It is here, having been originally prompted by Keble, that Pusey made his first tentative step in what became a definite retreat from his avowed ambition of introducing into English Biblical Criticism ideas that he had learnt in Germany. As the century wore on, witnessing the dilemma of fundamentalists on the one hand, in face of the discoveries of natural science, observing the incursions of the German critics on the other, Pusey would only have deepened his respect for Keble's teaching. The Victorian age, once blandly described as an age of faith, is now seen to be characterized by a deep concern for Christianity, but concern prompted as much by doubt and questioning as by simple adherence. It needs to be remembered that perhaps the majority of the influential intellectuals of the time were either unbelievers or professed a faith removed from conventional Christian orthodoxy.[17] Just as in early life Pusey encountered unbelief in his brother, Julian Hibbert and Maria Barker, so later he would not have been unaware that such teachers as Thomas Carlyle, J.S. Mill, George Eliot, J.A. Froude, Francis Newman, Matthew Arnold, Huxley and Spencer, were all propagating ideas calculated to unsettle if not destroy traditional Christian belief. By contrast, Keble's quiet and impeccably Anglican traditionalism, based on the 17th century Divines and the Fathers, must have appeared as an anchor sheet. In an age of immense economic and social changes, Keble, to whom 'all opinions differing from the traditional and all the fresh gains of the age in the region of thought and enquiry seemed . . . sinful inventions'[18], could only have encouraged Pusey along the path of caution. As Keble insisted –

> Whatever be the natural tendency of knowledge itself, so many temptations are called into action in the course of acquiring it, and still more in the display, which is nece-

ssary in order to make it useful to others, that it can hardly be considered upon the whole, more of an advantage towards the practice of piety than riches or honour or high birth.[19]

Initially, however, it was probably the problem of Church Reform in the early 1830s which brought Pusey and Keble close. Though Pusey at first showed himself in favour of moderate changes within the Church, his later disillusionment with the politicians probably led him to believe that Keble had been right all along in his advocacy of complete separation of Church and State. At least at the onset of the Oxford Movement, this was a policy seriously considered by Keble. He told A.P. Perceval:

> Anything, humanly speaking, will be better than for the Church to go on in union with such a state. And I think as far as I can judge, that this is becoming every day a more general feeling among Churchmen. But how to conduct a separation without producing a schism in the Church? Even *that* I am not sure that I should deprecate, if I were sure of getting rid of the right persons.[20]

Newman agreed with Keble, but he disliked the idea of saying so in print. 'It is so very fearful a responsibility', he said, 'to remove our Candle-stick from its present place . . . that I do hope the foes of the Church may have the burden of it instead of us'.[21] By 1836, however, Newman's views had become more radical. He told Pusey:

> Is it not very clear that the English Church subsists in the *State*, and has no internal consistenty (in matter of fact, I do not say in theory) to keep it together? Is bound into one by the imposition of articles and the inducement of State protection, not by ethos and a common faith? . . . Poor Keble's spirit was vexed for years, while he felt the evil but could not grasp it: he seemed visionary and eccentric while he was eating his heart, unsuccessfully attempting to analyse his own presagings, and to express a disapprobation which he could not help feeling. Are we not better off? Is

> not ours a state of hope? Have we not started the game? Is it not better to fight in light than in darkness? . . . Let us preach and teach, and develop our views into system, and in all likelihood we may be instruments in the preservation of the Church; and, if it loses in extent, if it is separated from the State, if it has certain portions torn from it, all this is most grievous, but still the better sort will be brought in to clearer and more complete Christianity and the Church will be purer.[22]

Like Newman, Pusey ultimately took up an attitude of obedience to established authority, but for some time he was not indisposed to consider that separation of Church and state, rather than a continuation of Erastianism, might be better for the Church of England. This notion, pressed by Keble and Newman, and closely paralleled by Lamennais' Liberal Catholicism on the continent[23], perhaps exercised the greatest influence on Pusey's outlook at the time of his bitter article in *The British Critic* in 1838 on 'The Royal and Parliamentary Ecclesiastical Commissions', in which he declared his fear that the Episcopate had been replaced by the Commissioners. Such feelings were probably exacerbated by the suspicion that certain of the Bishops, such as Bloomfield, were working hand in glove with the politicians. In 1836 Keble had been telling Pusey that he considered even Archbishop Howley – a Primate most other churchmen at least respected[24] – to be 'thoroughly Erastian' and unconsciously lending himself to 'the purposes of the enemies of the Church'.[25]

Though Keble's political views may have influenced Pusey's outlook, it is much more likely that he was drawn to Keble for reasons very similar to those experienced by Newman. In 1823 when Newman read Butler's *Analogy* for the first time, he thought of it as marking an era in his religious opinions; an event not unusual among early 19th century intellectuals[26] and one that probably also occurred in Pusey's own development. Later, Newman records that Keble recast for him two truths derived from Butler – those concerning the Sacramental System' and the principle of 'probability' – and it is not unlikely that the same happened for Pusey. It is undeniable that Pusey was immensely impressed by *The Christian Year*; his frequent mention of it in his unpublished lectures, 'On the types and prophecies of the Old Testament', of 1836 leaves no doubt that he imbibed Keble's ideas on Sacramentalism. This, indeed, is one of the keys to understanding the nature of Keble's influence over Pusey; it was the same as Keble had originally exercised to such effect on the contributors to the *Lyra Apostolica*. For these, as H. Scott Holland has related,

> ... the visible and the tangible were but symbols of a transcendent life, the vesture of the spirit, through which its motions made themselves felt. They rejected absolutely the notion of a material earth, isolated and complete, working by cast-iron laws, in the mechanical deadness of unintelligent force. On the contrary, it was alive, with a life not its own, which alone gave it meaning; and this life was personal, intelligent, sympathetic, communicable to man. In and through Nature, spirit spoke with spirit, man came in touch with GOD. The Church gave him the true clue by which to interpret the external world, through its sacramental use of material vehicles by which to realize spiritual power. Sacraments were no accidental form. They were in harmony with the being of things. The world was sacramental.[27]

It was not only in the sacramental sphere, however, that Keble exerted a great influence on Pusey; he also led him to an appreciation of some of the Nonjuring doctrines which were part of his own inherited teaching. Pusey told Keble in 1837:

> It was at Fairford, many years ago when I was thoughtlessly, or rather, I must say, confidently, taking for granted that the Stuarts were rightly dethroned, that I heard for the first time a hint to the contrary from you. Your seriousness was an unintended reproof to my petulent expression

> about it, and so it stuck by me, although it was some time before it took root and burst through all the clods placed upon it.[28]

Thus it was that Pusey preached his sermon 'Patience and Confidence shall be your strength', which advocated the doctrine of passive obedience in face of unjust authority, and emphasized the wickedness of those who resisted the tyranny of James II; a sermon reputed to be the first formally preached against the Revolution of 1688, since the time of Sacheverel.[29] Pusey told Keble:

> *Your* doctrine . . . which I preached on Nov. 5, takes with people whom one would not have thought, so valuable is the 'religio loci'. It seems as if true doctrine here still environed us, even when unseen that people held it, even though half unconsciously and that they needed but to be awakened to what they indeed held.[30]

Besides insisting on such themes as divine immanence in material creation and on the dangers of rationalism, Pusey was at pains in later sermons to stress another integral part of Keble's teaching – the achievement of true wisdom through self-discipline and submission to authority:

> Holy Scripture many ways, tells us that the light does indeed shine abundantly around all, but is seen by those only who have eyes to see; that a certain character of piety, and duty, and love, and humility, towards God and man, is necessary to enable us to see; that they who have not this, though they think they see, are blind, nay are the more blind, because they say, 'we see'; that God revealed His wisdom unto babes, but hides it from the 'wise and prudent'.[31]

Pusey had learnt from Keble that 'God is a God of peace, not of confusion, and is to be sought not in eager debatings and strifes, but in the secret chambers of our own hearts'.[32]

From 1837 onwards Pusey almost always turned naturally to Keble when troubled or in need of advice. A typical example of Pusey's dependence on the older man, even in the most trivial of events, arose over the question of whether he should contribute to a memorial to Dr Arnold in 1842. Until Keble wrote advising him what to do Pusey changed his mind no less than five times. This almost congenital indecision of Pusey's was a source of frequent trouble to him; on occasions, such as the erection of the Martyrs' Memorial in Oxford and the establishment of a joint Anglo-Prussian Bishopric in Jerusalem Pusey suffered more than his usual measure of mental pain, because he found himself somewhat out of step with both Keble and Newman, more opposed to the projects than he was initially. The extent, indeed, to which Pusey did come to rely not only on Keble, but also on Newman, might reasonably be considered excessive. He wrote to Newman:

> I wish I had got more into the way of acting for myself but it seems as if I were to lean on and trouble my friends (i.e. you) all my life. I decide for a time, and then I doubt about my decision; sometimes think it best to act upon first impulses, sometimes suspect them: and yet withal I only wish to do what is simplest, I believe, and yet do not know what it is. Early habit of leaning on others, seems to have impaired my power of deciding for myself.[33]

Newman may have been accurate in describing Pusey as 'a man of large designs', possessing 'a hopeful, sanguine mind' and 'confidence in his position', but one must qualify his statement that Pusey 'was haunted by no intellectual perplexities'.[34] Once Newman had retired to Littlemore, Pusey's moral peonage to Keble increased; especially on occasions of distress, such as the condemnation of his university sermon in 1843, the death of his daughter, Lucy, in 1844, and when his enormous feelings of personal guilt ultimately led him to adopt Keble as his confessor. The aggressive traits which developed among the younger members of the Oxford Movement, such as Ward and Oakley, were also topics that Pusey found it easier to discuss with Keble. The relationship, however, was not very reciprocal:

the only time before 1845 when Keble specifically asked for advice from Pusey was in 1841, when Keble's curate was refused ordination to the Priesthood.

Pusey's friendship with Newman was of a different kind. This may have been due partly to the fact that they were of an age, Pusey being only six months older than Newman, but the contrast between the relationship that Pusey enjoyed with Newman on the one hand, and Keble on the other, was deeper than a mere difference of age. In their early years together at Oriel, Newman and Pusey had not allowed their differences in outlook to affect their friendship. To Pusey, Newman appeared to embody the ideal of zealous practical Christianity; so much so, indeed, that L. Prestige has suggested that a synthesis of Pusey's two friends, Newman and Keble, would have provided a concrete illustration of the type of Christian that Pusey had advocated in his *Enquiry* into the theology of Germany.

It is possible that it was Newman who first introduced Pusey to the Anglican 17th century Divines in 1829. In order to lend an air of orthodoxy to his views on Biblical Inspiration at that time, Pusey drew up his first catena of passages from past Anglican writers, but it was Newman who originally searched the writings of Mede, Bull and Hall for such evidence, and, finding nothing, had advised Pusey to look at such works as Beveridge's sermons, Pearson on the Creed, Heylin, Chillingworth, and Laud's conference with Fisher. Pusey's replies to Newman do not suggest that as yet he was much acquainted with the Caroline Divines, and certainly the Pusey family library was not of much assistance to him:

> I have no doubt from looking over Andrewes that he has the same opinions as myself. Of Bishop Ken I can find nothing in our library but a popular Catechism and his poetical works, Jackson from what I have seen I like much. I shall procure his works as soon as I can.[35]

A short while later, Pusey was telling Newman that he had found some things to his purpose in Beveridge, but he thought him 'higher Church than I am'. He was unable to find any of the other authors listed by Newman, and asked if he might borrow copies from his friend. Coming from a man, soon to be in the vanguard of the Tractarian movement, whose proud assertion was that it taught doctrines which were those of a great tradition, such ignorance is remarkable. It demolishes any idea that Pusey had been brought up in a High Church tradition whose doctrinal pabulum was the teaching of the 17th century Caroline Divines. Pusey, in 1829, at least, might be considered the living embodiment or representative of 'the forgetful generation' mentioned by Newman in his dedication of his *Lectures on the Prophetical Office of the Church*.

Once a member of the Oxford Movement, Pusey had ample opportunity of learning from the past. Both in *Tract* 71 and in the Introduction to the *Prophetical Office* (1837), Newman was concerned to discover 'whether what is called Anglicanism, the religion of Andrewes, Laud, Hammond, Butler and Wilson is capable of being professed, acted on, and maintained on a large sphere of action'.[36] The Tracts themselves provided an important historical introduction to the High Church tradition. Tracts *25* and *26* contained extracts from Beveridge's sermons; *27* and *28* drew on the writings of Cosin and Bull, particularly the former's *History of Popish Transubstantiation*; *64* included excerpts on ancient liturgies extracted from Bull; *72* was based on Archbishop Ussher's writings concerning prayers for the dead, and *88* contained a translation by Newman of Andrewes' *Greek Devotions*. Tracts *74*, *76*, *78* and Pusey's *81*, (on Apostolic Succession, Baptismal Regeneration, the appeal to 'Quod semper, quod ubique, quod ab omnibus traditum est', and the doctrine of Eucharistic Sacrifice respectively), were all largely catenae of extracts from former writers.

Pusey's ignorance of the earlier Anglican divines is all the more strange in that he seems to have been unaware of their vogue (as yet a limited one) in the 1820s. In 1824, for example, the works of William Beveridge had been published again in nine volumes; in 1827 the works of George Bull had been republished; the following year there appeared Heber's edition of *The Whole Works* of Jeremy Taylor; 1829 had seen *The Life of Laud* by J.P. Lawson, and 1832 an edition of the writings of Charles Leslie in seven volumes. These were only a few of the books from 17th century and Non-juring sources which emerged while Pusey was a young don[37], but, unlike other future Tractarians, he appears not to have read them.

In his early friendship with Newman, Pusey had freely admitted his own ignorance of theology and clearly regarded it as a handicap. He went to some lengths to account for it, in an explanation which gives clues concerning his heavy reliance upon Keble and Newman. He told Newman in 1826:

> The labours for Oriel, the subsequent ill-health and weakness, the time expended on the Essays [for university prizes], the unfortunate circumstances of my friend [Julian Hibbert] and the consequent ensuing study of German, the subsequent application to Hebrew, Chaldee, Syriac and Arabic, have made my studies miserably desultory, and kept me from the core of Theology.[38]

Just as Newman was probably the person who made Pusey aware of the works of the Caroline divines, so it is possible that he was also the first to enlighten Pusey to the importance of the Early Church and the Fathers. Unlike Keble, resident first at Fairford and then at Hursley during the important years of Pusey's initiation into Tractarian ways, Newman had the advantage of living within easy reach of Pusey. He was, indeed, a frequent visitor to Pusey's home, an influence on the outlook of Maria Pusey, and a source of light relief to the Pusey children. From 1832 at least, when Pusey was writing his *Cathedral Institutions*, Newman was the one to whom Pusey turned for theological advice. When Newman returned the manuscript of Pusey's work, he took the opportunity to question Pusey's use of the word Catholic and his mode of describing Calvin as a Saint, and to give Pusey what amounted to a lecture on Primitive Christianity. Newman wrote:

> I am still of the opinion that the *great* evil of our want of Theological knowledge is its resulting in differences of opinion. Men say what they will about going by Scripture not tradition – but nature is stronger than systems. The piety and services of the Primitive Christians adds to their authority an influence which is practically irresistible, with those i.e. who are trained in right feelings and habits. And I think this was *intended* by the Author of all truth, and none but Primitive Christianity can bring this about, for other ages, if they have the high spirit, yet have not (of course) the authority of the first age. As to Scripture being practically sufficient for making the Christian, it seems to me a mere dream – nor do I find it anywhere said so in Scripture – nor can I infer logically that what is confessedly *the* sole oracle of *doctrine*, is therefore also of *practice* and *discipline*.[39]

Unlike Newman, who had set about reading the Fathers systematically as early as 1828, and on whom such Fathers as Clement and Origen of the Church of Alexandria had made a profound impression, Pusey seems to have studied the Early Church very little before he joined the Oxford Movement. Even as late as 1838, Pusey was complaining about the proposal that he should write a preface to the 'Library of the Fathers', since he considered that Newman and Keble knew 'ten times as much about the Fathers' as he did. Just as Newman in 1832 took it upon himself to explain to Pusey the significance of Primitive Christianity, so it is not unlikely that later he communicated to him those portions of the Fathers' teaching which had most aroused his own enthusiasm. These he had described as 'magnificent in themselves' and as coming 'like music to my inward ear'.[40] He chiefly valued those Fathers who taught that 'the exterior world, physical and historical, was but the outward manifestation of realities greater than itself'[41], those who insisted that 'Nature was a parable: Scripture was an allegory: pagan literature, philosophy, and mythology, properly understood, were but a preparation for the Gospel'.[42] Such notions reinforced what he had learnt from Butler's *Analogy* and Keble's *Christian Year* and predisposed him to regard the Church, her sacraments and hierarchical appointments, as symbols of heavenly facts.[43] Unless Newman passed on these ideas to Pusey, how else does one explain their vivid and repeated appearance so frequently in Pusey's 'Lectures on Types and Prophecies' of 1836? What Pusey seems to have done in his lectures is to have wed such thoughts as he received from Keble and Newman concerning the Fathers to his own obvious and greater knowledge of the Old Testament. For in the years when Newman had been studying the Fathers in detail, Pusey had been giving his attention to German theology and the original languages in which the Bible had been written. Whereas he eventually acquired a deep acquaintance with the Fathers, Pusey was probably first led to them by Newman.

After receiving trenchant advice from Newman on Primitive Christianity, it was but a short step for Pusey to request help from him concerning sermons, to assist in the distribution of the *Tracts*, to borrow books from him (significantly, at the end of 1833, Daubeny's *Guide to the Church*), and to ascribe to him the dedication of his first volume of sermons. Pusey was under no illusion as to the extent to which he was indebted to Newman whom he told in 1834:

> I have been learning, and trust, if it please God, all my life to learn of you (for through you I have learnt of our common Master) and I know not what you can have learnt of me.[44]

Though Newman is right to assert that, once Pusey had joined the Oxford Movement, he changed the character of the *Tracts*, making them less superficial in content, it is doubtful whether Pusey's own *Tract on Baptism* of 1835 would have been so weighty, had not Newman first prompted him to consider the importance of past Anglican divines and the Fathers. Before Pusey wrote his Tract, he had been anxious to learn Newman's views concerning the Sacrament of Baptism and wrote telling him so: it is possible, therefore, that Pusey was originally encouraged by Newman to consult the authorities he quotes so extensively in the Tract. Even though Pusey's capacity for work was enormous, it is extremely doubtful that he would have had the opportunity of discovering them for himself. In addition to the time Pusey was required to devote to his wife and the birth of four children, in the years immediately preceding the appearance of his *Tract on Baptism*, he was also heavily engaged with his Hebrew lectures, a full social round and the five year task of compiling the Arabic Catalogue for the Bodleian library. He had, nevertheless, found time to write the second part of his *Enquiry*, his *Cathedral Institutions*, four 'Letters' for the S.P.C.K., his *Tract on Fasting*, and to throw himself unreservedly into the University struggle over Subscription. All these activities had been undertaken in the face of frequent bouts of serious illness. Following his first breakdown in 1827 and 1828, Pusey was again ill from November 1830 to March 1831, and from the Michaelmas term of 1833 to Easter 1834. Unless Pusey was advised by Newman, how else can one account for his citation of such Fathers as Augustine, Jerome, Chrysostom, Basil, Gregory of Nazianzum, Cyprian and Tertullian, and such Anglican divines as Hooker, Taylor, Jebb, Bull and Beveridge, in the *Tract on Baptism*? Even in the period immediately following the appearance of the Tract, Pusey would again have been deprived of the chance to study the Caroline divines and the Fathers in any real detail, or to the extent to which Newman was familiar with them, by his work for the building of more churches in London, by his founding of a Theological Society in Oxford, and by the subsequent crisis over the appointment of R.D. Hampden the Broad Churchman, as Regius Professor of Divinity. Unlike W.F. Hook, who as early as 1823 was claiming to Pusey that he was becoming widely read in the Apostolic Fathers, and in 1836 was confessing his debt to the writings of John Jebb, the friend and pupil of Alexander Knox, Pusey was more conversant with the work of German theologians. By 1837, however, Pusey had extended his intellectual horizon; he then wrote to Hook recommending that he should read Bull, Skelton, Leslie and Potter. The previous autumn, indeed, Pusey had begun to feel sufficiently confident to challenge some of Newman's views in private.

2. Pusey's individual position

It is ironical that the first two subjects on which Pusey felt obliged to remonstrate with Newman, were two of the earliest in which his friend had originally been instructing him. In 1827 on the occasion of his brother Henry's death, Pusey had written to Newman from Germany asking whether prayers for the dead were in order. By September 1836, however, Pusey was less keen to publicize his earlier conviction that 'nothing ... can be found in Scripture against praying for the dead'[45], and instead, he was begging Newman to alter his Tract on Purgatory; prayers for the dead he now thought liable to arouse bitter controversy and scandal.[46] A few months later, Pusey was also doubting the validity of Newman's ideas on the invocation of saints; he could find little evidence of this devotion in the Ancient Church to warrant the prominence that his colleague gave it.[47] Roles were now somewhat reversed. A few years previously Newman had been informing Pusey about practices in the Early Church. Such disagreements, however, were small in comparison with more deep seated differences of outlook.

It is not unlikely that on joining the Oxford Movement, Pusey had been strongly impressed by at least two of the three propositions, which Newman claims to have adopted so confidently in 1833 – the principle of dogma in his battle with liberalism, and the truth that there was a visible church with sacraments and rites which were channels of grace.[48] The whole tenor, indeed, of Pusey's writings from 1835 onwards, suggests that he shared these ideas of Newman. On the third of Newman's points – utter antagonism to the Church of Rome – however, Pusey pursued a line which differentiated him not only from Newman, but, in certain respects from the majority of Tractarians. The view that

Pusey took of Roman Catholicism until 1845 was basically the same as he had held as a young don at Oriel. Unlike Newman, Pusey in later years never felt the need publicly to withdraw any violently anti-Roman Catholic remarks that he may have made; he did regret some criticisms, but for Pusey there was no equivalent paper to Newman's *Retraction of Anti-Catholic Statement* (1843). Even in his harsh original *Tract on Baptism*, Pusey had never doubted that Rome was of the true Church; he was careful to differentiate between her practice and theory:

> We must distinguish between the practical corruptions of the Church of Rome and her theoretical errors. For it often happens that she leads her members into error, and countenances corruption in them, where her statements in themselves are not very unsound: teaching us how much evil, what seems a little departure from the truth, may create.[49]

This tendency to criticize Rome in measured, rather than violent terms, was to remain with Pusey, and especially after 1844, when he shifted the standing ground for his theological opinions from Antiquity to the faith as defined by any Council which might be held to be Ecumenical.

Just as Pusey had maintained an unprejudiced view of Roman Catholicism from his earliest years, so, until the last stages of the Oxford Movement, he continued to express balanced views on Protestantism. Though he was prepared to 'amend' his original opinion that Protestant bodies on the continent were churches, and to declare to the Bishop of Oxford in 1839 that the title of Protestant belonged historically rather to Lutherans than to Anglicans[50], Pusey was much more interested in outlining the positive features of the 'Via Media'. This latter he described as 'a broad and tangible line', distinct enough to avoid Ultra-Protestantism on the one hand and Romanism on the other.[51] The clarity with which he held this view, probably explains his sense of shock, when Romanizing tendencies developed within the Oxford Movement among the younger men in the 1840s. 'The tendency

Romewards', he informed Newman, 'when I was first told it, did shatter me, and I felt like one who had been left ashore, and the tide sweeping by, I knew not whither'.[52]

Though Pusey recognized as much as Keble and Newman the shortcomings of Evangelicalism, this was a further subject on which he ever remained distinct from his friends. As much as Keble, Pusey would have deprecated the Evangelical tendency to debase scriptural truths into meaningless clichés by a facile bandying of biblical texts. Similarly, he would have agreed with Newman in deploring the Evangelical habit or 'commonplace mechanical way ... in which the great doctrine of His (Christ's) death and the benefit of His blood-shedding is thrown to and fro, at best as if a spell or charm, which would surely convert men'.[53] Nevertheless, Pusey was not blind to the good qualities in Evangelical teaching, as were so many of his friends.

In his attitude to the English Reformation, Pusey can be clearly seen pursuing a thoroughly independent line from other Tractarians. As early as 1835 Hurrell Froude was complaining to Newman concerning Pusey's views.

> I have ... to grumble at you for letting Pusey call the Reformers, the Founders of our Church ... Pour moi, I never mean, if I can help it, to use any phrases even, which connect me with such a set.[54]

From this and similarly hostile opinions of Froude, which only came to light on the publication of his *Remains* in 1838, it is possible to estimate the pain he would have felt had he read Pusey's earlier laudatory words on the Reformation in his *Enquiry* of 1828. Eleven years later, Pusey was still insisting to Keble that 'whatever faults there were, we should never have been "Apostolicals" without them (the Reformers)'. He was certain that 'we owe our peculiar position as adherents to Primitive Christianity to them, besides other blessings'[55] not until 1844 was Pusey to change this view. He refused a subscription to the Martyrs' Memorial in 1838 only because he feared the scheme was largely 'a hit against' Newman. Keble, by contrast, was opposed to the Memorial in principle and wrote to Pusey that he could not understand how Cranmer could be reckoned a 'bona fide' martyr, that he was not prepared to express public dissent from Froude's view of the Reformers as a party, that if the monument were confined to Ridley he might consider it, but that as things stood it would require episcopal authority to make him subscribe.[56]

It is clear that much as he was devoted to and influenced by Newman and Keble, Pusey in many ways felt more kinship with older high church figures. It was for this reason that he could write in 1839 to Newman of his pleasure at meeting Joshua Watson at Brighton. (Until then, Pusey's only direct contact with Watson had been when they worked together in 1832, in seeking to secure the election of W.H. Mill, Principal of Bishop's College, Calcutta, to the Professorship of Sanskrit at Oxford.) Pusey, indeed, was more than delighted at his encounter with the old high churchman.

> I cannot say how cheering it was to be recognized by you as carrying on the same torch which we had received from yourself, and those of your generation who had remained faithful to the teaching. We seemcd no longer separated by a chasm from the old times and the old paths to which we wished to lead people back: the links which united us to those of old seemed to be restored.[57]

Similarly in 1840, when looking over some of the letters of Rose, lately deceased, Pusey saw in Rose shared characteristics which separated both from Newman to whom he wrote:

> In his [Rose's] mind defence of and rallying round and developing the Church *as she is* was so prominently *the* object, as almost to exclude the thought of any improvement in the Church, that you especially felt that the business of the present generation was not to change, or to compass changes, but to develop and enforce; preparing the way, or sowing the seed of improvement hereafter. In a word R. would be fixed on the present, so as to be

> absorbed in it, in making sure our present position, and would be a little fearful of any advanced posts being sent out: you would see our main business to be with the present; but with an eye to the future ... Apart from all criticism, they [Rose's letters] set before the eyes, what his view as to our position in the Church at this day is, and her needs, and in principle I should agree with what I read.[58]

These words of Pusey accurately sum up the cleavage which gradually divided such men as Rose and other conservative high churchmen, such as William Palmer of Worcester, from the majority of the Tractarians. Many of Rose's ideas were akin to those which Pusey expounded in his *Cathedral Institutions*, particularly in their advocacy of resuscitating the Church as it existed. The differences between the Tractarians and the old high churchmen went deeper than questions of tactics; in part they were reflections of subtle differences in politics and theology. Whereas the Tractarians were largely convinced that the High Church party's former allies – the Crown, the Bishops and Tory politicians – had proved themselves broken reeds[59], the conservatives disliked the idea of disestablishment. In theology, the old high church figures also preferred the traditional teaching of the Caroline divines to that of more radical Non-Jurors, and they were content to appeal to Antiquity only to justify Anglicanism. To many of the Hackney Phalanx, for example, Newman and Keble's publication of Froude's *Remains* appeared as 'a sort of manifesto of the "Apostolical" party; it represented a repudiation of the whole pattern of Church revival upheld by Rose and Palmer'.[60]

It was Pusey's personal dilemma that, as a result of his background, he was in close sympathy with much of the customary and static outlook of the old High Church party, yet emotionally and intellectually attached to the dynamic Anglicanism of Keble and Newman. Since he also disagreed with his two friends on certain fundamental issues, however, he fitted easily into no particular section of the party. For a long time, Pusey endeavoured to appeal to all sections of the

High Church in its variety of groupings, such as the Clapton Sect, the Bisley School and the radical Newman wing. In his *Letter to the Bishop of Oxford* of 1839, Pusey attempted to reassure people that the Tractarians were aware that their office was not to reform the Church, to add or take away from her, but to obey her; to study her character, to see how they might increasingly bring out and realize her teaching and principles.[61] He maintained that 'we must have acted up more to the theory of our Church as she is, before we attempt to alter any ritual belonging to her'.[62] Even in the early 1840s, Pusey never lost hope of preventing a break-up of the cause, and he seemed unconsciously to hope that Newman would do likewise; a tendency most apparent from the end of 1841 onwards, when Newman was on his 'Anglican death-bed'. Newman wrote:

> A common friend of ours broke it all to him [Pusey] in 1841, as far as matters had gone at that time, and showed him clearly the logical conclusions which must lie in propositions to which I had committed myself; but somehow or other in a little while, his mind fell back into its former happy state, and he could not bring himself to believe that he and I should not go on pleasantly together to the end.[63]

For Pusey logic was not everything; he had learnt this in great measure from Keble. It is probable that in adopting this attitude Pusey was being neither naive nor dishonest. Though extremely dependent on Newman and devoted to him, Pusey never considered himself a member of what he termed 'N's tribe of friends'.[64] Pusey's background, position in the university, early experience of Germany, and interest in affairs outside of Oxford, all rendered him frequently different in secular and religious outlook from Newman. Only at the very end of the Oxford Movement did Pusey cease to occupy a seemingly ambiguous place within the Tractarian party; in 1844 he then began to move into a recognizably extremist position.

3. Tractarian doctrine

Pusey's indebtedness to Keble and Newman on the emotional and intellectual plane explains in part his willingness to join forces with the Tractarians, despite his differences from them. The ideas which the Oxford Movement sought to propagate, nevertheless, also exerted an attraction for Pusey; he would have appreciated that 'the power of the Movement's religious ideas sprang from somewhere deeper in men's souls and minds than their contemporary ideas of ecclesiastical expediency'.[65] Influenced as he was by current affairs and controversies within Oxford, Pusey was undoubtedly convinced that the doctrines being disseminated by the Tractarians provided the remedy for the age.

Confronted with the Latitudianarian teaching characteristic of the Church of England in official circles in the previous century – a period Pusey referred to as the 'Saeculum tepidum' – and aware of the infidelity (as he deemed it) which had gradually infected the majority of continental countries in the 18th century, Pusey saw the Oxford Movement as a revival of truth.[66] He admitted that the Evangelicals had arisen in opposition to 'lukewarmness', but he deprecated their preaching 'too nakedly the two doctrines – a corruption of our nature and natural helplessness; the need of our Redeemer'.[67] Whilst he believed equally with the Evangelicals that man needed God, he preferred to emphasize the doctrine of our being 'in Christ'; for him this entailed being in the Church, especially by participation in the sacraments:

> To dwell *in* God is not to dwell *on* God only. It is no mere lifting up of our affections to Him, no being enwrapt in the contemplation of Him, no going forth of ourselves to cleave to Him. All this is our seeking Him, not His taking us up; our stretching after Him, not our attaining Him; our knocking, not His Opening. To dwell in God must be by His Dwelling in us. He takes us out of our state of nature, in which we were, fallen, estranged, in a far country, out of

> and away from Him, and takes us up into Himself. He cometh to us, and if we will receive Him, He dwelleth in us, and maketh His abode in us.[68]

It was in his insistence that union with God principally took place by way of the sacraments, within an Apostolic and traditional Church, that Pusey parted company with the Evangelicals and took his place amongst the Tractarians. 'Although all shall not be saved who partake of the Holy Sacraments, there is no revealed method of salvation from original or actual sin . . . without Baptism; without the Holy Eucharist there is no life'.[69] He maintained that

> The two Sacraments . . . are unlike everything else even in the intense fulness of the Christian life. Other gifts of God are means of grace; prayer, fasting, almsgiving, reading of God's Word, the rehearsal of our Belief, contrition for wrong committed, the blessing given by the Priest in the name of God, meditation upon God. But the Sacraments are more.[70]

Pusey's accentuation of the importance of the Sacraments stemmed from his manner of regarding the Incarnation. Tractarians as a whole, indeed, made this the central dogma of Christianity; their attitude to the Church and sacrament was conditioned by their treatment of them as 'extensions of the Incarnation'.[71] It is doubtful, nevertheless, whether many of the Tractarians ever approached the Incarnation with the sense of awe which characterized Pusey.

> 'He emptied Himself', He the Eternal Son of the Eternal Father, God of God, Light of Light, Co-equal with the Father, Who hath neither beginning nor end, but is Himself 'the Beginning and the End, the First and the Last', Uncreate, and the Creator, Infinite, Almightly, dwelling Ever-blessed in the Infinite Love of the Father, worshipped by Cherubim and Seraphim, and all the Host of Heaven and the Heaven of Heavens, became What He was not, Flesh . . . It surpasses all thought, it amazes, it confounds, to think of God becoming man; the Infinite enshrined within

> the finite, the Lord of all blended with His servant, the Creator with His creature! It is a depth of mystery unsearchable. We must shrink with awe when we pronounce it. Of old they fell down and worshipped, when, in our Creed, they uttered it – 'God was made Man'.[72]

Thus it was that Pusey could proclaim humility as the foundation of all Christian virtues – 'by humility alone canst thou reach that Rock, which shall not be shaken, that is Christ'.[73] It is also not difficult in view of such utterances, to understand how it was that Keble, who was revered for his humility, could exercise such a powerful influence over Pusey. The acute sense of the reality of the Supernatural, which permeates the whole of Pusey's outlook, accounts also for the serious manner in which he regarded the smallest of things; it also partly explains the strong element of moralism in his thought; a feature not merely Tractarian, however, but one shared with the majority of participants in religious movements in the 19th century, and a quality perhaps thoroughly English.[74]

The documents which probably reveal Pusey most convincingly as a Tractarian, are his unpublished 'Lectures on Types and Prophecy' of 1836; for some unaccountable reason they were mentioned only once, and then briefly, by Liddon, and it was not until recently that their importance was appreciated by historians.[75] The first outstanding note of the Lectures, both in style and content, is their romantic quality; Frederick Faber was typically effusive in his initial response to this fact. He told a friend:

> Pusey commenced his lectures yesterday with Noah and I was really so carried away by the majesty of his interpretations, that I could scarcely conceive him uninspired. It seemed as if a live coal from the altar had been placed upon his lips, and that the words he spoke were not his own.[76]

4. Romanticism

Whatever the precise relationship between the Romantic and the Tractarian movements[77], it cannot be disputed that four out of the six characteristics, which Professor Lovejoy lists as comprising Romanticism, and which exercised such a profound influence on the educated classes of Europe between 1730 and 1830, are clearly found in Pusey's Lectures. These qualities were –

i A craving for infinite values or infinite objects for thought or for the imagination to contemplate or for the will to aim at.
ii A love of mystery and otherworldliness.
iii An awareness of the duality of man's constitution.
iv A preoccupation with the inner life and a sense of man's corruption.

Of the two remaining features listed by Lovejoy, there are few indications that Pusey shared them.

v The notion that man ought to be of his own time, to express in his life or art the characteristics, ideas and the spirit of his age.
vi An interest in medievalism.[78]

Tractarian appreciation of the English Romantic writers is well known.[79] In an age, indeed, when romanticism not only affected leading minds of the day, but was to a large extent a popular even vulgar movement[80], it was natural that Pusey should have been influenced by it. In his youth as we have seen Pusey avidly read the works of Byron and he was also on visiting terms with the families of Scott, Coleridge and Southey. Much more significant, however, was the fact that Pusey always held that the real source of the Oxford Movement was to be found in *The Christian Year*.[81] Here, according to Y.T. Brilioth lay the connecting link between Romanticism and the Oxford Movement.[82] The manner in which Pusey appealed in his Lectures to nature as 'the emblem of the spiritual' is particularly reminiscent of Keble's work. Similarly, Pusey's insistence on the objective quality of nature's symbols is almost an echo of ideas found in Keble's *Lectures on Poetry*. This is clear when Pusey writes –

> Instances of . . . nature in conveying moral and religious truth will have been felt by everyone; and they will have

felt also, that these religious meanings were not arbitrarily affixed by their own minds, but that they arose out of and existed in the things themselves: and if a different meaning is found in the same object, this will be, because in fact each thing contains several such relations, or has several such characters impressed upon it, whereof, according to their peculiar characters or susceptibility, different minds have perceived different sides. A proof that this expressiveness really lies in the object and is not the work of imagination (otherwise than as imagination is employed in tracing out the mutual correspondence of images with their reality . . .) is furnished by this, that when the religious poets (as Wordsworth or the author of *The Christian Year*) have traced out such correspondence, the mind instantly recognises it as *true*, not as *beautiful* only, and so belonging to their minds subjectively, but as actually and really existing (objective). As the Christian poet just alluded to well said –

'Every leaf in every nook,
Every wave in every brook,
Chanting with a solemn voice,
Mind us of our better choice'.[83]

When discussing the nature of religious belief, Pusey seemed fully aware that, like all Tractarians, he was fighting on a double front: against rationalism and anti-dogmatism on the one hand, against the intellectualism of older orthodoxy on the other.[84] It was perhaps for this reason that he employed Romantic conceptions of human nature having spiritual depths extending beyond the intellect, and insisted that religion should cater for them in a vital way.

Our conviction also is of a compound character and made up of various emotions: in moral subjects it cannot be mainly intellectual: in Divine things, awe, wonders, and absorbing sense of infinity and of purity, or of holiness infuse conviction more directly than reasoning: nay, reasoning in that it appeals to one faculty only, and that for a time is erected into a judge, and so, as it were sits

> superior, constantly goes directly counter to the frame of mind wherein belief is received. The chance sight of a flower illumined by the sun's rays or of the starry heavens. 'The moon and the stars which God has ordained' impress the feeling of God upon the soul more than any artificial reasoning from final causes.[85]

It was for this same reason that Pusey attacked both contemporary exponents of 'the so-called historico-grammatical interpretation' of the Bible and the shallow interpreters of the 18th century; to Pusey's mind they failed to appreciate the importance of mystery and vitality contained within biblical language.

> It follows that a sense is to be sought and found in words and phrases, deeper than that which is required from the mere context, and not only so, but that neglect to do this was blameable, and neglecting a treasure which God has deposited in Scripture below the surface, and burying the talent committed to them in the earth.[86]

Much as these ideas give Pusey a kinship with the romantic reaction against rationalism of the previous century, and much as they show him falling very much into line with Tractarian thought as it was expressed in *Tract 79*, ('On the Introduction of Rationalistic Principles into Religion'), his main concern was to advocate a dynamic and typological interpretation of the Bible.

5. Types and Prophecy

When Pusey was composing his Lectures in 1836, modern critical methods of biblical research were largely only matters of hearsay in England, and, if studied, generally with suspicion. Pusey himself had long abandoned the idea of revising the Old Testament in the light of what he had learnt in Germany, and, on the whole, he now deplored the outpourings of the German critics. In view of this, the startling fact remains that, in his 'Lectures on Types and Prophecy', he sought to propagate at least one important discovery that he had probably made in Germany; he now saw the task of biblical scholarship to be, not one of interpreting supposedly infallible and often obscure oracles, but of tackling the Bible in terms of history, especially in regard to prophecy. Unlike so many of his contemporary English theologians, Pusey appreciated that the fulfilment of prophecy in the Bible involved more than the fruition of words and predictions. What he wanted, indeed, was nothing less than a return to the classical Christian approach to prophecy as exemplified in St Augustine, and shorn of the medieval and later tendency to search, in the narrow sense, for clues and patterns in the biblical text. In this wish, Pusey was anticipating present day methods of visualizing prophecy not as a detailed fulfilment of predictions, made years previously, but the gift of individuals to discern the inner significance of historical events within the whole scheme of salvation history, displayed typologically through the Old Testament. Perhaps many Churchmen, of all shades of opinion, were as aware as Pusey that traditional theology regarded earlier events in the Bible as 'types' of later, or New Testament history as the fulfilment of Old Testament 'types', but probably few of them at that time considered that real eschatological analogies existed behind typology, in the broad sense that Pusey was advocating. He was adamant that the history of the Old Testament, its events and institutions, as a whole, was prophetic; it was mistaken to consider isolated and particular sayings.

> Holy Scripture does not favour our mechanical views of prophecy, as containing so many items, as it were, as there are striking passages; as though prophecies admitted of being counted up, and the entire evidence of prophecy was to be weighed according to the number and contents and tangibleness of these several predictions. Rather the whole previous dispensation of the O.T., its people, its individual characters, its rites, its sayings, its history was one vast prophetic system, veiling, but full of the N.T.[87]

Pusey was equally certain that as a remedy for the errors which resulted from viewing prophecy in the narrow sense, it was necessary to view everything in the world as a type or symbol of heavenly realities. In his declaration that 'The world is full of types . . . The words of a child are constantly typical of the future developed beings: they speak greater truth than they themselves . . . know'[88], Pusey can be seen wedding Keble's ideas on sacramentalism to his own knowledge of the Old Testament. When children were being prophetic in this manner, Pusey considered that they spoke 'in reference to some particular occasion but indefinitely; they are aware of something kindred to that whole Truth and have some glimmering of it, but it they grasp not'.[89] For this reason, Pusey unconsciously also paraphrases Wordsworth, and suggests that a child's 'indefiniteness adds to its reality, comprehensive from a power within it; they are in truth the words of God, in the mouth of a little one, so lately come from its Maker's hand'.[90] He then proceeds to link such ideas to his views on prophecy in the Bible.

> In like manner the sayings of the O.T. tho' they often have not the distinct outline of truth, which belongs to the development, have in them continually a depth of shade, which impresses the mind in the midst of its indistinctness, yet more forcibly and has more religious awe than would the mere outline, tho' even so distinct.[91]

To Pusey's mind, typology in both the Old Testament and the world at large were deliberate gifts of God to man; they were the prescribed methods by which God led man to Himself. Not content with viewing individuals in themselves as types, however, Pusey went on to suggest that developed characters should be seen as 'the type of some ideal good or bad'; thus he cites Nero and Domitian as 'emblems' of cruelty, Scipio of self-commanding justice, Plato of contemplation and Xenophon of practical wisdom. 'The other visible creatures of God's Word,' he said, 'and the efflux of his Spirit . . . present a continual harmony with an order of things above them; they possess in themselves a relation to things unseen'.[92]

Pusey's conviction that much of prophecy was deliberately of an indistinct nature, accounts for his hostility to the more radical of the biblical critics.

> When moderns then attempt to translate into plain terms the figurative language of Holy Scripture, and to substitute abstract, and as they would fain have it, clearer forms for these types of typical language of the O.T., they uniformly by this transmutation evaporate such of their meaning. We have not, it is true, visible propitiatory sacrifice, a visible theocracy, a visible temple; but it is still thro' the medium of these figures that we understand (as far as we do understand) the reality: we have no better way of understanding the main truths of the Gospel than thro' these very figures, 'the sacrifice of Christ', 'the Kingdom of God', 'the temple of the Holy Ghost'; and he who would lay aside these types and typical language and understand the mysteries of God without them, would be acting contrary to the teaching of Scripture and so very wrongly and foolishly. Men think that they gain in clearness, but they lose in depth; they would employ definite terms in order to comprehend that which is infinite.[93]

It is very clear that by 1836 Pusey had thoroughly imbibed the Tractarian notion that clarity and intelligibility were to be eschewed, if they narrowed or limited the apprehension of things divine. Two years later, he was telling W.F. Hook that in his opinion Issac Williams' *On Reserve in Communicating Religious Knowledge* was the most valuable of all the Tracts.[94] The doctrine of a reticence, prompted by respect for the depth of religious truth, was much misunderstood by many of Pusey's contemporaries. Even though Samuel Wilberforce might speak of it as one of the 'peculiarities' of the Tractarians[95], there is no doubting that the 'Disciplina Arcani', so well understood by Keble and Newman[96], was making a strong impression on Pusey when he wrote his 1836 Lectures.

> Everyone has been aware how in mixed society, he has often had pleasure in uttering words, which in his own mind related to some holier subject, than he thought it expedient either for himself or others to speak of more plainly; yet one, who knew him well, would know the veiled meaning was his real one, and that it was for the sake of that, that the words were uttered. . . . One might even say that no deep saying was ever uttered which was not capable of many applications and a variety of meanings, which might very possibly float before our minds together or severally, of which one remains the highest and of that one the rest are fainter and interior representations.[97]

At one stage in the Lectures, Pusey can also be witnessed making a tentative step in the direction of formulating a theology of history; he proclaimed, for example, that 'Sacred history is the key to profane. The veil is then raised, which ordinarily covers the connection of events with God, their First Cause'.[98] His main concern, however, remained with prophecy in the Old Testament. 'I would rather by directing attention to what has already been authoritatively explained, lead men (if it might be so) gradually back to the old paths, which I see to be the safer and the firmer and to lead to a higher wisdom and insights into Holy Scripture'[99]; for Pusey this was synonymous with the theology of Bishop Bull and the ancient Church, particularly of Augustine.[100]

It was Pusey's belief, therefore, that the biblical revelation was given through the use of types, symbols and sacramental action in their broadest sense; such a view may have been acquired by Pusey through his long and intense study of Semitic languages in Germany, and from his friendship with Keble, who ever believed that 'there is a receiving of our Lord in his Scriptures' and a 'perception of our Lord's presence, through the veil of the letter'.[101] To Pusey's mind, the controversies which had divided Christendom were the result of arbitrary selection of certain images, or over-emphasis on certain aspects of revelation at the expense of others. For this reason, he stressed in his Lectures the importance of the

Fathers, who 'from their vivid perception of the relations of the several Christian truths (one with another), glide imperceptibly from the mention of the one to the other, or speak of the one under the terms of the other'.[102] As examples of this, he cited the way in which Augustine passed from the mention of the one sacrifice on the cross to the daily refreshment through Christ's blood, which derived from it, and the ancient method by which the sacrifice of the Eucharist was connected immediately with other sacrifices, such as those of prayer, thanksgiving, alms and oblations.

As far as Pusey's own intellectual development is concerned, his Lectures of 1836 reveal him to have been a creative writer within the Movement, alongside Keble and Newman. No longer can it be maintained that Pusey made no intellectual contribution to the Movement – a view which one might adopt from Newman's silence on the subject, and from Owen Chadwick's assertion that Pusey was not a speculative theologian.[103] This is not to deny that after 1845 Pusey's writings became erudite and controversial and lost their imaginative appeal. The 'Lectures on Types and Prophecy', however, belong to the period of prosperity within the Tractarian movement; they were written and delivered at a time when the troubles of the 1840s and the controversies of the next two decades, such as the Gorham Case and that over *Essays and Reviews*, were not in sight. Not until the appearance of *Lux Mundi* were fertile ideas, comparable to those of the 1830s, to appear within Anglo-Catholic circles again. A reading of Pusey's Lectures shows how superficial was Fairbairn's description of the Oxford Movement, at least in 1836, as 'less the child of a great love than of a great hate of what its spokesman and founder called "Liberalism"'.[104] Much as Pusey had come to adopt Keble's and Newman's distrust of liberalism in the 1830s, he was also participating in 'the renascence of wonder'. In common with other Tractarians, such as Frederick Faber, who could proclaim to a friend that 'I *feel* Berkeleyism must be true',[105] Pusey shared a vision, aesthetic in origin, but for a time integrated into a deeper awareness of its relevance and significance to man's moral and intellectual perceptions.

5
EVANGELICALISM

1. Pusey and Pietism

In 1934 Archbishop Brilioth, in his study of the connections between Evangelicalism and the Oxford Movement, asked the question 'Would it be untrue to call Pusey one of the great English Evangelicals?'.[1] At first sight, such a question might come as a shock, particularly if one thinks of Pusey in his ultimate role as leader of the Anglo-Catholic party after 1845, but there are considerable grounds for believing that Pusey had more in common with Evangelicals than is generally supposed.[2] As early as 1828, in the allusive writing contained in his *Enquiry* into the theology of Germany, Pusey had recognized (what he deemed) a kinship between English Evangelicalism and Pietism. There can be little doubt, indeed, that the characteristics he thought common to both movements, played no small part in his own intellectual development; his closest friends in Germany had all been influenced by Pietism, and the correspondence between Pusey and Friedrich Tholuck in the 1820s and the 1830s was redolent of warm feelings and a mutual sense of purpose. Tholuck wrote:

> With every new communication of your struggles and your works, increases my attachment, my reverence for you and your Church. Your letters are edifying to me, they build truly the belief in me that the Lord has now a Kingdom on earth. They spur me on in similar struggles to hope with confidence for success. Thus your beautiful words: it is so that now everything great has to be brought about by a few, by entire self-denial. Just so it is in Paris, where all Christian undertakings (when I was there in 1825) lay in the hands of three men, and yet out of this has grown a tree

> under which the birds of Heaven dwell – not quite so in Berlin, but partly there also. Quite so it is also at home in Halle.[3]

By this time, however, the movement as originally promoted in Germany, had undergone profound vicissitudes; the Pietism of his friends was subtly but significantly different from that which Pusey had applauded in his *Enquiry* but one cannot doubt his encouragement of intercourse with the continent in his early years. He informed Tholuck that he would be pleased to receive anyone he cared to send from Germany, and he undertook to encourage promising Theologians to visit him.

The origins of Pietism were international and complex; it was a movement which showed signs of having been partly influenced by Calvinism, as found in Dutch Precisism, by English Puritanism, and also by an ancient core of mysticism found in Lutheranism. Behind it might be found certain 17th century devotional books, such as John Bunyan's *Pilgrim's Progress*, Richard Baxter's *Saint's Everlasting Rest*, Johann Arndt's *Wahres Christentum*, and particularly the *Practice of Piety* by Lewis Bayly, which was translated into at least five continental languages.[4]

In Germany, Pietism reached its zenith under the guidance of Spener (1635–1705), who had followed in the footsteps of Arndt, Valentin Andreae and Johann Gerhard; it was then a movement expressly opposed to what Pusey called Lutheran 'orthodoxism'. As a Preface to an edition of Arndt's sermons, which he wrote in 1675 and issued later under the title *Pia Desideria*, Spener outlined what might be termed the Pietist programme in the shape of six points:

i. the necessity of establishing 'collegia pietatis' for Bible reading and scriptural edification.
ii. the conception of the universal priesthood of believers, involving the duty of mutual instruction, inspiration and reproof.
iii. the practical nature of Christianity especially found in mutual love and service.

iv. the evils of religious controversy and an insistence on charity towards unbelievers and heretics.
v. the importance of piety as well as learning in candidates for the ministry, and the recommended reading of such books as the *Theologia Germanica*, Tauler's *Sermons* and the *Imitation of Christ*.
vi. the imperative need to make preaching simple and practical.

In his *Enquiry*, Pusey had prominently and enthusiastically described the work of Spener and his immediate disciples; he detailed Spener's deprecation of what appeared to him as an over-emphasis upon the theoretical aspects of religion, and how he preferred to stress personal piety and to relate theology to practice. Above all, Pusey recognized Spener's concern to cultivate all portions of the Christian system, including the doctrine then deprecated, that regeneration implied a transformation of character, evident on good works, through a vital union with Christ. It is significant that at the precise time that Pusey was engaged on a close study of Spener's teaching, he was explaining his own views on justification to his fiancée; the resemblance between Pusey's opinions and those of Spener was remarkable. Pusey told Maria Barker:

> My father and myself hold *in principle* the same opinions; both, that is by faith in Christ, not for our own merits, that we are justified; both that works are indispensable; my father, however, from hearing and seeing the abuses of preaching faith . . . *without works*, connects no other idea with the 'being justified by faith only' than by Faith exclusive of works, not only as not entitling us to salvation, but as being in no way necessary to it.[5]

From his practice of separating 'the things to be believed from the things to be practised', the elder Pusey, unlike his son, was unable to conceive of works as the fruits of faith; he regards them as 'duties'.[6] Pusey, however, having read Spener, was able to view works as 'the natural results of thankfulness and love towards God', and to state that 'for the difficulty whether works or faith are to be the subject of our final trial, the answer seems to me that they are inseparable'[7].

Throughout his account of early Pietism, Pusey was at pains to insist on Spener's orthodoxy and his attachment to the Church.

> He [Spener] distinguished between the faults of the individuals and that of the Church; he explained that though many preachers might in many ways fail in delivering the revealed truths, yet that the Lutheran Church possessed in her symbolical books the right doctrines, and on that account and of the due administration of the sacraments and of public worship, it was certainly the 'true visible' Church.[8]

It was probably because Pusey considered that his German friends, such as Tholuck, had largely recovered Spener's sense of the role of the Church that he could take such an optimistic view of the situation in Germany in 1830:

> The anticipated day has now for some time dawned, the vital warmth of spring is now returning: the spiritual world in Germany is putting off the dreary garb of winter; it is now starting up in the fresh vigour of renovated life . . . the crisis is past: there must be, and is, very different progress towards a better state; yet still there is everywhere progress: the stern dominion of Rationalism is broken and gone.[9]

Pusey was well aware that Pietism of the generation after Spener had declined; he had explained this process in his *Enquiry*, and it was Spener's successors that he had perhaps compared allusively to the English Evangelicals of whom he had heard. To his mind, however, his German friends appeared to have recovered something of the original Pietist spirit. After the Enlightenment and the upheavals of the Napoleonic wars, indeed, a quiet Pietism of the unlettered folk (a type admired by Pusey) did regain its strength; it influenced theology and preaching, coincided with philosophical development and went hand in hand with Romanticism. Perhaps most significantly in any consideration of Pusey's links with Pietism, it revived an interest in the processes of historical growth, the role of the Church, ancient devotional literature, and the Confessions of the Reformation.[10] Even though Pusey was ultimately disillusioned with affairs in Germany, it is possible that he appreciated that, in this New Pietist revival, his friends were endeavouring to transform an individualistic Evangelicalism into rejuvenated institutionalism. It is not, therefore, so difficult to understand Pusey's adherence to Tractarianism from 1834 onwards; until then, he had not found in England a type of High Churchmanship which satisfied his heart as well as his mind. In Germany, the fervour of his friends' devotions, so diametrically opposed to the emotionless religion he had encountered at home, at school and at the university, would have appealed to Pusey; his warm friendship with the Evangelical Newman, during his early days at Oriel, indicates that he felt a need for warmth in religion, even though he could not assent to the Evangelical tendency to lay stress on particular doctrines to the detriment of others. Pusey would have understood Grundtvig's description of the old High Church party in 1843 as 'the embalmed corpse of the beauty of the House of the Lord'[11], this came very close to Pusey's picture of it in 1828, which so upset H.J. Rose.

In addition, however, to finding in Germany a conception of religion which catered for all his needs, intellectual and emotional, Pusey seems also to have acquired a general outlook on life reminiscent of Spener. Liddon, indeed, suggests that 'in Pusey's feeling about Spener there is something presentimental', and that in character they closely resembled each other.[12] Pusey certainly steeped himself in Spener's writings and the biographies of him by Von Canstein, Knapp and Hossbach; he was of the firm opinion that 'A view of his [Spener's] deep piety, humility, charity, his practical judgment and character, cannot but be improving'.[13] Pusey also went to some lengths to show how it was not Spener, but later Pietists, who permitted the movement to degenerate into a phraseology from which the spirit had departed, who allowed private edification to decline into blatant hypocrisy, and who encouraged the 'adiaphora' controversies to reappear over whether worldly pleasures, such as dress and dancing, were sinful in themselves. More than a small portion of Pusey's *Enquiry* was taken up with illustrations of Spener's prudent handling of situations, including his condemnation of the publication of 'accounts of conversion, regeneration and renovation'; to Spener's mind, 'although there is but one way, in which all the children of God are led to salvation, there are many paths along this one way, by which he [God] leads different persons according to his wisdom'.[14] Such, indeed, was Pusey's admiration of Spener that he probably modelled his own behaviour on that of his hero; in time Pusey acquired so much of the gentleness he revered in Spener, that he himself was referred to as the 'Saint Barnabas of the [Oxford] Movement'.[15]

As a young man, Pusey had been a shot, was well known as a rider, had followed the hounds and indulged in novel reading, but from the time of his visits to Germany and his encounter with Pietist-influenced friends, he showed himself even more than usually reluctant to embark on what he termed 'ephemeral pursuits'. Whereas in 1824, he probably shared at least some of his friend John Parker's opinion that it was absurd of the Bishops of Chester and Lichfield, (Charles Blomfield and Henry Ryder), to forbid their clergy to attend such things as plays and balls[16], Pusey now found it depressing even to visit London, where people in general seemed oblivious of otherworldly matters. More and more he became the critic of luxury and eventually, among the Tractarians, perhaps the chief advocate of works of piety and charity.

> Alas, in this wealthy city [London], [he was then to say] with its frightful contrasts of extreme luxury and extreme misery, and luxury and misery either way of thousands of everliving beings, who once were made brethren in Christ, yet in life are strangers and estranged, loathing and loathed by one another, there is not one work of piety or charity, – the building houses of God, relieving God's peculiar care,

> the fatherless and the widow, tending Christ in His sick members, guarding those frail but hallowed temples of the Holy Spirit, the baptized children of the poor, on which a hundred fold more energy, than now is, should not be employed, for which sacrifices a thousand fold should not be made. Alas, in this wealthy city, Lazarus lies neglected many thousand times.[17]

Small wonder it was that Pusey had earlier praised the work of the Pietist Francke for his founding of orphanages, or that he himself, in later life, was to do much for the introduction of Sisterhoods into the Church of England.[18] Pusey's concern for the poor and his insistence on mutual love and service, so reminiscent of Pietist thought, ultimately found expression in such sermons as 'The Danger of Riches', 'Why Dives Lost His Soul'[19], and perhaps most eloquently in 'God With Us'. In this latter, he demanded 'gigantic efforts' on behalf of the poor:

> We know not too often of their existence; our fair houses are like painted sepulchres, hiding, by a goodly outside, from our own sight, the misery, and hunger, and cold, and nakedness, which we love not to look upon, but will rise in judgment against our nation, if we heed it not . . . We should treat their needs with reverence, not relieving them coldly, and as a form, but humble ourselves in heart before their patient suffering.[20]

It was probably Pusey's appreciation of the valuable features that the English Evangelicals shared with the Pietists that made him initially reluctant to join the Tractarians. Even as late as 1852, he was informing his cousin, Shaftesbury, that he wished not so much to oppose Evangelicalism, as 'to supply its defects'.[21] At the onset of the Oxford Movement, Pusey also told Newman that he considered he was being 'too hard on the "Peculiars" as you call them. You should conciliate them'.[22] In joining the Tractarians, therefore, it is not unlikely that Pusey hoped to foster an objectivized and institutionalized form of Pietism, such as he had experienced from his reading of Spener and found practised among his German friends. It is clear that he was not seeking simply for High Churchmanship or straightforward Evangelicalism, but rather for what he termed 'Catholic principles'.[23]

2. Origins and definitions

What was this Evangelicalism, within the Church of England, that Pusey admired but considered a maimed form of Christianity, and how had it arisen? By way of definition, Evangelicalism has been termed 'a school of Protestants' which held that 'the essence of "the Gospel" consists in the doctrine of salvation by faith in the atoning death of Christ, and denies that either good works or the sacraments have any saving efficacy'[24]. Even so, bald definitions are inadequate; too frequently the Evangelical Revival as a whole is still simplistically thought of as a solid, unified movement, first created, then led by John Wesley; too rarely had it been appreciated that 'the ethos of Anglican Evangelicalism was largely formed by men who owed little or nothing to Methodism and stood increasingly apart from it'.[25] In addition and perhaps equally important, it has now been proved that in the 18th and early 19th centuries 'the norm of Evangelicalism [in the Church of England] lay with the Moderates, with Venn and Simeon, Hey and Wilberforce, not with Toplady and the Hills'.[26] By and large this remained the case, even though mid 19th century controversies led many Moderates to adopt attitudes that earlier Evangelicals would have considered too intransigent. In theological terms, the bulk of educated Anglican Evangelicals were usually moderate Calvinists; the Evangelicalism of such as the Clapham Sect, for example, Pusey would in all probability not have found uncongenial; it was that of radical extremists that he deplored. In order to prove this, however, it is necessary to examine briefly the small but clear-cut group of theological concepts that the moderate Calvinists clung to, and to observe their effects on behaviour; only then, can one determine how it was that Pusey could claim to Shaftesbury in 1852 that he shared 'the fundamental truths' comprising Evangelicalism.[27]

The first promise of moderate Calvinism was belief in the doctrine of Total Depravity. Its adherents taught that the image of God in man had not been defaced but effaced by the Fall, and it naturally followed, therefore, that if man was basically evil, he could do nothing for his own salvation; he could be justified only by faith, God's free gift to his chosen; his heart being totally corrupt, needed the drastic change of conversion before it was suitable for God's service. To the Evangelicals, love and mercy were attributes of God, but justice and holiness, inseparable from God's perfection as Almighty, opposed to all moral impurity, were evident characteristics revealed in scripture. Because God's transcendent holiness was mirrored in the eternal Law, as realized in the Ten Commandments and man's conscience, they strived unceasingly 'to throw men down by the Law and to raise them again by the Gospel'; this they considered 'the preaching of the word'.[28] It was by being driven, as it were, from Sinai to Calvary, that the repentant sinner who experienced conversion, came to an understanding of the economy of Salvation. Without conversion, the Gospel was not fully meaningful and a man's heart remained unaffected by it; only Christ had ever satisfied the demands of the Law, and, to one who was converted, Christ's righteousness became an imputed gift; he was now able to participate in the New Covenant, saving faith having come to him (through no merit of his own) in a sudden or gradual awakening, by means of 'afflictive providences', preaching, prayer or Bible study.

Justification, however, was not the end of the matter; it was but the serious start of a work which required the whole of life to complete, even though Moderate Calvinism usually included the comforting doctrine of Final Perseverence.

Such, very crudely summarized, were the basic doctrinal teachings emphasized by the Anglican Evangelicals and, even in their developed form, they were frequently bitterly criticized. Their tenet of Justification by Faith alone was feared by some (by Pusey's father for example) as solafidianism; the doctrine of election was thought to weaken man's moral responsiblity. Their doctrine of the Holy Spirit, especially in connection with conversion, was distrusted by the opponents of Evangelicalism as smacking of 'enthusiasm'. Anglican Evangelicals in the main however were fully determined to prove that their critics were mistaken. Not only did their sermons usually stress the dangers of Antinomianism, but the operations of the Holy Spirit and the connections between faith and holiness were topics treated with especial care; good works were continually emphasized as the necessary fruits of a faith which justified and all religious impressions were tested by their scripturalness. 'Privilege and Duty, Imputed Righteousness and Personal Obedience – too often laid aside by Protestant extremists – were always preached conjointly by the Moderate Calvinists'.[29] Thus it was that they regarded good works as springing from an internal principle of love in the heart.

> In the vocabulary of the great evangelicals, heart-religion was something very different from the introspection of the mystic and still further from the sentimental *religion du coeur* of Rousseau's *Emile*. It was distinct from the uncontrolled emotionalism of a revival meeting, and far deeper than the particular 'frames' or feelings of day to day religious experience ... Vital religion claimed all man's faculties and not least his affections ... The essence of heart-religion was its engagement of the whole man, the unified self, complete in all its functions and attributes, in the service and love of God. Religion was a surrender of the whole personality, not a small section of activity marked off from the remainder of life.[30]

It is true that the pith of the Evangelicals' sermons was often narrow and limited to a repetition of the evangelical 'scheme', but this was largely due to their distrust of erecting dogmatic structures over and above (what they considered) the plain Scriptural basis of their teaching. This, however, not only often forced their sermons into an intensely practical vein, it made some among the Evangelicals hold to the title of 'Calvinist' with regret, since it implied too metaphysical and systematic a version of the simple scriptural 'Gospel Scheme'. They sheered away from some traditional Calvinist doctrines such as Reprobation and Supralapsarianism.[31] Though holding to particular election, they nonetheless held that Christ had died for all men, and not (as High Calvinists asserted) merely for the elect. Cling as they might to such central doctrines as Original Sin, Justification by Faith and Regeneration by the Holy Spirit, in the Calvinist controversy between Arminian and Calvinistic Methodists the major Anglican Evangelicals (with the exception of Toplady and Berridge) had taken no part. By the end of the 18th century they distinguished themselves sharply from Methodists and Dissenters, and held firmly to the rules of Anglican church order. Their moderation and their aversion to ecclesiastical irregularity were reflected in the pages of the *Christian Observer*, founded in 1802 as a vehicle for their views.

By the turn of the 19th century, the Evangelicals within the Church of England approximated to a cohesive party, possessing a degree of unity through local parochial and clerical societies and on the national scale with the formation of the Church Missionary Society. The advent of the French Revolution and subsequent Napoleonic wars increased their distrust of the political outlook of many Dissenters, and their accurate belief that 'Sectarianism' was multiplying; this in turn compelled the Evangelicals to assert their own churchmanship. A new emphasis appeared in their outlook on discipline, liturgy, respect for infant baptism, set forms of prayer, besides qualified defences of the episcopate and the establishment. The Clapham Sect's participation in politics encouraged them to become patriots. 'Up to the Revolution Evangelicalism had fought for every yard of its advance in Church and Society. Now the way was made straight'.[32] Fears of political convulsion, and insecurity concerning the changes in the social fabric of Britain (results of the industrial revolution), brought about a change in the outlook of the middle and upper classes; a recognition of the seriousness of life and the importance of moral earnestness, especially in the domestic sphere, began to dawn on them; they were ripe for conversion. Edmund Burke's *Reflections* may have encouraged this attitude, but it was also a tribute to Evangelical preaching and the writings of such Evangelicals as Hanah More, Wilberforce, and Arthur Young. 'The moral improvement which can be traced in the quality of English life between the latter part of the eighteenth century and 1830 was mainly due to them [the Evangelicals]'.[33] In the meantime, Evangelical theology had become even more moderate; Wilberforce was of the opinion that every year he became more 'impressed with the unscriptural character of the Calvinistic system'.[34] This is not to suggest, however, that the right wing members of the party ceased being Evangelical simply because they sometimes adopted the language and sentiments of the High Churchman; they often assumed these traits as a protest against the pretensions of the radical elements in the party.[35] In all probability, it was not the Evangelicalism of such as Simeon and Wilberforce and their moderate successors that Pusey would have found distasteful; he was much more likely in the first three decades of the 19th century to have been opposed to strident elements, who were followers of Edward Irving and Henry Drummond. In much the same way, indeed, that the *Christian Observer* school of Evangelicals viewed with concern the rise of pentecostal trends and the spirit of Pharisaism within the party after 1820, so Pusey had deprecated the appearance of more or less conscious hypocrisy among the Pietists who succeeded Spener. He would equally have appreciated that too much concentration by the radicals on the invisible True Church bred complacency towards administrative ills within the visible Church. He would have shared the dissatisfaction felt by the offspring of Wilberforce concerning the narrowness of the theology of militant Evangelicalism. No small number of the educated children of the moderate Evangelicals, such as Henry and Robert Wilberforce, George Ryder and Leslie Stephen, left the Evangelical party completely. Nevertheless, just as he had applauded the advent of Pietism in Germany as a reaction against Lutheran scholasticism, so he ever gave credit to Evangelicalism for having been in its origins a protest against prevalent rationalism.[36]

3. Eirenic proposals

To the end of his life, Pusey asserted that he could ever maintain with Evangelicals that 'I believe all which you believe; we only part where you deny'; this he termed his 'formula', and it sums up his attitude.[37] In 1839, when discussing Evangelical teaching with his friend H.V. Elliott of Brighton, Pusey could inform him that '*we* [the Tractarians] . . . look upon your views as imperfect, that you have taken up a portion of the truth only, and so, that if you receive the whole, your views must of necessity be modified; but we have no occasion to speak against you'.[38]

How had Pusey arrived at his view of Evangelicalism? Despite his father's distant Flemish refugee origins, Evangelicalism was not indigenous to the Pusey family; the elder Pusey, indeed, found certain aspects of its teaching distasteful. Neither as a schoolboy[39] nor as an undergraduate, had Pusey found religion in any particular form an abiding influence. In all probability, his first significant encounter with Evangelicalism was made at Oriel, in his early acquaintance with Newman. Though Newman saw that his friend was not then one of 'God's children', Pusey valued the relationship thus begun; in a sense, it perhaps paved the way for his discovery of similar qualities among his Pietist-influenced German friends. From 1826 onwards, Pusey also became acquainted with Robert Wilberforce; he corresponded with him from Germany and discussed the question of Robert's following him into the field of Biblical scholarship and Oriental languages.[40] On Pusey's return from the continent, Robert introduced him to the Wilberforce family at Highwood. There may have been other encounters with individual Evangelicals; contrary to previous widespread opinion, it is now known that the party was not small in numbers or influence at Oxford throughout the period of Pusey's intellectual development.[41] Pusey's own sister, Charlotte, was to marry R.L. Cotton, the Provost of Worcester, and one of the leading Evangelicals in the university. It is very probable that Pusey also sympathized strongly with his Evangelical cousin Ashley's labours to alleviate the sufferings of the poor. Nevertheless, the problem remains of determining how Pusey became aware of Evangelical theology.

In 1833, before he joined the Oxford Movement, and when he was chiding Newman for being too hard on his former colleagues, the Evangelicals, Pusey informed him that he himself was thinking of writing a paper to conciliate them. Because this was the occasion on which Pusey formally became a Tractarian, and because his first Tract was *On Fasting*, it has generally been supposed that this was the paper he had referred to in his conversation with Newman. This may be the case, especially as fasting was practised by some Evangelicals, and the Tract itself in its emphasis on personal and experimental factors contained overtones of Arndt and Spener. Much more significant, however, to the question of discovering the sources of Pusey's theoretical knowledge of Evangelicalism, were the letters to Pusey from Anne Tyndale, the Evangelical wife of the Rector of Holton near Oxford; a correspondence which H.P. Liddon overlooked. During the months immediately preceding his entry into the Oxford Movement, Pusey was resident at Holton and, indeed, he preached at Tyndale's church. Besides exchanging letters in which Anne Tyndale and Pusey asked each other questions concerning High Church and Evangelical teaching, they also passed each other books and Tracts; Pusey sent her the first tracts emanating from Oxford, and she sent him Evangelical papers (including a definition of the term Evangelical in which stress is placed on the need for 'a conciliatory spirit' in the Church), some of which she had written herself. This procedure lasted at least two years and, as a result, Pusey would have gained an insight into Evangelical doctrines and the manner in which some Evangelicals arrived at their opinions.

In what was perhaps the first of her letters, Anne Tyndale gives proof to the now accepted view that many Evangelicals were prepared to welcome and co-operate with the Tractarians in the early 1830s. In the defence of orthodoxy and the Articles, in the struggle against liberalism and rationalism, certainly the leaders of the two movements were united; as yet, the controversies over the Real Presence, the Eucharistic Sacrifice, Romanism and Ritualism had not arisen, to say nothing of Baptismal Regeneration and Gorham.[42] 'I feel anxious to tell you', wrote Mrs Tyndale in 1833, 'the thankfulness it excited in my mind to see the *sap* circulating between the two parties into which the *British Magazine* divides the Church of England. I mean the High Church and the Evangelical, and to see in each, the love of Christ the constraining principle'.[43] It was with regret that she found the sentiments expressed in the first Oxford Tract 'too refined' and puzzling.

> If it [Apostolic Succession] is the only accredited means of conveying Spiritual instruction to the Church, in what a dreadful state of famine the Church must be whenever a graceless man is appointed to a bishopric or a Ministry. The Succession having been so perfectly preserved would appear to me rather to be an interesting and curious circumstance as it relates to *Ecclesiastical* History or history of the *External* Church, than as it relates to the Spiritual history of the Church of Christ, which has been fed by many *other* Holy Shepherds, who we may suppose Christ would not have blessed had they been working contrary to his will.[44]

A few days later, and significant in view of the fact that Pusey was himself to write a tract stressing the importance of Baptismal Regeneration, Anne Tyndale was endeavouring to answer Pusey's request for 'some statement as to the connection of regeneration (regarded as a privilege) with baptism'.[45] Whether she and Pusey were aware at the time or not, her answer revealed that on this topic she stood theologically to the left of such representative Evangelicals as Simeon, Wilberforce and J.B. Sumner, all of whom did not confuse Regeneration with Conversion. She told Pusey:

> In the Evangelical School Regeneration means *only* a renewal of the heart by the influence of the Holy Spirit, either *before* baptism, *after* Baptism, or *at* Baptism, varying in different characters, and in some characters, altho' baptized never taking place at all.[46]

She was uncertain, however, whether she and Pusey were using the word Regeneration in the same sense; for her part, she had always regarded baptism as 'an outward and visible sign of His gracious disposition to adopt infants into his family, but further than this appears to be a great mistery' (*sic*).[47]

When Pusey sent her J.W. Bowden's Tract *On the Nature and Constitution of the Church of Christ* (Tract number 5), Anne Tyndale found it 'very difficult to believe that those Ministers who care nothing for God or Christ or Salvation are really ordained by the Holy Spirit'.[48] Nevertheless, just as she was ready to listen to Pusey's views on baptism, so she was willing to encourage his friends if it meant that 'Christ should be glorified in his Church', so that the Church would be addressed as truly beautiful 'when once the stones really become living stones'.[49]

After Pusey had joined the Oxford Movement, his correspondence with Anne Tyndale continued in its eirenic vein; they seem to have shared a common view as to the role of the Tract writers. She asked him:

> Is not the Ecclesiastical Kingdom that which the High Churchmen as a party are the most anxious to support, if we except a few individuals? Is not the Spiritual Kingdom that to which the attention of the Evangelicals is chiefly directed? The only cause of division is perhaps that each takes a part instead of the whole. The Oxford writers seem anxious to take both and in proportion as they do this I expect to see the Evangelical party flock to them. I think I understand now why you do not look upon Milner as giving much *ecclesiastical* information; his is a *Spiritual* history.[50]

Concerned with the problem of unity, Anne Tyndale had been able to applaud Newman's Tract on *Thoughts on Alterations in the Liturgy . . . The Principle of Unity*; she hoped that Pusey's friend would go on with his 'testimonies to the Spirit of Unity', her own ideas having always centred on chapter IV of the Epistle to the Ephesians.[51] On the subject of frequent Communion, however, she had doubts. It seems that in common with many Evangelicals (amongst whom Holy Communion was often referred to as THE Sacrament), she valued it in proportion to its rarity, and she feared 'running the risk of its being done formally'. Should there not be 'a great change in the habits and manners of Christian families' and in 'the present style of living', before people 'will be sufficiently liberated from the cares which now choke the work, to receive the Communion profitably', she asked?[52]

Having experienced friendly relationships with Evangelicals such as Anne Tyndale, and witnessing their deep concern for the cause of religion, it is not difficult to understand Pusey's words thirty years later:

> Ever since I knew them (which was not in my earliest years), I have loved those who are called 'Evangelicals'. I have loved them, because they loved our Lord. I have loved them, for their zeal for souls. I often thought them narrow; yet I was often drawn to individuals among them more than to others who held truths in common with myself, which the Evangelicals did not hold, at least explicitly. I believed them to be 'of the truth'. I have ever believed and believe, that their faith was and is, on some points of doctrine, much truer than their words. I believed and believe, that they are often withheld from the clear and full sight of the truth by an inveterate prejudice, that that truth, as held by us, is united with error, or with indistinct acknowledgement of other truths which they themselves hold sacred. Whilst, then, I lived in society, I ever sought them out, both out of love for themselves, and because I believed that nothing (with God's help) so dispels untrue prejudice as personal intercourse, heart to heart, with those against

whom that prejudice is entertained. I sought to point out to them our common basis of faith.[53]

4. Shared fundamentals

What were the affinities in both thought and behaviour that Pusey shared with the Evangelicals, and how did he attempt to make up for (what he deemed) deficiencies in their teaching? Despite the clear differences between the two movements in respect to history and tradition, and what he terms 'an undeniable change of emphasis from the subjective to the objective of faith', Brilioth maintained that there were four matters in which Evangelicals and Tractarians closely resembled each other in the sphere of doctrine and on points of practical significance. Just as early Tractarians had rested firmly on the Prayer Book, so he thought later Evangelicals were continuing this tradition in their campaign against the Ritualists. On the doctrine of Holy Communion and the Eucharist (as a pleading of the sacrifice on the Cross), he considered that the two movements were not contrary, and in their basic attitude to Scripture he thought they scarcely differed. Brilioth also found affinity between the renewal of Anglican preaching, which accompanied the first phase of Tractarianism, and the emphasis which Evangelicals placed on preaching the Word[54]. Among the Tractarians as a whole, he further claimed to have discerned three types in their attitude to Evangelicalism. First there were such men as Keble, Froude, Isaac Williams and Church, who regarded the Oxford Movement simply as a reassertion of old ideals and who showed little interest in Evangelicalism. Secondly, there were the followers of Newman, many of whom had been reared as Evangelicals, but who were ultimately carried beyond the Oxford Movement in their religious development. Finally, there were those who never denied religious affinity between Tractarianism and Evangelicalism; of this last group, Brilioth suggested that Pusey was the chief representative.[55] Unfortunately, Brilioth did not develop this last point. Pusey's rapport with Evangelicalism went even deeper than Brilioth had managed to convey in his illuminating but brief study.

Perhaps above all, Pusey would have appreciated and shared the Evangelical 'thirst for holiness'; he would have echoed Simeon's remark that 'Progress in holiness is above all things to be desired',[56] and he would have assented to Wilberforce's idea that 'the nature of that holiness in which the true Christian seeks to progress is no other than the restoration of the image of God in his soul'.[57] The emphasis on holiness, indeed, was the prime feature which all Tractarians shared with the Evangelicals. As a generalization, it is true that 'like its predecessor the Evangelical Movement, it [the Oxford Movement] was more a movement of the heart than of the head'[58], and (in a modified sense) 'an impulse of the heart and conscience, not an inquiry of the head'.[59] Pusey, however, had undertaken this quest for holiness before he joined the Tractarians; his first sermon of 1828 had as its text 'Follow peace with all, and holiness without which no man shall see the Lord'.[60]

In later years, it was Pusey's preoccupation with the gravity of post-baptismal sin that also lent his thoughts on 'the fewness of the Saved' a certain resemblance to moderate Calvinism. In Pusey's case, however, he was led to such views by Saints Paul and Augustine:

> What is the very name of Christians in St. Paul but 'the elect', i.e. those 'chosen out of' the greater mass who remained; and of those thus chosen, there is yet a smaller body, which, when the larger part are cast away, shall be 'the chosen'. Again, the name by which our Lord calls His disciples, is 'a little flock'. He prays for them who are chosen out of the world. They are but as a heap of corn, small compared to the chaff from which it is sifted.[61]

Pusey's conviction of the enormity of sin also enabled him to see the need for Conversion; the manner in which he tackled this issue (in what he termed 'its wide and narrow sense') would probably not have offended the right wing Evangelicals:

> For in its widest sense 'conversion' is a turning towards God; and if, by His mercy we have been preserved from being turned away from Him, yet none of us can say, that we have been, or are turned to Him as fully as we might be . . . But besides this, Conversion may be taken in a narrower sense, for the first turning of the soul to God after it has been estranged from Him.[62]

He was not unaware of the frequent connection between misfortune and conversion; he may have known of this in the personal lives of Newman and Manning. 'It is . . . mostly amid terror and amazement', Pusey said, 'that men are restored to God. God has impressed a law on the natural world also, that healthful cure can, for the most part, only take place through bitterness and suffering'.[63] At certain points in his sermon on 'Conversion', Pusey seemed to forget that he was trying to inculcate a sense of balance and sobriety into the topic; he then adopted the language of a revivalist preacher:

> Fear, exceeding fear of Hell is one of the most usual ways in which God brings us back to Himself . . . Judgement to come is preached, and they, whom we should least expect, or have least deemed it needful for them tremble. But God 'seeth not as man sees'; 'the wind bloweth where it listeth', the Spirit descendeth as 'a Spirit of burning' . . . Those around know not, or learn, as it seems, by accident, what is working within. But day after day He brings before them the fear of Judgement . . . He brings before them endless misery, years after years still the same, so that they wish they had never been born. Others of elder years, night after night, He has terrified with visions of Hell . . . Others He has kept waking day and night, with Hell ever plain before their eyes . . . Others He has kept, year after year, upright, performing their duty to Him and to man, but hopeless of their salvation. He has written it on the wall, in the midst of gaiety and dissipation, as in Belshazzar's feast, so that the memory of that fearful hour should live on in the soul for ever and ever.[64]

Pusey's stress on sin and the necessity of constant consideration of the Four Last Things, was doubtless a tendency which emanated from his own psychological make-up, but it was a feature he shared with Evangelicals. There can be no disputing the fact that he emphasized at least his own total depravity. He was equally convinced with Evangelicals of the vital importance of the Atonement. In his Preface to Surin's *The Foundations of the Spiritual Life* (1874 edition) Pusey acknowledged that it was through Evangelicalism that 'a vivid and energetic, however partial, preaching of the corruption of human nature, and of the Cross . . . by the Providence of God broke in upon an age of torpor and smooth easy ways of religion'.[65] An insight into how he considered Evangelicals had taught only part of the truth, is contained in his sermon 'The Cross borne for us, and in us'; in this he spoke conjointly of the value of the Cross and the Sacraments:

> The whole of the Gospel is the doctrine of the Cross, but that two-fold; the Cross borne for us, and the virtue and power of the Cross by the Sacraments communicated to us, and henceforth to be borne *by* us.[66]

In a similar way, Pusey appreciated the significance of preaching; it would have been with the emphasis that some of the Evangelical party placed on it, to the detriment of other things, that Pusey would have quarrelled. He might not have agreed that it was through preaching the Word that the saving work of the Spirit chiefly operated, but he was immensely aware of its importance; he would have assented to Simeon's notion that the object of preaching was 'to humble the sinner, to exalt the Saviour, and to promote Holiness'.[67] On one occasion, indeed, he expressed a similar idea but in even stronger language than Simeon. 'God's servants', Pusey said, 'have a two-fold message to deliver, – of terror, and of peace; of an offended God, and a Just Judge; of life and death; of heaven and hell; of everlasting joy, and of the never-dying worm, the never extinguished fire'.[68] As a member of the Tractarian movement, however, and as a disciple of Keble, Pusey would have appreciated equally as well the sentiments expressed by Isaac Williams:

> If people were now asked, what was the most powerful means of advancing the cause of religion in the world, we should be told that it was eloquence of speech or preaching; and the excellency of speech consists in delivery ... Whereas, if we were to judge from Holy Scripture, of what were the best means of promoting Christianity in the world, we should say obedience; and if we were to be asked the second, we should say obedience; and if we were to be asked the third, we should say obedience.[69]

It is well known that in 1840 Pusey wrote his celebrated answer to the question 'What is Puseyism?' under a series of thirteen headings[70], the first six of which he regarded as ideas stressed in Tractarian teaching, and the remaining seven as those which indicated 'the broad line of difference between the views so designated [Puseyism] and the system of Calvin'. Significantly, however, he spoke of Calvinism as having been 'only partially adopted in our Church'; he was of the opinion that it was not 'for the most part held by conscientious and earnest-minded persons' in the Church of England. He also emphasized his conviction that 'there is less difference between right-minded persons on both sides than these often suppose – that differences which seemed considerable are really so only in *the way of stating them*'. Such sentiments clearly suggest that Pusey felt affinities to exist between himself and at least the moderate Evangelicals; he believed that such Evangelicals only blamed him for (what they considered) his too high estimate of Tractarian tenets. Pusey's feeling of kinship with right-wing Evangelicals, and their fear that he gave too much consideration to matters only relatively important in their eyes, were natural results of the manner in which he had developed intellectually since the late 1820s. As we have seen, before Pusey formally joined the Oxford Movement, many of the views which he had expressed at the time he was writing his *Enquiry* into the theology of Germany, were of a kind that would not have offended some Anglican Evangelicals in the least. 'When I first began to desire and seek . . . wisdom, I set out with the assurance, that it was to be found in the Holy Scriptures, and nowhere else; they alone being able to make us wise unto Salvation'.[71] These words of Thomas Scott in 1779 were not unlike Pusey's utterances fifty years later. Though Pusey's thoughts on Inspiration brought him into collision with the radically-minded *Record* in the 1840s, and though he had by then fully imbibed the role that it was 'the Church to teach, the Bible to prove', his devotion to Scripture remained. In his insistence on the broad and comprehensive character of the Bible, Pusey also equalled in the intensity of his convictions such Evangelicals as Charles Simeon. Pusey's efforts to improve the training of men for the Ministry was another field in which he resembled the Cambridge divine. The remarks which Pusey had written in his *Enquiry* concerning the place of the episcopate in the Church, were reminiscent of those uttered by such Evangelicals as Thomas Dykes, who 'loved the episcopal form of government, but did not regard it as indispensable to the existence of the Church'.[72] Pusey's early love for his German friends and his respect for the Protestant churches, almost echoed some of the sentiments expressed by T. Haweis in his *Plea for Peace and Union* of 1796. In his readiness to recognize the virtues of the 16th century reformers, Pusey would have found kinship with all Evangelicals until the mid 1840s. Having studied Spener, he had a grasp of Evangelical teaching on Justification by Faith, and the role of Good Works.

After the revolution that occurred in his thought and behaviour in 1835, Pusey undoubtedly modified many of his former opinions and attitudes; as his theological outlook evolved, he especially gave greater attention to such Sacraments as Baptism, the Eucharist and Penance, and to Tradition. But, though his views may have altered largely owing to the influence of Keble and Newman, we also know that, within the Oxford Movement itself, Pusey occupied a very individual position. This state of affairs was accurately observed by Pusey's Evangelical friend, H.V. Elliott in 1839 when he told Pusey:

> I love the fair, gentle and humble spirit, Pusey, which distinguishes your books from others of the same school, in many of which there is, I am sorry to be obliged to think, abundant bitterness and what is more, secret bitterness. Again, you speak out: others are often so obscure that they seem to leave a back door open to get out of their own propositions ... I will only add one more thing. Your books have made me pray more than I ever did in my life before for the spirit of truth, unity and concord in our beloved Church – and the whole Catholic Church.[73]

It was perhaps as much as anything this spirit of tolerance which in later years led Pusey to defend so vigorously the activities of the Ritualists, even though he was not one himself; in the initial stages of the revival of ceremonial, he had been careful to warn against 'points of singularity' and 'matters of personal distinction' in the younger Tractarians. The manner in which he warned the enthusiastic J.F. Russell against such things, was reminiscent of the moderate Evangelicals' advice to their own radicals on the dangers of self-indulgence and vanity. Pusey told Russell:

> It seems beginning at the wrong end for the ministers to deck their own persons: our own plain dresses are more in keeping with the state of our Church, which is one of humiliation.[74]

Equally with the older Evangelicals, Pusey possessed their passion for souls, but just as much he also recognized the deceitfulness of emotions. As early as 1829, Pusey had endeavoured to explain to Keble how he regarded the role of emotion in religion, and those aspects of it which he deplored:

> On the province of 'feeling' in Religion, I fear that I shall be widely mistaken: it would be almost too much to expect that a distinction should be made between 'feelings' and 'feeling': the one the faculty of the mind, the other the outward manifestations of that faculty – the emotions. It is I think the employment of the latter as a test of religion,

> which has caused so much mischief and self-deception and misery: while the neglect of the former appeared to me also to have been injurious to Religion by causing the intellect to be alone considered.[75]

Eight years later, (albeit still aware of the value of 'heart-religion'), he deprecated over-emphasis on externals in liturgy. What he most wanted was concentration on the truths of religion. 'The Low Church [by which he meant the Evangelicals'] theology', he told Russell, 'has frequent mention of the cross, and we see that it has degenerated oftentimes into mere words: but as easily may the representation of it (on altars and vestments) become a mere shadow'.[76] On the other hand, Pusey was well able to applaud people's acceptance of 'Catholic views', especially, as he informed his friend Tholuck, if they were 'leaving the narrowness of the so-called Evangelical party; or, often, adding to their previous warmth and energy, the depth and reverence which belong to the old Church's view of the Incarnation, as connected with the Sacraments'.[77]

Perhaps the greatest fundamental characteristic that Pusey shared with Evangelicals was his religious seriousness.[78] In the same way that the moderate Evangelicals had endeavoured to differentiate between 'real' and 'nominal' Christians, ever since Joseph Milner had done in his *History of the Church of Christ*[79], so in a similar way did Pusey. The practical conclusions that Pusey reached in his observations, were not unlike those of Wilberforce, who in 1823 had expressed himself very positively:

> One of the main differences ... between real Christians and nominal consists in the cases in which they respectively apply religious principles. Even nominal Christians apply them on great occasions; real Christians apply them on small, that is on all and thus a habit is formed.[80]

In the view of the historian David Newsome, Wilberforce was convinced that 'real' Christians were thus marked off from others by the possession of the quality of 'seriousness', which showed itself in one's bearing and demeanour.[81] This 'gave to Evangelicalism its spirit of dedication and its fire of zeal, and also established a kind of mint-mark whereby the faithful could be immediately discerned'. In the Preface to his sermon 'The Day of Judgement', Pusey can be seen deliberately inculcating this notion of peculiar earnestness:

> What is lamentable is that one sees in so many even well-minded persons . . . [that] they seem to act, at most, as though they were under a sort of general law; they acknowledge, that they are to avoid certain classes of action (as those forbidden in the Ten Commandments), that they are to perform certain others, such as acts of mercy and charity; they are aware that they are to act, in the main, on certain motives, but they seem to have no notion that they are responsible to God in all the details of their actions. They seem to act as to their time, incomes, expenses, dress, tables, speech, and so on, as if they were their own masters, not as having received all they are and have, and having of all to give account before God. It is plain on the very surface of society, that people are not even aiming to live under an habitual sense of their responsibility to Almighty God. Religious people, for instance, often speak in a religious way about religion, and in a wordly way about wordly things; as if religion and the world had each their proper sphere; as though religion ought not rather to pervade and sanctify every thing[82].

Thus it was that Pusey was considered by some Evangelicals to have adopted part of their programme. W.F. Hook gleefully told Pusey:

> The bitterness of the Leaders of the old Evangelical Party 'is to be traced to the fact of *your* having taken the wind out of their sails. They were considered the *really* pious people in our Church; the High Churchmen were represented as ungodly: this is no longer said, hence the

> rancour of the *ungodly* Evangelicals, under whose influence there are not at present many godly men.[83]

Pusey was not doing this for selfish or party reasons, however; in the manner of Spener, he was endeavouring to incorporate (what he deemed) the positive features of Evangelicalism into a wider framework of doctrine.

6
NATIONAL AND UNIVERSITY AFFAIRS

1. The Church in danger

In an article in *The Edinburgh Review*, it was once said of Pusey that he was 'a fossil, embedded in his library, and the only events which befell him were mere domestic incidents'.[1] A more recent writer, and one more kindly disposed to Pusey, has suggested that it should rightly have been said of him that 'he had one foot in heaven and the other foot in the third century A.D.'.[2] A study of Pusey's interest and involvement in national and university affairs during his early manhood, however, makes it quite clear that he was only too well aware of what was happening in the outside world, and that his feet were fully in the 19th century. Even during the years when he was most involved in the Tractarian movement, Pusey regarded his Oxford activities simply as 'an effective means of bringing to the vivid consciousness of members of the Church of England, Catholic truths, taught of old within her'.[3] He thought of the Oxford Movement merely as a phase, albeit an important one, in the life of the Church as a whole and at no time were his ideas and interests limited only to Tractarian concerns.[4]

As we have seen, from the moment of his birth into upper class surroundings, and throughout the whole of his school and undergraduate days, Pusey encountered members of his own family and friends to whom politics were a passion. As a young don, Pusey had gained himself a reputation as a Liberal. From his earliest years, Pusey also enjoyed an especially intimate relationship with his elder brother Philip. When the latter became an M.P. in 1830, Pusey took a lively interest in all his activities. Philip's avowed ambition in parliament was not 'to make speeches', but to foster 'practical legislation'; this wish was inspired by his attention to constitutional and financial topics, as well as his deep concern for experimental farming.[5] Besides being the close friend of Peel and Gladstone, however, Philip Pusey was also on social terms with other influential figures of the day, such as Samuel Rogers, Monckton Milnes, Lord Spencer, Samuel Wilberforce, Lord Stanhope, Carlyle and Grote[6], many of whom Edward Pusey met at his brother's house. Relations between the Puseys and the Chevalier Bunsen were more than usually close. From his first meeting with Philip Pusey at the Palazzo Aldobrandi in Rome (where Philip and his wife lived in the early 1820s), Bunsen, the minister of the Prussian legation to the Holy See from 1823 to 1839, was welcomed into the whole Pusey family circle as an intimate friend. He later wrote to his wife:

> I wish I could give you an adequate idea of the love and admiration I feel for [Philip] Pusey: *admiration* for his extraordinary statesmanlike judgment, wherever he is, on the ground of his parliamentary life and business, in which he moves as a fish in the water; not less for his admirable temper and character: and *love*, for his unspeakable goodness to me.[7]

Thus it was largely through his brother and Bunsen that Pusey was able to keep himself fully informed of events on the continent[8] and in parliament. Already, however, his cousin Lord Ashley was in the Commons and his uncle, the Earl of Radnor, sat in the Lords.

For all his devotion to academic matters, none of his contemporaries doubted that Pusey was immensely interested in current affairs. In December 1829 he approved the founding of King's College, London, and he assumed that his friend Tholuck would share his delight at the prospect of Church reform. He wrote:

> You will be glad to hear that a Commission has been instituted to reform our Ecclesiastical Laws, with a view to a more regular, speedy and effective discipline of the Clergy, which will be a great blessing to us.[9]

It was largely politics, indeed, which ultimately led Pusey to throw in his lot with the Tractarians when he became alarmed for the safety of the Church at the hands of Whig politicians. Politics contributed in no small measure to the enormous change which came over Pusey's outlook in the early 1830s.

In 1830 itself Pusey was fearful of events in Europe. After the uprising in Paris, revolutionary fever had spread to the Swiss Cantons, to parts of Germany and to Belgium; it showed itself initially in England in the form of agricultural discontent and the outbreak of revolt among farm labourers[10], which was harshly suppressed by the government. Soon, however, popular agitation for parliamentary reform broke out, particularly during the prorogation of parliament from October 1830 to November 1831. The fury of the rioters was aimed especially at the established Church, twenty-one of whose bishops had voted against reform. Such a decision by the bench had the effect of uniting Catholics, Dissenters and demagogues more closely with the Whigs; an alliance which had begun in the 1820s in the agitation for the repeal of the Test and Corporations Act and Emancipation. The grievances of the Dissenters were genuine; they felt keenly the hardships imposed on them by the state in such matters as the registration of births, marriage, burial, church rates and higher education.[11] Their inability to obtain redress on all these points, ultimately made them bitter opponents of the establishment. From the early 1830s onwards, but especially when they became disillusioned with the ministries of Grey and Melbourne, Dissenters began their radical attacks on the Church of England. Extreme, but influential in his attitude towards the established Church was T. Binney, a Congregationalist minister, who declared it 'a great national evil' and 'an obstacle to the progress of truth and godliness in the land'; 'its end', he said, 'is most devoutly to be wished by every lover of God and man'.[12] In 1834 the Congregationalists established a Voluntary Church Association precisely for this purpose. Five years later, Radicals and Dissenters joined together in a Religious Freedom Society; this union had appreciable effect in parliamentary elections and within the Chartist movement.[13] The campaign against the Church of England received a major fillip in 1841 with the publication of *The Non-Conformist*, and, three years later, when Edward Miall, another Congregationalist minister, used the British Anti-State Association to promote the election of further Dissenters to parliament.[14]

Until 1834, Pusey, though fearful of the direction national events were taking, was not blind to the need for Church reform nor opposed to political innovation. In 1831 he urged Hawkins, the Provost of Oriel, to persuade the Hebdomadal Board at Oxford to do something at least about the issue of Parliamentary Reform and not simply oppose it.[15] Of the Ecclesiastical Inquiry Commission appointed in June 1831, Pusey considered that the Church had much reason to desire such an inquiry and that it seemed unlikely to lead to evil results.[16] Rather like Grey himself (in whose cabinet of fourteen members only four sat in the Commons), Pusey believed that unless the privileged sections of society were prepared to adapt and to improve, national catastrophe might ensue. Fear of revolution was a commonplace emotion among intellectuals in the early 1830s[17], but for the moment Pusey showed no signs of antagonism towards a ministry likely to be influenced in its legislation by the Benthamite philosophy of 'Utility' and the economic doctrines of Adam Smith and Ricardo, with their emphasis on *laissez-faire*. It was only when the government seemed bent on deliberate and 'scientific' interference to achieve a harmony of interests within the nation, that Pusey was offended.

He would have agreed that 'old opinions, feelings – ancestral customs and institutions are crumbling away, and both the spiritual and temporal worlds are darkened by the shadow of change'[18], but in his *Cathedral Institutions*, published in 1833, Pusey endeavoured to show how ancient institutions might be adapted to meet the needs of the age without being destroyed. Until Pusey joined the Oxford Movement and became more open to the influence of the ultra-Tory views of Keble, he was not opposed to political change, though he was concerned to insist that the precious fabric of the constitution, including the Church, should not be rent, and that alterations should be gradual. Even in 1836 when Keble expressed surprise at Pusey's 'general approbation of the pending Church Reform'[19], Pusey asked why no clergy spoke out against it except those who were members of Chapters.[20] Though in 1833 Pusey could recognize the spirit of the age, he was not as alarmed as some of his friends:

> The two characteristic evils of our times are *excitement and superficialness*, either reproducing the other. Great progress has been made in the intellectual cultivation of one, perhaps of several portions of society; much fallow land has been broken up, and it may please God hereafter to make this also productive unto good. But the immediate effect of so sudden and rapid a change must, of necessity, be detrimental as well to the higher degrees of intellectual improvement, as to a sober state of feeling and a calm estimate of things . . . In proportion, then, as every class of society advances in secular knowledge, or intellectual cultivation, in that degree do they themselves need a balance of increased religious knowledge.[21]

Newman saw things rather more hysterically. 'Though all holy interests and the cause of the Church', he told Pusey, 'seems to lie at the mercy of bad men who have not the faith, yet we know the triumphing of the wicked is short. No good ever came . . . from seizing on consecrated things'[22].

Though Pusey did not join the Oxford Movement at its inception and though he did not seem to regard Keble's Assize Sermon of 14 July 1833 as being of particular significance, his concern for the fate of the Church equalled, and his knowledge of ecclesiastical politics excelled, that of most of the early Tractarians. The factor which ultimately drove him into the Oxford Movement, besides fear for the University at the hands of Dissenters, was what he considered the increasingly Erastian tendency of successive governments, especially their 'attack on property'.[23] In his *Cathedral Institutions*, in which he endeavoured to indicate how the efficiency of cathedrals might be increased by making them the nuclei of seminaries, Pusey 'gave the lie direct'[24] to Lord Henley, Peel's brother-in-law, whose *Plan of Church Reform* had advocated that Chapters be reduced. At the same time, Pusey's paramount concern was to ensure that in any proposed reform of cathedrals the rights of property and trusts be safeguarded:

> It is manifestly of the utmost importance that we should, in these days, have definite and distinct notions upon the subject, and to these notions adhere uncompromisingly, – that not only should we not yield one jot or tittle of *right* to any *expediency*, however apparently pressing, but that we should take heed that our views of right be not unconsciously warped by a reference to expediency, – that our rule of right be not crooked.[25]

Such ideas were calculated to appeal greatly to the instincts of the country gentry.[26] It was when the preponderantly Whig Ecclesiastical Commission, appointed in March 1835 as successor to that established by Peel, seemed to be disregarding these principles, and when his own notions of how reform should be conducted were ignored, that Pusey linked forces with the Tractarians. He had fully explained his view in 1833.

> The present reformers of the Church appear to have begun at the wrong end. Our first object ought not to be, to ascertain how much one might by any possibility curtail, but how much one ought to retain; what offices the good estate of the Church demands, if not in their present, at least in some kindred form; what duties, in fact, besides those of the parochial Clergy and of Episcopal superintendence are required for the healthful condition of the Church.[27]

These are not the words of a person opposed to reform, but of someone prepared to adapt to the changed nature of society. In a different way, Dr Arnold retaliated against Henley by producing his pamphlet *The Principles of Church*

Reform, in which he suggested the opening of the doors of the Church of England to Dissenters; this scheme was dubbed by *The Times* an ecclesiastical Noah's ark; a remark which did injustice to much of Arnold's insight into social and ecclesiastical abuses.[28] Hearing of Arnold's ideas, Newman wrote to Pusey expressing his alarm lest Arnold was 'opening the door to alterations in *doctrine*'[29], and William Palmer considered the whole period as one of unmixed evil:

> Nothing was heard but dissatisfaction with the Church – with her abuses – her corruption – her errors! Every sciolist presented his puny designs for reconstructing this august temple built by no human hands.[30]

After the publication of *The Extraordinary Black Book* in 1831, however, it would have been difficult for anyone to have been unaware of ills in the Church. Though Tractarians like Palmer were later to exaggerate the abuses in order to exalt the achievements of the Oxford Movement, it is to Pusey's credit that his main concern was to inject a wholesome sense of moderation into the debate in the early 1830s. It is not likely that he took a complacent view of such revelations as that the bishops controlled 1,500 out of 11,700 benefices, and that a benefice was often regarded as an item of property and auctioned. He would certainly not have been surprised to learn that about 4,000 of the clergy's freeholds were not worth more than £50 per year and individuals were therefore compelled to resort to pluralism. Similarly, he would probably have appreciated that pluralism accounted for 6,000 benefices being without a resident incumbent, and that the curates who performed pastoral duties in such parishes were often paid less than labourers in their flock. In time, indeed, Pusey was to prove just how much he recognized that the Church was making inadequate provision for the spiritual needs of the mass of the population, especially in the North. Whereas once the Province of York had been poor and under-populated, with only 2,000 parishes and six bishoprics, compared to Canterbury's 18,000 parishes and twenty dioceses, the situation by the early 1830s had altered out of all recognition. The increase in the country's population as a whole, from twelve million in 1811 to sixteen and a half million in 1831, (by 1851 it increased to twenty-one million), had found the established Church largely unprepared. In Sheffield, for example, the population rose from 35,840 in 1811 to 59,011 in 1831, and similar increases were to be found in Manchester, Liverpool and Leeds. In addition there were rarely sufficient free seats for the poor; new Ministers often depended on pew rents for their income, and the rich sometimes objected to sitting alongside the poor.[31] Among all the Anglican churches put together in Sheffield in 1821, there were not as many as three hundred sittings for the poor[32], and such figures were not unusual.[33]

Pusey's awareness of the Church's problems was quite clear in 1833; when he debated the question of Church rates, for instance, he was alive to the issues involved. His advocacy of Separation rather than Indifferentism, however, reveals the movement of his mind along lines very removed from those of Arnold. He informed Gladstone that he had no objection to a tax on the richer clergy or any reduction in their income for the sake of parishes dependant on them:

> But if the Church Rates were to be abolished here I had much rather have the maintenance of the material Churches left to the Christian feeling of the public, than either to see a levy made for the support of *all* places of worship (for one could not conscientiously contribute to the support of an Unitarian Chapel) or to have it raised by a tax on the Clergy.[34]

Pusey further expressed his opinion that if funds of the Church were to be applied differently, they should be employed for the benefit of parishes in large towns. Taxation of the poorer clergy, he was sure, should 'not be resorted to except [in] an extreme case.[35] It was Pusey's tenacious hold on what he considered were the rights of property, however, which destroyed his sense of balance, and which embittered his future relations with Ecclesiastical Commissions; this was made evident in his reactions to the Irish Church reform bill. Just as much as the Tractarians, Pusey feared that similar measures might be enacted in England, but his chief worry was subtly different from theirs. He told Gladstone:

> I see not what right the State has to offer *our* [the Church's] property for sale, any more than that of the Marquis of Westminster. In England, I suppose, the great evil of such a measure would be the loosening the tenure of our property, and thereby of property generally.[36]

What Pusey showed himself unable to appreciate was the scandalously excessive number of clergy in the Church of Ireland in proportion to laity. Even after the suppression of ten sees, there still remained twelve bishoprics in the Irish Church, and only Chapters to which no care of souls was attached had been abolished. Similarly, incumbents and curates were only suspended in parishes in which no church service had been performed for three years[37]. Even sadder was Pusey's apparent ignorance of the sheer lawlessness which had arisen in Ireland, partly as a result of grievances against the established Church. In 1832 alone, nine thousand crimes had been committed, including 568 acts of incendiarism, 190 cases of cattle maiming and 242 murders.[38] Pusey might well tell Gladstone that 'whether one looks on the strife of men or of the elements, all for the time seems chaos'[39]. As far as he could see, however, improvement in the Church would come if only neglected duties were once again undertaken:

> All that I should wish would be that Sir Robert Peel should not so far commit himself or so divert Cathedral Property from its original purposes . . . There is a mode of applying Chapter to improve small livings, which I not only think just, but which ought I think to be made compulsory . . . In all such cases, if they have neglected their trust, or from circumstances been unable to realize it, I think that the State ought to enforce its execution; and I should be glad to see a Bill on the plan of the Archbishop's *enabling* Act,

> requiring Chapters to endow their poorer benefices in certain proportions, according to the Population.[40]

A year later, however, Pusey's moderation on the whole question of Church reform had hardened into intransigence. The widespread sale of church patronage following the Municipal Corporations Act, the appearance of Unitarians and Dissenters on town councils, the Registration and Dissenters' Marriages Act, and the general Tithe Commutation Act, were all events likely to commit Pusey more strongly to Tractarianism. Two bills introduced by Lord John Russell (one to remodel English sees in respect to size and income, and the other to suppress cathedral preferments and sinecure benefices) probably finally convinced Pusey that the Liberals were indulging in sacrilege; a view taken by Newman three years before. This attitude of Pusey's earned him a firm rebuke from his brother, who supported the bills and who considered Pusey's opposition precipitate. By now, however, events in Oxford had also contributed towards the revolution in Pusey's outlook.

2. University issues

Oxford in the early 1830s reflected on a lesser but equally virulent scale, almost all the strain felt by ancient, unreformed and privileged corporations throughout the country; before the Royal Commission began its work in 1850, the university was a microcosm of those institutions under fire from the Radicals and Dissenters. Just as the established Church faced mounting criticism from Unitarians, Presbyterians, Congregationalists and Baptists, so did Oxford. In Pusey's mind the Church and University were historically and traditionally inseparable; an attack on the university was equivalent to questioning the fundamentals of his faith. When the Whig success at the polls in 1830 encouraged those outside the Anglican Church to embark on a campaign of abuse against the university[41], it was unlikely that Pusey would remain indifferent. Denied the benefits of higher education at Oxford and Cambridge for so long, Dissenters were stimulated by the reform of parliament to claim an unbridled right of entry into what they called the 'national universities'. In the opinion of many senior members of Oxford university, including Pusey, if the Dissenters met with success it would be tantamount to a violation of Oxford's 'legal and prescriptive Rights'; it would 'subvert the system of Religious Instruction and Discipline, so long and so beneficially exercised by us', and 'by dissolving the union between the University and the Church of England' would 'impair the efficiency, and endanger the security of both'.[42] To the Radicals, the university system was encumbered by Subscription (in addition to oaths, fees, tithes and preferments), but Pusey saw the matter differently. His uncle the Earl of Radnor, who was not only the head of the Bouverie family but one of the leading opponents of Subscription in the House of Lords, asked Pusey for an explanation of his views. Pusey informed him that Subscription was 'a solemn and influential act'[43]. In a sense, therefore, it was the Dissenters and their allies the Radicals, as well as such men as Sir William Hamilton, J.S. Mill, Arnold and Conop Thirlwall (all of whom sided on this issue with the Nonconformist claims), who drove Pusey into the arms of the Tractarians and beyond the Protestant High-Churchmanship of the Hebdomadal Board. When this latter body seemed prepared to bow to pressure from a government which found Subscription a useful device to distract Dissenters from the problem of Church establishment, Pusey reacted as to a clarion call. 'You will have heard', he told Newman at the end of 1834, 'that the Heads of Houses have decided by a majority of one to displace the Articles from Undergraduate subscription: I will gladly join in any measure, which can be adopted to fight the battle in Convocation'.[44] It now mattered little to Pusey that parliament had received 1003 petitions from Dissenters, and that the Duke of Wellington had advised the Hebdomadal Board to 'overhaul every university and college statute, to abolish what was obsolete and bring regulations and practice into harmony'[45]. Pusey was bent on destroying arguments that the religious content of Oxford education was insignificant, and that no harm would come from the admission of Nonconformists; it was to this end that he published a Flyleaf of twenty-three *Questions*[46] and worked alongside Newman. Thereafter, Pusey was a member of the Tractarian party; no longer did he have any hesitation. As though to prove his allegiance, Pusey soon published his *Tract on Baptism* and inaugurated the reign of austerity in his family; his role in the subsequent Hampden affair was a logical conclusion to his change of outlook.

Ever since R.D. Hampden had declared that he was not opposed in principle to the admission of Dissenters, but thought it was only a matter for the university to settle, he had been an object of suspicion to the Tractarians. When he was therefore appointed a professor of Divinity by Melbourne in 1836, Pusey joined in the outcry and the attempts to declare his theology unorthodox, especially on the interpretation of formularies:

> In our present state it was enough to shew that Dr. H.'s system, as a system, went counter to that of the Articles, to shew the leprous spot, and warn people to flee infection. There is somewhere a very valuable rule of Vincent of Lerins, to this effect, 'When a heresy first appears, put it down, if you can; afterwards, if it gains head and you must, enter into arguments' . . . the conflict is moral, not intellectual.[47]

The conflict with Hampden also compelled Pusey to revise his ideas on the whole question of ecclesiastical appointments. He told Gladstone:

> The Church must now make some great effort or is lost, i.e. corrupted in and through its spiritual heads: the Clergy are, I believe, about to prepare petitions to the King, to ask him to take his Ecclesiastical appointments into his own hands, and consult the Ecclesiastical authorities and the elder Bishops of the Church upon them. This was the old plan . . . and though Ministers were oftentimes (of old also) troublesome, worldly, and interfering, yet this modern

plan, wherein Ministers are virtually the Patrons, and the King a cypher, did not come in until the middle of the last century; so I see not why we should not hope that with a struggle we might again recover the old system.[48]

Henceforth, it was inevitable that in all later university controversies Pusey would side with the Tractarians; even though he might adopt different attitudes in private, he was too closely allied to Keble and Newman to reveal his differences in public. In 1838, for example, when he was initially prepared to support the Martyrs' Memorial project, he explained to Newman that 'even if I should be satisfied with any plan myself, I would not join in anything which did not satisfy you'.[49] At times, indeed, Pusey's devotion to the Tractarian cause was a source of annoyance to his friends. 'I do not at all enter into the notion that we are a sort of Jack the Giant Killer or Knights Errant to attack all nuisances and offences'[50], complained Newman. On other occasions, Pusey's anxiety to aid his friends was embarrassing; when he wrote a *Letter* in support of Isaac Williams' candidature for the Professorship of Poetry, it only succeeded in spoiling Williams' chances by making the contest take on a religious hue involving party loyalties. It was in the same spirit of unworldly wisdom that Pusey precipitated himself into a controversy in 1843 concerning a sermon of his on the Eucharist.[51] The following year, despite attempts by others to dissuade him, Pusey insisted on opposing the nomination of B.P. Symons to the Vice-Chancellorship on theological grounds. Whereas Gladstone considered such a scheme 'a *mad* one'[52], Pusey told his brother, 'I use no concealment now, if I ever did, that I think Dr. S. ought to be opposed as a protest against heresy and heretical decisions'.[53] To his opponents, Pusey's words would probably have been construed as spite, since Symons had been one of the six doctors who had condemned his sermon the previous year. In all probability, however, Pusey was merely continuing the task he had originally taken up on the issue of subscription; he was concerned for (what he deemed) the purity of doctrine, and, having bitterly regretted some of the remarks which he himself had expressed in his *Enquiry*, he was now displaying the zeal of a convert.

Not quite all Pusey's energies were spent in controversy; he still found time, in addition to his routine academic work, to lend strenuous support to Charles Marriott's efforts to open a college for poor scholars in the university.[54] From the late 1830s onwards, however, Pusey had felt increasingly impelled to assume the role of official apologist for the Oxford Movement; an office made necessary when support for the Tractarians from all the parties declined, in face of the relaxation of external threats on the Church, and the rise of Romanizing tendencies in the right wing of the movement. In attempts to allay suspicion, Pusey spilt much ink writing his *Letter to the Bishop of Oxford* in 1839, his *Letter to Dr. Jelf on Tract XC* two years later, and his *Letter to the Archbishop of Canterbury* in 1842. Valuable as were these labours, the prosperous days of the Oxford Movement in the university were irretrievably numbered by the early 1840s. When 'Newman . . . had done his work. He had broken the back of the [39] Articles',[55] influence at Oxford gradually shifted to the Tractarians' rivals, the Liberals and Evangelicals. In the next decade, the attention of the majority of the university was held less by theological niceties, than by the need to implement the University Reform Act of 1854. Pusey's support for the founding of Keble College in the 1860s, was a gesture of recognition that secularism and 'scepticism' could no longer be fought with the weapons so successful in the past.

3. The Ecclesiastical Commissions

For all his involvement in rather narrow university concerns, Pusey stood out in sharp contrast from many of his fellow Tractarians in the 1830s and 1840s by his keen interest in affairs outside of Oxford, and by his grasp of the political complexities in any matter concerning church and state. He exhibited these qualities perhaps most clearly in his article on 'The Royal and Parliamentary Ecclesiastical Commissions', originally published in *The British Critic* in 1838. A recent writer has described this article as presenting 'the melancholy spectacle of a high-principled clerical mind almost unhinged by excitement and morbidity'[56], but, as a contemporary criticism of church reform, its value remains great; neither is it a totally negative document.

In February 1835, the Prime Minister, Peel, had instituted an Ecclesiastical Commission in which he himself was the driving force; the Commissioners as a whole comprised the two Archbishops, three bishops, four cabinet ministers and three non-ministerial men. When Peel's 'hundred days' came to an end, and Whig ministers replaced Conservatives on a reconstituted Commission, Bishop Blomfield of London assumed Peel's mantle of dominance. The first report of the Commission was issued in March 1835 and was concerned chiefly with reform of the episcopate; the main section of its second, issued in March 1836, was devoted to cathedral and collegiate churches; the third and fourth reports of May and June 1836 were largely extensions of the previous two.

Until the appearance of the second report, Pusey considered that on the whole no real harm had been done to the Church; more relevant was the useful work that had been neglected. He was critical, however, of the presence of laymen on the Commission. What had they to do, he asked, with 'the more equal distribution on episcopal duties', and how could they know how 'cathedral and collegiate churches might be rendered most conducive to the efficiency of the Church'?[57] The speed in which the Commission had arrived at its decisions also drew Pusey's fire. Six weeks, he argued, were insufficient for 'remodelling almost every diocese of the Church of England, for re-distributing and re-moulding it'.[58] What especially pained him was the Commission's failure to recommend an increase in the total number of bishoprics. 'Nothing but the increase of the 'total number of bishoprics' would afford any real remedy', he declared.[59]

> It was impossible that any scheme should even palliate the existing evils, which should attempt to portion out the

> population of England and Wales among twenty-four bishops, the same number which the Church had three centuries ago, when Westminster and Liverpool were villages; our manufacturing towns, commons; and Lancashire a moor.[60]

As a theologian deeply read in the practices of the Early Church, Pusey undoubtedly appreciated the traditional role of a bishop more than many of his contemporaries; he recognized that the increase in population required more bishops. Parliament thought otherwise. By the Established Church Act of 1836, which embodied many of the Commission's recommendations, Parliament had abolished livings held *in commendam* with sees, placed incomes of bishops on a sliding scale according to seniority, and incorporated the Commission as a permanent body; it had not, however, increased the number of sees above the existent twenty-four. Though it created new bishoprics at Ripon and Manchester, it had united the sees of Bristol and Gloucester, and St Asaph and Bangor. Perhaps the recommendation of the Commission which most incensed Pusey (it was included in the Act but repealed two years later), was the union of the see of Sodor and Man with that of Carlisle. This Pusey termed 'wanton destruction', and his anger betrayed him into even more exaggerated language:

> The extinction of the diocese of Man was unjustifiable on every principle of honesty, generosity, and ecclesiastical polity; it was an Erastian act, oppressing and spoiling a weaker neighbour; it re-enacted the abolition of the Irish Sees, and made the English Church the Spoiler.[61]

Pusey's real quarrel, however, was with the Commissioners who had drawn up the second report. According to him, this latter went *beyond* the objects of the Commission and in parts contravened its terms. 'Instead also of considering "the state of the several cathedral and collegiate churches in England and Wales" to render *them* most conducive to the efficiency of the Established Church, it spoke of their *endow-*

ments!' When Pusey went on to write of the Commissioners' lack of respect for the piety of founders, cathedrals' past services, the sacredness of trusts, the rights of property or vested interests of posterity, he was clearly still partly motivated by ideas which had coloured his correspondence with Gladstone in 1833, and with his brother two years later. The essential difference in Pusey's outlook was the element of fierceness which now clothed his words:

> The Commissioners seem to have borrowed a hint from the treacherous act of Medea, when she cut in pieces the aged King, limb from limb, and seethed him, and boiled up his flesh, in order to restore him to the freshness and vigour of youth.[62]

He was equally convinced that, as a result of the establishment of a standing Commission, 'the Episcopate is the creature of the state, to be modelled, re-modelled or broken in pieces, as it wills'[63]; a reproach that was not met until 1840, when the Dean and Chapter Act changed the membership of the Commission to include all the bishops of England and Wales, the Lord Chief Justice, five other judges, the deans of Canterbury, St Paul's and Westminster, and six lay persons.

As Pusey was bent on pointing out, he was not opposed to reform in itself, and he was prepared to indicate what he thought were abuses needing remedies:

> . . . a legislative is much wanted for the Church, and the want is felt; we have no authoritative canons, no discipline, no means of adapting ourselves to the altered state of society and population, – none of commanding the energies of powerfully-stirred but un-regulated minds, which since not employed by the Church are turned against her, – no means of finding nor of securing any adequate knowledge in our candidates for orders, – none of educating the increasing middling classes; and the education of the lower, which, as being less costly has almost alone been attended to, is, on account of our neglect, passing out of our hands; uniformity among the clergy is thought im-

> possible; the solemn worship of our Church is neglected because we have but few daily to offer it. We have our old institutions awakened or awakening from their slumbers, into which they were cast by the Revolution, and diffusing good as far as they extend, but no means of extending their usefulness beyond their present confined limits; on the other hand, we have the fresh activity finding vents for itself, since it is undirected, confusing the Church, if within her, weakening her if without; societies taking the initiative for every purpose under the sun: if the Lord's-day is to be decently observed, we have a society; if animals not to be cruelly treated, a society; if Church rates to be opposed or defended, a society; if Church legislation, a lay society; and the ultimate end of these societies is to obtain acts of parliament, instead of canons; societies are our Episcopacy, and newspapers our rules of faith.[64]

To the problems of training for the ministry and the provision of education for the middle classes, Pusey devoted much attention. In itself, he was also not opposed to parliamentary legislation. He would probably have recognized the virtues of the Pluralities Act of 1838, by which a cleric was forbidden to hold more than two benefices (and then only with the permission of the Archbishop of Canterbury), neither of which was to have a population exceeding three thousand nor a joint value of above £1,000. What Pusey feared, however, was an excessive assumption of power by the Commission: 'it will be our legislative', he said, 'executive, the ultimate appeal of our bishops; it will absorb our Episcopate; the prime minister will be our Protestant Pope'.[65] He was not alone in thinking such things; others such as Charles Merrivale, considered that Blomfield was certainly exhibiting tyrannical tendencies.[66] It was with the Commission's methods that Pusey most quarrelled; in his awareness of the pressing need for social adaptation, he was probably the equal of Blomfield and Peel.[67] Pusey only insisted that measures taken to provide ecclesiastical facilities in the new large towns and to place finances within the Church on a more equitable basis, should not be achieved by (what he termed) 'spoliation'. It is even possible that Pusey may have seen more deeply into things than Blomfield. He would never have committed Blomfield's error of supposing that the Commission had saved the Church of England.[68] Pusey was well aware that much of the life of the Church was unaffected by the decisions of Commissioners. His interest in the activities of the Ecclesiastical Commission and his appeal for structural reform to the externals of the Church, however, rendered him untypical as a member of the Oxford Movement. His concern for conditions in the large, industrial, new towns made him even more unusual among his contemporaries.

4. Social problems

Pusey's Tractarianism was not of the kind which R.W. Church suggests gave no thought to influencing the middle classes, or remedying the ignorance and wretchedness of the great towns[69]; in these senses, Pusey's outlook was utterly distinct from that of Keble, Newman, and the majority of the members of the Oxford Movement. Much as Pusey shared the theological views of his colleagues, his constant efforts to draw attention to conditions in the slums of the industrial towns, were exerted over and above the usual Tractarian concentration on the themes of the corporate nature of the Church and of the Incarnation.[70] Nothing, indeed, so much demolishes the myth that Pusey was an academic recluse or remote university scholar, as the record of his labours on behalf of the working population. It must be admitted immediately, however, that Pusey did not possess what might be loosely defined as a social policy in relation to industrialism. His view of such problems as poverty and economic ills was, nevertheless, grounded on certain fundamental principles. He believed passionately that the Church of England had a moral obligation to remind men that the poor were creatures with hearts and souls and were not to go unrelieved or to be downtrodden. Pusey propounded no plans for the economic or social reorganization of society, but he frequently questioned the motives of those responsible for administering society, and he invariably threw light on the dangers to individuals and communities when cities were left in a 'heathenish' condition. Even in this field, Pusey was in a minority among his fellow Anglican clergy; discussion concerning the spiritual destitution of the lower orders was commonplace in religious circles, but the number of clergy prepared to do anything about relieving their squalor was pitifully small. G.S. Hall of Bradford, the advocate of factory reform, had laboured hard to secure the passage of the Ten Hours Act, but Law of Chester was the only bishop who was known to have set foot in a factory.[71] Bishop Barrington of Durham (1734–1826) had supported Robert Owen in his co-operative schemes, and other individuals, such as Hook in Leeds and Stanley of Alderley, had investigated Chartism and Socialism, but Arthur Wade, the Vicar of Warwick, was described by the Owenite *Pioneer*, as 'the only one of the beneficed servants of the Most High who had consistency and virtue sufficient to enlist him in the cause of poverty and oppression.[72] Until the advent of Christian Socialism, the record of clerical assistance in the battle against the evils of industrialism was meagre in the extreme. Many of the clergy were assiduous in administering charities, visiting the sick and almsgiving; others were active supporters of the National Society, even though they may have often regarded education merely as an extension of religion and as a means of keeping the poor in their place. The majority of churchmen, however, were usually negative in their attitude towards political, economic and social change until at least the late 1840s.

Much of the outlook of the clergy in the Church of England was probably rooted in their own social origins. Except in the industrial towns where they sometimes rose from the middle classes or even humbler ranks, many clerics were the sons of gentry; almost half the episcopate were of noble birth. Though entry to the clerical profession was open to all, the frequency of poor livings often made patronage (and therefore the need to remain on good terms with one's patron) necessary for survival; in new churches income so often depended on pew rents that an incumbent felt obliged to cultivate the wealthier members of his parish. Although the clergy were not as a whole associated with any one particular financial or social group in the country, they frequently possessed strong links with the landed interest; these in turn would have influenced any social teaching they may have imbibed. Their denunciations of commercialism and industrialism as harbingers of unnatural inequalities might be interpreted as echoes of the fears felt by the landed classes. Many of the clergy were also Justices of the Peace only too anxious to repress popular agitation. In their private lives they were often more interested in secular activities, such as sport, antiquities and drinking, than in theology or the pursuit of 'causes', which they associated either with politics or the more 'enthusiastic' Evangelicals. Few among the latter, however, ever argued for drastic social reorganization; Wilberforce, J.B. Sumner and Shaftesbury were all traditionalists in their attitude to class structure. As a party, Evangelicals rarely evinced an interest in economic explanations of poverty, the social origins of vice, or the medical necessity of sanitation; their dislike of many pleasures and recreations now deemed innocent, increased the dreariness of the lives of those they attempted to assist. The great issues for which they campaigned so effectively were primarily regarded as moral ones; their private acts of charity were inseparable from their thirst for souls.

In view of this general state of affairs, it is remarkable that Pusey, the son of an aristocratic landowner and very early in life Hebrew professor and Canon of Christ Church, should ever have bothered about the plight of the working classes. In a sense, it is true that much of Pusey's concern centred on the spiritual and moral vacuum among the poor in the same manner as the Evangelicals[73], but he sometimes went beyond this and criticized the economic and social framework which commerce and industry flourished. What were the conditions he deplored?

When criticizing the Ecclesiastical Commissioners' failure to increase the total number of bishoprics in England, Pusey had complained that their oulook was more suited to the time when Lancashire had been merely a moor. He at least recognized that the region had changed out of all recognition. In the early 19th century, Lancashire contained three fifths of all the establishments in England concerned with the spinning and weaving of cotton; at its centre lay Manchester, containing one hundred factories and indistinguishable from a surrounding network of suburbs, with a total population approaching half a million. In its turn, Manchester was the chief among an even larger accretion of industrial towns, such as Bolton, Preston and Chorley, but all of them were uniformly smoke-blackened, inhabited largely by workers and petty tradesmen. Whereas the middle-class cotton-factory owners lived outside the towns, the workers dwelt in a conglomeration of lanes, alleys and courts near the factories themselves. In 1841 in Manchester alone, 18,000 people lived in cellars, almost no house contained a water closet, 248 of the streets were unpaved, and 352 of the roads contained stagnant pools of water and heaps of refuse.[74] Conditions in Liverpool were worse. In that town, 40,000 lived in cellars and 60,000 of the houses (built back to back) were contained in close courts, with an inadequate water supply and no lavatories. This pattern was repeated in other industrial towns besides those of Lancashire; it was a familiar sight in Birmingham, Bristol, Leeds and Glasgow. London was the same in such areas as Limehouse, Spitalfields and Whitechapel; in Bethnal Green, for example, 30,000 people endeavoured to live in an area half a mile square. In time, and as the investigations of such as James Kay, Neil Arnold, Southwood Smith and Edwin Chadwick bore fruit in government legislation, so conditions improved, but meanwhile Pusey at least did not remain indifferent.

Long before E.P. Hood and Henry Mayhew were exposing the extent of squalor in England's large cities in the 1850s and 1860s, Pusey had raised the subject in his *Cathedral Institutions* of 1833.

> We cannot pass through, or hear of, a single manufacturing or commercial town, or a single mining district, with-

> out its being forced upon our minds, that a large portion of that population, the sinews of our national strength is left ungratefully in a state of Heathenism.[75]

In his *Tract on Fasting* of the same year, he challenged his readers to consider the poverty and ills around them:

> Let them but observe generally the glaring contrasts of extremest luxury and softness, and pinching want and penury; between their own ceiled houses, and the houses of God which lie waste; or let them only trace out one single item in the mass of human wretchedness, disease, insanity, religious ignorance, and picture to themselves what a Christian people might do, what the primitive Christians would have done to relieve it.[76]

Sharing fully the axiom that the presence of the Church brought light and civilization to distressed areas, Pusey then wrote his article 'Churches in London' for the *British Magazine*, describing the crying need for new churches in the metropolis. Thereafter, he served for many years on Blomfield's committee, which was set up to fill this vacuum. The extent of Pusey's concern about the degradation which accompanied industrialism and flourished in the absence of religion, comes out clearly in his 'Churches in London':

> [Our ancestors'] spirit is fled: we have come to the dregs of time . . . Our old towns and cities are recognised from far by their towers and spires, hallowing all the landscape . . . Our modern towns have *their* characteristics – the chimneys of our manufactories, and the smoke of our furnaces. And we 'boast ourselves in the multiple of our riches', and our wisdom, and our enlightening, and our skill in the mechanical arts, and our knowledge in physical sciences, and the Bibles which we print; while the only true wisdom we have not known . . . Shall we inure ourselves, as to a thrice-told tale, to hear of the myriads who subsist by breaking the Seventh or Eighth Commandment; of quarters of our metropolis which are 'sinks of iniquity'; of 'hells' in our Christian city . . . Shall we hear, day by day, of

> drunkenness, debauchery, brutality, profaneness, reigning among those who were once made 'members of Christ and heirs of heaven', and turn on the other side as if it concerned not us? . . . It concerns us all. London, as the heart of our social system, must be, and is, day by day more manifestly circulating health or disease, religion or profaneness, the fear of God or atheism, in every corner of our land.[77]

Thereafter in sermon after sermon, preached not only in Oxford but in such places as London, Bristol, Brighton, Ilfracombe and Leeds, Pusey re-iterated similar themes. Not content simply to emphasize that his audiences should forge their luxuries and comfort in the interests of the poor[78], however, Pusey also questioned the ethical basis of particular social and economic practices. In his sermon 'The Value and Sacredness of Suffering', originally published in 1841, Pusey made a direct allusion to the Poor Law Amendment Act:

> Recent changes have turned the compulsory provision for the poor into a measure of restriction and police. Such is the law of the land, and it is not our business to speak against it. It may be made wholesome. Would one could think the change arose in the desire only of correcting misuse of that provision, not to save ourselves at the expense of the poor! Such savings would be a nation's curse.[79]

On the Day of Humiliation for the Irish Famine of 1847, Pusey took the opportunity not only of condemning the widespread prevalence of luxury and self-indulgence among the upper and middle classes, but of demanding that workers should receive just wages:

> In its turn luxury is the parent of covetousness; and covetousness of unjust gain, and of the grinding of the poor. We *will* not limit our self-indulgence; and so in order to obtain it cheaply, we pare down the wages of our artizans. They who have seen it, know that full often the very clothes we wear are, while they are made, moistened by the tears of the poor.[80]

At times, there can be no doubt that Pusey showed especial concern for the religious poor. 'I never see the patience of the religious poor', he was to say in the 1860s, 'their self denial, their endurance, without thinking that they are among the most stupendous proofs of the stupendous grace of God'.[81] It was for this reason that he so strongly advocated the abolition of pew rents in the 1830s[82], and took an interest later in the Free Church Society established to achieve this. His preaching in aid of the Oxford Diocesan Society for the Religious Education of the Poor in 1837, and at Ilfracombe for the building of parochial schools in 1844, were evidence of the close connection he saw between religion and education. Similarly, his encouragement of Anglican Sisterhoods in slum areas, and his construction of St Saviour's at Leeds, were instances of his efforts to bring religion to the working classes.[83] In so far as Ritualists from 1845 onwards carried religion to the poorest people and the most squalid regions, so they may be regarded as heirs of Pusey's position. Though he might not share their devotion to colourful ceremonial and medieval music and architecture, Pusey was aware of the need for such men as W.J.E. Bennett, Bryan King, Charles Lowder and Upton Richards. They may have owed much to the Camden Society and its successor the Ecclesiological Society, but they were also indebted to Pusey.

Nevertheless, Pusey was alive to the needs of the irreligious poor. In 1845 Pusey was persistently trying to persuade his brother to place the needs of the poor before the country, as he had previously in his book *The Poor in Scotland, compiled from the Evidence taken before the Scotch Poor Law Commission*. 'Let it be if it please God', Pusey told Philip, 'the business of your life in whatever way He may put into your hands to benefit the poor, writing, speaking at Agricultural Meetings, in the House of Commons, watching opportunities'.[84] Pusey was delighted when his brother was planning to embark on a fact-finding tour of Ireland with Gladstone:

> The case . . . of the Irish peasantry seems to me very strong and though their murders and cruelties should not be

> palliated, their combinations seem [to] me to have been founded on the preservation of their families from starvation, because the possession of land is their sole dependence since they have had neither employment nor poor rate to look to.[85]

It was in this same spirit that Pusey could write with so much feeling against the opposition of a section of the Tory party to the repeal of the Corn Laws; he described Bentinck's attitude as 'madness' and thought it a great 'wretchedness . . . to see men so blinded by anger and so reckless'.[86]

Nor was Pusey interested solely in relieving the ills of the poor; after 1846 he also proved himself a loyal supporter of Nathaniel Woodard's schemes to provide schools for the offspring of the middle classes. Woodard, 'the chief emissary of Puseyism in secondary education'[87] had probably first become acquainted with Pusey when he was at Oxford from 1834 to 1840. Woodard's notion that it was the Church of England's neglect of the middle classes that was at the root of much of the discontent in England during the tumultuous 1840s[88], was one which appealed strongly to Pusey. As early as 1838, Pusey had drawn attention to the need to provide education for the class that increasingly developed a consciousness of its own in the face of Chartist threats, and with the success of the Anti-Corn Law League. It is not surprising, therefore, that Pusey showed a lively interest in the schools that Woodard established.[89] In the meantime he concentrated his own efforts on securing a proper training for the clergy so badly required in the new towns and later in the Woodard Schools.

5. Training for the ministry

In the early 1830s, facilities for preparing men for the ministry in the Church of England were meagre. Apart from the universities, there were no institutions such as theological colleges where graduates might receive specialized instruction. For non-graduate students there was no provision, except St David's College, Lampeter (founded in 1822 to replace the seminary of Ystrad Meutrig), St Bees' College in Cumberland, or the Church Missionary Institution, established in Islington in 1825.

Before Pusey tackled the subject of clerical education in his *Cathedral Institutions* of 1833, isolated individuals, such as Bishop Randolph, the author of The *Clergyman's Instructor*, and Henry Raikes in his *Remarks on Clerical Education* (1831) had attempted to remedy the situation, and one or two bishops had alluded to it in Charges.[90] In 1812, Thomas Jones had founded the Clerical Education Society, and four years later the London Clerical Education Society was established, with Daniel Wilson as its secretary. Nevertheless, what was lacking was an overall and systematic course, which might replace individual and often amateur methods of educating ordinands. Too frequently there existed the complacent notion that the general education for the B.A. degree at the universities, was sufficient instruction for future priests. To Pusey's mind, however, instruction in theology should commence on graduation; he deplored the practice whereby those seeking orders were required only to attend one short course of twelve lectures from the Regius Professor of Divinity before being ordained.[91]

In order to place clerical education on a sound footing, Pusey proposed that twelve cathedrals should become the nuclei of theological colleges serving the whole country.[92] By reason of their library facilities, their staffs and proximity to diocesan bishops, Pusey considered them eminently suitable for the purpose. Under the guidance of experienced clergy, the students could receive expert instruction for two years, especially in the practical field of catechetics, the management of schools, and in visiting the poor and sick. Pusey thought that the colleges attached to the cathedrals in this manner, should consist of about seventy or eighty students under five professors.

It was not until the end of 1838, however, that Pusey's ideas bore positive fruit; the first theological college to be founded was at Wells, and Chichester was opened two years later.[93] In the meantime Pusey had been active at Oxford; in

1835 he instituted a Theological Society in the university and the following year he housed and supported a few promising graduates (the first was J.B. Mozley), in order that they might remain at Oxford to further their theological studies. Pusey was also in correspondence with Archbishop Howley concerning the possibility of persuading the university authorities to introduce a special examination in divinity for ordinands, to be taken two years after their first degree.[94] If the Church was to make any impression on Victorian society, Pusey fully appreciated that the clergy should be professionally educated.

Linked with his wish to see better trained priests, was Pusey's frequent preoccupation with the shortage of clergy. Between 1811 and 1871, when the population of England and Wales increased from 10 to 23 millions, the number of active clergy rose only from 16,000 to rather more than 19,000.[95] 'We are crippled everywhere', Pusey told his brother, '... it is useless to build new Churches without an enlarged supply of Clergy. What is wanted everywhere and for everything is, – not funds, but men'.[96] By 1846, indeed, so aware was Pusey of the sheer practical difficulties that the Church faced in its attempts to meet the changed nature of society, that he preferred to make the best of establishment (albeit remaining eminently critical of its disadvantages), and to talk less of separatism from the state. His theological outlook having also developed towards ultra Anglo-Catholicism by then, Pusey could sympathize too with the difficulties facing the Roman Catholic Church in Ireland. He was now prepared to condone Roman Catholic bishops in the House of Lords, and to accept the idea of government endowment of their colleges and payment of their clergy, provided it was not to the detriment of the Church of Ireland.[97] So convinced was Pusey that Christianity was vital to the health of the nation, he could inform his brother that 'I do not see anything amiss, or any principle violated, in doing anything *positively* for the R.C.s'.[98]

6. Christianity and politics

What were the underlying principles which influenced Pusey's outlook and behaviour in relation to political action? In very broad terms, throughout the course of history, two observable and opposite attitudes have been adopted by Christians in regard to politics. These in turn reflect a fundamental difference in theological outlook among them. On the one hand, there are those who maintain that faith saves men *from* a lost world and for whom political commitment is of secondary importance, and on the other, there are those who claim that faith requires them to change and integrate with the world. Sometimes these contradictory viewpoints are present simultaneously in Christian Churches, at others one tendency dominates over the other. The assumption that Christianity is relevant to politics was never made in the Early Church, and was held by only a few in the post-Constantine Roman Empire. By the Middle Ages and for many years after the Reformation, however, it was generally supposed that the Churches had a right, (even though it was not always practicable for them to exercise it), to voice an opinion in political (and economic) concerns. But by the 18th century this idea was no longer tenable in England; the Churches' business was then held to be simply the religious life; the clergy (it was deemed) no longer possessed any authority by reason of their role as priests, to make their views accepted in secular subjects.[99] In 1836, however, Pusey could be found attempting to adopt a middle position between the two extreme points of view, and it was one which largely influenced his conduct thereafter. 'I would only gently disclaim', he said, 'the supposition that Divines are not judges in political matters'.[100] Pusey was prepared to acknowledge that details were not the concern of the clergy, and that only the 'moral and religious portion' of any subject was their business. Nevertheless, since they were 'abstracted from the ideas of glory, national honour, dignity, pride etc', he believed that they were often able to form better judgements than politicians.[101] On questions such as whether a war were just or unjust, for example, he thought the clergy better judges.[102] He was also afraid that the idea of removing 'all clerical interference in matters of politics' would make politics 'irreligious and . . . encourage notions of self-satisfaction and expediency in the governing body'.[103] It was the especial duty of the clergy, he said, to act as 'Watchmen' and 'to observe the evil tendencies of their times'.[104] It is against this set of principles that Pusey's interventions in politics need to be considered; they were the backcloth to his devotion to the rights of property owners, his defence of university privileges, his pleas for action in the great towns and his concern for clerical education; they also in part account for his interest in specific parliamentary measures.

Frequently Pusey was not averse from attempting to foster or to secure the defeat of bills being debated in parliament; he also occasionally lobbied on an intensive scale. In 1839, for example, he informed Keble of his desire for agitation in the form of clerical petitions for the repeal of Mortmain Act[105], 'as being a slur upon giving property to the Church', and for 'National Compensation for the sacrilege at the Reformation'. The first of these he thought could be obtained easily if the Church asked for it, and the second would not only relieve the wants of the Church, but would 'remove a national sin'.[106] A year later, when parliament had its own ideas concerning the needs of the Church, Pusey entered into an earnest correspondence with his brother on the Ecclesiastical Duties and Revenues bill; a measure which attempted to reorganize cathedral establishments and their property. Although the passage of the bill met with universal indifference in parliament[107], it was guaranteed by the nature of its contents to hold Pusey's interest. His diligent investigation of the bill also revealed his astonishing business acumen and grasp of detail; qualities which were later to astound some of his colleagues on the reconstituted Hebdomadal Board at Oxford, after the university reforms of 1854. He was fully determined to take advantage of the fact that Philip Pusey had been asked to present an Address on the bill to the House of Commons. His ideas, however, continued in the same vein as that of earlier years. The first point that Pusey instructed his brother upon, was that parliament should not confuse redistribution of funds in a cathedral with their alienation; he was not opposed to readjustment of property, but 'this is a very different thing from alienation; remodelling within, from removal to without'. Next, he wanted his brother to argue that any money removed from a particular cathedral should be applied to the needs of the diocese in which the cathedral was situated. He also urged that the present bill be delayed; he considered it too vague in its direction, too radical in its handling of property, and took too little account of the opinions of those within the Church who opposed it.[108] Even Pusey, however, seemed to realize that such ideas were unlikely to be accepted; he was aware that Peel also 'feels the alienation to be a "dangerous principle" . . . only that he thinks it more dangerous to leave our great towns as they are'.[109] In the event, when the bill became law, it ordered a gradual reduction of all nonresident prebends (over 360) and sinecure rectories (68). The number of canons was limited to six at Canterbury, Durham, Ely, Oxford and Westminster, five at Winchester and Exeter, two at Llandaff and St David's, four everywhere else. As a result, an annual sum of between £360,000 and half a million pounds became available to supplement poor livings and to assist new parishes in the large cities.

Shortly afterwards, Pusey had much occasion to consider the connection between politics and religion, owing to the projected establishment of an Anglo-Prussian bishopric in Jerusalem. On the one hand the bishop was to cultivate friendly relations with the Orthodox Church, and on the other he was to promote conversions among the Jewish people. Nominated alternately by the Prussians and the English Crowns, and supported by both, he was to be responsible for Anglicans as well as Protestants in Jerusalem.

The whole behaviour of Pusey was curious from beginning to end in the controversy which quickly engulfed this plan and which divided so many churchmen in their opinions. On 1 July 1841, Pusey met the chief Prussian negotiator, Bunsen, at his brother's house and was persuaded to support the project; rather in the spirit of Archbishop Howley and Bishop Blomfield, Pusey had high hopes that the Prussian Protestants would benefit from an alliance with Anglicans.[110] In September, indeed, he discussed the Jerusalem bishopric with the Archbishop and he continued to approve of the scheme.[111] By November, however, Pusey had misgivings; he claimed to have been astonished at discovering that the bishop's congregation amounted to only four persons, and, in a protest which he sent to the Bishop of London via Richard Jelf, he informed Newman that he had embodied 'all your strongest language as my own'.[112] When Newman himself, subsequently protested to Archbishop Howley on the recognition of Lutherans and Calvinists implied in the establishment of the new bishopric, Pusey approved his friend's action. By the time Pusey wrote his own *Letter to the Archbishop of Canterbury* in the following year, he had fully imbibed the fears of Newman.

The Jerusalem bishopric episode was, indeed, a good example of how the marriage of politics and religion could breed dissension among individuals and parties within the Church of England. Amid the many actors claiming a role in this tragicomedy, Pusey's part was a sad one; his initial sympathy for the idea shows how naive he could be in the face of Bunsen's skilful charm, and his later disapproval suggests how impressionable he was to the arguments of Newman. In theory and as conceived by Frederick William IV, the project was imaginative and visionary; in reality it engendered too many petty ambitions and private feuds.[113] Initially at least, the British government supported the plan for political and economic reasons; Palmerston was at first only too willing to gain a footing in an area where British interests were threatened on the one hand by Russia and on the other by Mehemet Ali. But by July 1841, these dangers had receded. In the meantime, however, Ashley and the Evangelicals backed the scheme as a method of cementing an alliance between Protestants and of dishing the Tractarians. These latter were riddled by scruples and talked feverishly of schism and dangers to the Apostolic Succession. Some High

Churchmen such as W.F. Hook were in favour of the bishopric, others like A.P. Perceval had doubts. Even the gentle Howley complained of the speed in which the plan was conducted; only five months intervened, from the arrival of Bunsen to discuss the matter to the consecration of the first bishop, Alexander. Newman later spoke of it as 'the third blow' which finally shattered his faith in the Anglican Church.[114]

In 1841 Pusey was particularly active in his self-appointed role as 'Watchman' of the activities of politicians; he was concerned about the attempts made in that year and the following one to introduce bills into parliament to legalize marriage with a deceased wife's sister, and he asked his brother to keep him informed of events.[115] Already, indeed, he had been campaigning against such a measure, had written a 'letter on the Proposed Change in the Laws . . .' in the *British Critic*[116], and had informed Benjamin Harrison, Chaplain to the Archbishop of Canterbury, of his wish to see 'some counter demonstration of abhorrence and disgust.[117] From now until 1907 (when the law was eventually altered), this controversy was to reappear constantly on the Victorian scene, and the arguments concerning the interpretation and validity of Leviticus 18 mounted incessantly.[118] In Pusey's mind, there never was any doubt about the matter:

> If the Levitical decrees are abandoned, there remains no safeguard (save where and as far as the Church holds her ground), except man's natural instincts. But what are these instincts? Are they one uniform, distinct, powerful voice of nature, making herself heard equally under all circumstances, in every moral or religious condition, so that she cannot be mistaken . . . All experience tells us the contrary.[119]

Not content, however, to point out the dangers when 'Single stones are pulled out first' and 'The thin edge of the wedge is introduced first'[120], Pusey also endeavoured to bring to the public's notion how the whole weight of Scripture bore on this subject, and had been interpreted in this way by the

Church down to the Council of Trent. This he did by sending reprints of his original article in the *British Critic* to all Archdeacons and members of both Houses of Parliament[121], by giving lengthy evidence to the Royal Commission established to investigate the controversy, and subsequently by publishing his evidence when advocates of a change in the law introduced another bill into the Commons in 1849. In the debates which revolved around this particular bill, Gladstone took a leading part, having previously been furnished with ample material for his speeches by Pusey.[122]

Linked very closely to this controversy in the opinion of Pusey, was his fear of the terrible consequences that he thought would ensue should Parliament cease to pay heed to the laws of the Church. 'Chartism, Socialism, Pantheism', he declared, 'show what is to be expected as to the civil, moral, religious, condition of the world which throws off the Church'.[123] Thus it was that he was so embittered when he learnt that Gladstone was prepared to support the right of Jews to sit in parliament in 1847; in his biography Liddon recorded Pusey's displeasure, but carefully omitted to quote the harsh anti-Semitic language in which Pusey vented his anger. Whereas Pusey was prepared to acknowledge a certain amount of good in Mohammedans, Unitarians and even Rationalists[124], he became quite unbalanced on the subject of Jews:

> it does, of course, give me great pain when one knows of a religious man, and one's friend joining in an irreligious act, which one looks upon as a renunciation of Christianity on the part of the State and a preparation for its final apostacy. When such acts take place, I can only wish that Oxford were disfranchised and that the Clergy had no votes; that we might cease to have any share in the election of a Parliament, which admits those who must, if Jews, be blasphemers of our Lord ... It is very painful, (as I have myself both seen and heard) to know of the devilish pleasure which it gives a Jew to utter blasphemy. They seem like persons possessed, and are so. The sort of laugh I

> have seen in uttering blasphemy was no other than Satanic ... Their authentic books are full of frightful blasphemies. By virtue of their now false faith, they must blaspheme our Lord ... if they are infidels they blaspheme God too.
>
> I do not know whether you are prepared to see a Jew sit with his hat on, or jeer at prayers which in his heart he does not believe, offered in the Name of Him whom his fathers crucified ... or whether you are prepared to give up this fragment of our being a Christian Legislature.[125]

Despite this obvious prejudice, however, no one can say that by 1850 Pusey was lacking sufficient experience to hold his place as leader of the Anglo-Catholic party in the Church of England; his multifarious activities and interests in the previous two decades not only made him unusual among Tractarians, but were to serve him in good stead in the years ahead.

7
PUSEY AND MISSIONARY ACTIVITY

1. Faint beginnings

Perhaps the most significant event in the life of the Church of England in the 19th century, was the establishment of a world-wide Anglican Communion; it was also one in which Pusey showed considerable interest. Until Holland and England became global commercial powers in the 17th century and were able to challenge the naval superiority of Spain and Portugal, Protestant and Anglican activity in the missionary field had been meagre.[1] The Reformers had said little on the subject; and up to 1648, Protestants on the continent were often fighting for their existence, and Anglicans were involved in a long struggle with Puritan radicalism; both were dissipating their energies in theological controversies or were mesmerized by the notion *Cuius regio, eius religio*.[2] Missions supported by the non-Roman Catholic Churches only really began with the appearance of the Pietist movement, and when King Frederick IV of Denmark employed missionaries in India. It was these and their successors who were used first by the Society for Promoting Christian Knowledge from 1728 to the 1820s, and then by Anglican bishops in India until 1861. Though these German missionaries officiated from the Book of Common Prayer, baptized and celebrated the Lord's Supper according to the Anglican rite, they had never received episcopal ordination.[3] This did not prevent Pusey from referring to them in general, and to C.F. Schwartz (1724–1798) in particular, as 'Apostolic men', even though he considered that their efforts lacked the support of a Church system.[4]

Except for the work of the S.P.C.K. and the Society for the Propagation of the Gospel in Foreign Parts, founded respectively by Thomas Bray in 1698 and 1701, the Church of

England as a body remained feeble in missionary consciousness and zeal until the 19th century.[5] Although the American colonies were well populated by the end of the 17th century and England had added Canada and large parts of India to her empire by 1763, the religious needs even of colonists had been little considered by the Crown, government, or Anglican Church, apart from conventional utterances in Royal Charters, Letters Patent and colonial documents in general. In 1770, Cook had further claimed New South Wales for England, but up to and including the time that Britain formally lost her American colonies (1783), there was still no diocese or Bishop of the Church of England outside the mother country. (S. Seabury, Bishop of Connecticut, was consecrated by Scottish bishops in 1784.) Technically, and as laid down by Charles I in an Order in Council, all British subjects overseas were under the ecclesiastical jurisdiction of the Bishop of London.

At the end of the 18th century, however, a variety of forces coalesced to bring about a profound change in this picture of general indifference or apathy towards missionary activity. The new outlook was primarily engendered by the Evangelical Revival, which found one outlet for its energies in the formation of such missionary societies as the Baptist Missionary Society (1792), the Church Missionary Society (1799) and the British and Foreign Bible Society (1804). This outburst of religious impulses also coincided with public interest roused by geographical advances, with the emphasis in Britain on commerce and the search for markets due to the industrial revolution, and with improved communications. Intellectual currents, based on ideas of political freedom and emanating from the American and French revolutions, had given birth to changed conceptions of humanity; the anti-Slavery movement had brought an increased awareness of Christian responsibility towards the non-European peoples. In the years to come, the imperialistic policy pursued by successive British governments in Africa and the Far East, and the absence of any general war in Europe for over a century after 1815, were also by and large to assist the efforts of missionaries.[6] Nevertheless, and despite the strained relations which often existed between the society and the episcopate until 1841[7], it was undoubtedly the Evangelical C.M.S. which made the greatest contribution to Anglican missionary work in the 19th century. Only from the end of the 1830s did the S.P.G., which by its constitution was the nearer to being an official Church organ for missionary activity, participate seriously in the Victorian expansion.

On the whole, Pusey initially approached the subject of missionary affairs out of obedience to what he thought of as Christ's explicit commission to preach the Gospel to all nations: later, he concerned himself with it out of a sense of responsibility for the spiritual need of those peoples comprising the British Empire, or for ecclesiological reasons associated with the idea of *plantatio ecclesiae*.[8] Until the late 1830s, indeed, his concern for the missions did not amount to much. As a young don at Oriel, he regularly paid his subscriptions to the S.P.C.K. and S.P.G. and had spoken with Newman about the work of the missionary Henry Martyn, a Chaplain to the East India Company who had died in 1812.[9] In 1824 Pusey and his brother, Philip, were endeavouring to rouse interest in the establishment of schools in Ceylon, and in the following year were discussing the necessity of support for Bishop Heber's efforts in India.[10] Pusey's outlook may have been influenced to some extent by his friend W.F. Hook, who at this time was an ardent member of the S.P.C.K. and S.P.G. and was showing an early interest in the Church in America. He was especially delighted to inform Pusey of his acquaintance with 'a venerable and respected Prelate of the American Church – Bp. Hobart, Bp. of New York ... a *worthy* successor – as far as uninspired man can be so – of the Holy Apostles'.[11] Four years later, Pusey was condensing S.P.G. reports for Hook's benefit, describing exaggeratedly the new Bishop's College in Calcutta (established for the training of men for the ministry) as 'the mightiest (engine), I think which has ever yet been raised for the systematic extension of Christianity[12], and dilating on an increase of conversions in Ireland.[13] Neither Hook nor Pusey realized at this time that just over fifteen years later, and probably as a result of their link with Hobart, both of them would be fostering dialogue between the Church of England and the American Episcopal Church.

2. Missions and the Church

In the United States, Tractarian views followed as controversial a course as in England.[14] Owing to the early activities of such men as Hobart, who was an intimate of the Hackney Phalanx and who had been greeted in Scotland as 'Seabury redivivus' during the visit mentioned by Hook, High Church doctrines had gained a firm hold in America.[15] In 1833, Newman wrote to his sister during his Mediterranean tour and told her that he had been given such a promising view of the American Episcopal Church, that 'we mean when turned out of St Mary's, to go preaching through the Churches of the United States.[16] His consciousness of the value of the American Church was to increase to such an extent that, five years later, in a sixty-two page essay in the *British Critic*, he stressed its three great advantages; its Catholic doctrine, its independence of the State, and its very existence, which removed from the Anglican Church the charge of childlessness.[17]

For his part in the 1840s, Pusey was actively corresponding with Hobart's disciple, Bishop G.W. Doane of New Jersey. In the year of *Tract XC* Pusey seemed particularly indebted to Doane; he dedicated a sermon to him, 'in grateful acknowledgement of the Christian charity which believed all good when the world censured; and when those near seemed estranged, owned us from afar as sons and brethren'.[18] Pusey also discussed with Doane the possibility of introducing Anglican monasticism into America and advocated that the American episcopate should communicate with English Colonial bishops. These latter, Pusey told Doane, 'are nearer to you than to us and it seems to belong to the oneness of the Church, that there should be some sort of intercourse with you'.[19] It may, therefore, have been due to Pusey that Doane did in fact correspond with G.A. Selwyn, the Bishop of New

Zealand[20], who (Pusey had informed Doane) was 'carrying out the system of our Church, in a way in which it has not been developed yet.[21]

Previous to Pusey's efforts, Hook had written a Preface to the English edition (1838) of *The Early Life and Professional Years of Bishop Hobart* by John McVickar, and had invited Doane to preach in 1841 at the consecration of his parish church in Leeds. A recent writer has testified to Samuel Wilberforce's tremendous interest and work in forwarding missionary activity, and in promoting the idea of a mission Church.[22] Wilberforce gave expression to these in his *History of the Protestant Episcopal Church in America*, published in 1844, but perhaps as much as Wilberforce, Pusey and Hook were aware of their importance. Hook may even have appreciated before Wilberforce the significance of sending out 'missionary bishops'[23], and in 1838 Pusey fully realized the value of the American Episcopal Church. In a sermon of that year, which he preached for the S.P.G., Pusey referred to it as 'a choice vine ... passing far beyond the bounds of the provinces, which were our immediate colonies; multiply her Bishoprics continually ... forming Churches of God, where some years past were literally a wilderness'.[24]

It was in this same sermon, or rather two sermons preached at Melcome Regis on the same day and entitled *The Church the Converter of the Heathen*, that Pusey propounded in their most highly systemized form, his views on missionary work in the Church. In order to do this, he first asked Newman for 'any book about primitive spreading of the Gospel, or that of the Middle Ages, or of our own Church', and he questioned whether Cave's *Primitive Christianity*, Stillingfleet's *Origines* or Bingham contained such information.[25] Not long afterwards, Pusey asked information of Benjamin Harrison Chaplain to the Archbishop of Canterbury concerning any circumstances in the founding of the S.P.G. and its history which illustrated its 'Church character'. He also enquired about the needs of the society, and said he was anxious to see whether there was any correspondence in principles between the establishment of cathedrals in England

and colleges overseas, such as Codrington College in Canada and Bishop's College in India.[26] Pusey also expressed too his hope of instituting Missionary Scholarships at Oxford.

The 'Church character' of the S.P.G. was the first point that Pusey was at pains to emphasize in his sermon. He deplored the fact that, though the S.P.G. (which then incorporated the missions of the S.P.C.K.) had been for one hundred years the only missionary society in the nation, it had of late been supported less than others.

> For its [the S.P.G.'s] *very* excellence . . . is not, like those recently set up, popular in its constitution, does not give persons control over it, simply because they contribute to its funds, but remains under the direction of those, who are set over us in the Lord; the Bishops of the Church, and those called in by them to their aid; as the Apostles whose successors they were ever known to be, called in the seven Deacons.[27]

Much as Pusey recognized that other societies had played an important role in missionary activity, he considered also that they set forth the truth imperfectly, and he lamented their presence in areas served by the S.P.G.

Closely linked with his stress on the need for missionaries to be under the control of the episcopate, was Pusey's condemnation of 'the easy unsacrificing multiplication' of copies of the Bible. He was critical of the prevalent view that

> the mere circulation of the printed Bible would convert the heathen; that it was but necessary to persuade men to accept the Bible, and that the reading of it, without any previous knowledge of its contents, or any one to explain it, that the written word without a preacher, would turn men from Satan to God.[28]

In a passage where he was probably criticizing both the C.M.S. and the British and Foreign Bible Society, Pusey expatiated upon what he called 'two defective theories'; the indifference to bishops and the free spreading of the Bible.

> The desultory way in which Missionaries are sent out, not responsible or, in the best cases, scarcely responsible, to Bishops, under no control over them, departs as widely from the Apostolic and Scriptural plan of converting the heathen, as that of circulating the Scriptures only.[29]

In Pusey's mind, '*The* Missionary Society set forth in the Prophets, by our Lord and by His Apostles, is, the Church'.[30]

> Nothing which depends upon individuals has that permanency, which can supply the needs of successive generations . . . No! For the wants of mankind, an institution is needed, unvarying in its main character, independent of man, and not subject to his caprice or changing will, supported by God, abiding in Him, and His permanency imparted to it; and such an institution He has given us in His Church.[31]

It was for this reason that Pusey was anxious that a distinct branch of the S.P.G. should be established for Canada. In September 1838, he informed Harrison that some evangelicals had formed a Canada Society on the principle of retaining the selection and control of missionaries in the hands of the society; this he thought contrary to tradition:

> It is the wisdom of the Church to absorb everything into itself keeping the direction itself, but availing itself [of] and directing to right ends and in a right way, every feeling which arises. The S.P.G. ought to have availed itself of this feeling on behalf of Canada.[32]

A year later, Pusey was telling Harrison that, whenever possible, the S.P.G. should only collect money and let Colonial Bishops find their own missionaries; if this were impracticable, the selection of missionaries should still remain in the hands of the authorities and not of the society. 'If the S.P.G. could reform itself in this way', he told Harrison, 'as Joshua Watson says the others must follow in time; but now the Church Societies countenance in a degree the un-Church or anti-Church'.[33] Pusey was quite clear in his own mind that

in the English church and endeavour to promote holiness. He claimed that he had been doing all he could 'to back and soothe' others within the Anglican Church, especially and positively by the assertion of 'our ... grounds and our duties'. Negatively, however, he could not say anything against 'the formal decrees of Rome i.e. the Council of Trent'. His reading of 'the Acts of S Perpetua and Felicitas' had completely shaken his disbelief in Purgatory. The invocation of saints in the Early Church he had discovered was more common than he had supposed. He was troubled by Anglican indifference to the intercession of the Blessed Virgin, since this was believed in by both the Orthodox and Roman Churches. He told Manning:

> I hardly know, however, wherein you would differ from me. I suppose you must yourself believe that the C. of Trent must be accepted by us, if it were not for the further practical system. I suppose too that you cannot look upon our present as any other than a provisional state. You too must think that we ought to remain in our present insulated state no longer than we can help it, that if we (our Church) could obtain terms which she could accept, she ought to accept them ... In a word, were I in authority, and inter-Communion were offered, on the terms of the reception of the Council of Trent, leaving us (as Roman Controversialists say) all matters of discipline, including the Cup, our Liturgy in our own tongue, I should do, I believe, what in me lay to induce people to accept it.

Pusey then recorded again his debt to Thorndike for having broken in on his 'acquiescence' that a particular Church had a right to reform itself, and he repeated his belief that there had been 'too much human element' in the Reformation. Though Pusey appreciated the value of the Eastern Church, he was certain that 'our immediate business and duty is with the Western Church'. Concerning the Thirty Nine Articles, he said that he could satisfy himself about each one individually, but that he disliked 'the tone of the whole', and he could hardly imagine St Anslem or St Augustine signing them.

Nevertheless, Pusey expressed his conviction that God intended the Church of England as an instrument for some good.

> And so I desire to give what strength God may give me, in working for her and for souls in her. It is a fearful crisis we are going through, but my hopes rise with it.[97]

Such was Pusey's outlook after a decade of evolution; the views he expressed to Manning were also the ones he was to retain for the remainder of his life. On the departure of Newman from the Anglican Church in 1845, it appeared to many that Manning rather than Pusey was better fitted to assume his role as leader of the Anglo-Catholic party; confidence in Pusey seemed shattered owing to defections among the clergy at St Saviour's, Leeds, a church built at Pusey's initiative and expense, and to many people he was an object of suspicion.[98] From the Gorham Judgment in 1847 and onwards, however, Pusey came into his own; his development, both intellectual and emotional had come to an end; he took up the reins of leadership with the years of preparation behind him.

APPENDIX: PUSEY'S HISTORY OF THE THEOLOGY OF GERMANY

1. Dispute with H.J. Rose

In 1828 Pusey turned aside from his revision of the Old Testament, solely in order to write his *An Historical Enquiry into the Probable Causes of the Rationalist Character lately predominant in the Theology of Germany*. This work was intended as an answer to H.J. Rose's *Discourses on the State of the Protestant Religion in Germany*, a book which had been published in 1825, and which aroused fierce antagonism among Pusey's friends when it was translated into German the following year. Apart from Schleiermacher, Pusey found no one in Germany who spoke favourably of Rose's *Discourses*. 'The rest', Pusey told Newman, '. . . of all the different shades of opinion and earnestness, unite in condemning it. The strongest against it are the most Christian'.[1] In its German translation, Pusey was informed that Rose's book was doing considerable harm as 'a narrow, partial, bigoted, shallow work', and Pusey himself was of the opinion that 'in England its effects, though not so important, will still, I fear, be prejudicial, especially from the unbounded praise which persons, knowing nothing of the subject, have thoughtlessly bestowed upon it . . .'[2] Reluctantly as Pusey was to engage in controversy, he was ultimately persuaded by Sack, Lücke and Nitzsch to write a history of German theology from the time of Luther onwards; a work they thought Pusey well qualified to perform and which would disprove the accuracy of many of Rose's statements. In order to assist him, Tholuck gave Pusey permission to use the notes of some lectures he had delivered in 1825, entitled 'A History of Theology of the 18th century, together with the principles of Supernaturalism and Naturalism', and Sack agreed to write an introduction to

Pusey's *Historical Enquiry*, outlining his opinion of Rose's *Discourses*. From the very beginning, however, Pusey's dispute with H.J. Rose was subject to considerable misunderstanding.

Having paid a visit to Germany in 1824, Rose had returned to England profoundly shocked. J.W. Burgon suggests that it was 'the phenomenon of German Protestantism, as the system was to be seen at work in Prussia, which shocked his [Rose's] piety, aroused his worst fears, exercised his intellect'.[3] Rose found in Prussia, 'a rationalizing school, of which the very characteristic was the absolute rejection of a Divine Revelation', and which furnished him with sufficient evidence, 'for raising his voice in solemn warning to his countrymen, at a time when, in high places, the fires of faith and love were burning low'.[4] Be that as it may, however, Pusey, equally aware of rationalistic developments in German theology, considered it his duty to defend his friends from some of Rose's more indiscriminate assaults. Pusey deplored with Rose any loss of hold in Germany on the fundamentals of Christianity, particularly concerning the Person and Nature of Christ, but he deprecated Rose's suggestion that this was due to 'the absence of control' in religion. (By the word control, Rose meant restraint on speculation exercised by subscription to Confessions of Faith, by ecclesiastical forms of worship and by guidance and discipline from ecclesiastical superiors.) Possessing a greater knowledge than Rose of all the varieties of German rationalism, their strengths and weaknesses, as well as their connections with one another[5], Pusey set out to place them in their correct historical perspective, and, at the same time, to indicate that Rose was mistaken in regarding the Protestant Church in Germany as a mere shadow of a name, with religious indifference in almost all its members. Whereas Rose attributed rationalism in Germany to an absence of 'control', Pusey traced it to the rise of Lutheran 'orthodoxism', (a term by which he meant 'a spurious or blind and unimagining orthodoxy'[6]), to the decline of Pietism, and to the penetration of theology by anti-Christian philosophical ideas. Above all,

Pusey hoped 'to shake the despotism which Mr Rose's opinions were rapidly gaining in this country [England]',[7] for, as he told his friend Tholuck,

> I cannot render my countrymen a greater service than by shewing them the dangers of a stiff spurious orthodoxy, and the benefits of the bold but Christian course, (or rather bold *because* purely Christian course) which German theology is now taking.[8]

No more than Rose did Pusey underestimate the possibility that England might soon experience crises in religion. 'I have for some time', he told Tholuck, 'feared that we have a fearful ordeal to go through; many of the phenomena which ushered in the struggle with unbelief in Germany seem to be gathering here'[9], but this made his dispute with Rose even more urgent.[10] When Pusey wrote in his *Enquiry* of the German theologians who maintained a rigid and inflexible hold on orthodox beliefs and who neglected spiritual values, he probably had in mind the English High and Dry churchmen; in describing the Pietist successors of Arndt, Andrea and Spener, with their narrow conceptions of theology, he was possibly thinking of English Evangelicals. Thus it was that Pusey continued to adhere to comprehensive views in his own theological outlook and to eschew all party labels for himself. It was the quality of optimistic tolerance in his opinions, however, that roused the strongest suspicion in his critics. When Pusey spoke of a 'new era' beginning in the theology of Germany, or when he stressed the value of 'blending . . . belief and science'[11], he immediately encountered opposition from such as Rose. Anxious only 'to look for what is of good, and calculated to promote God's great design for man, where others seem to see an unmixed manifestation of evil'[12], Pusey was thought to be an ally of the rationalists. Any investigation of Pusey's *Enquiry*, however, reveals the prejudice of his critics, and, much more, it manifests the true nature of Pusey's outlook in the years from 1828 to 1830.

2. The rise of 'orthodoxism'

It was in the period immediately following the death of Luther that Pusey considered the seeds of future German unbelief had first been sown, and the *Enquiry* opens with an explanation of theology at that time. According to Pusey, Luther had been prevented from developing his reformation principles fully, with the result that his successors, lacking his authority and firmness, had been unable to prevent the German Church from being torn by harsh polemics over doctrinal niceties. Protestant Princes, in an effort to obviate discords, instituted minute and detailed confessions, but these only gave rise to scholasticism and further disputes.

> Certain it is, that the measures employed to produce uniformity, miserably impeded the progress of the Reformation, buried in great measure the hardly won evangelical truth under a load of scholastic definitions, and converted the Gospel truth itself, when it shone dimly through, into matter of speculation, instead of motive for practice.[13]

The inevitable outcome of these controversies and of the imposition of narrowing Confessions of faith, particularly of the Formula of Concord in 1580, was the development of a rigid theological pattern in which 'the conviction of the intellect becomes in itself the end; the heart is forgotten in the exclusive employment of the understanding'.[14]

Pusey then proceeded to trace this pattern and its effects on the German Church in general. In the field of biblical interpretation, he saw that the chief and almost exclusive aim had become the justification and defence of the Symbolical books. False ideas were also held, such as that all parts of Scripture were of equal value, all having been supposedly dictated by the Holy Spirit. The difference between the Law and the Gospel was obliterated, and the sense of biblical words came to be derived from that attached to them in the symbolical books. 'The Scriptures thus handled, instead of a living Word, could not but become a dead repository of barren technicalities', and even historical passages, in which no religious truth was contained, were not admitted to include error.[15] Pusey then pointed out how, not only were the principles of scriptural interpretation perverted, but the study of the bible itself came to be neglected. Doctrinal theology also, he asserted, encouraged 'the extremest dryness of scholastic formalism', and moral theology exercised no influence upon the Christian life.

> Abounding . . . in technical formulae . . . in straw splitting distinctions, in endless problems and deductions, the systems of the age were rather a massive repertorium of all which might be accumulated on doctrinal theology, than a clear exposition itself.[16]

The study of history was also neglected; what existed was either a mere justification of Protestantism, or an account of contests between Lutherans and the Reformed and a catalogue of heretics. In the universities it was extinct. As a result of all these things, the 'crown of theology' or Pastoral theology suffered an equal decline; pulpit and catechetical instruction becoming vehicles for the exposition of dry and polemical data. The Thirty Years' War, particularly in the 1630s, only exacerbated the already bleak state of religious life in Germany.

Having deeply studied the rise of 'orthodoxism' in Germany following the death of Luther, Pusey was full of admiration for the 16th century reformers and suspicious of Articles of Religion. In the second part of his *Enquiry*, he complained that Rose had represented him as being almost a 'fanatical enemy of all Articles and Confessions, and all restraint'.[17] At about the same time, Bishop Blomfield had also felt obliged to write at great length to Pusey on the subject of Articles of belief, pointing out that he considered it a fundamental principle of church policy that Articles were absolutely necessary.[18] To a certain extent, Rose was accurate in his description of Pusey; the attitude Pusey was to adopt in the later Subscription and Hampden controversies points to a complete revolution in his thinking from that of the years 1828 to 1830. In these early years, Pusey was unwilling to credit Articles with the same value as his contemporary fellow high-churchmen.

> I thought it a dangerous supposition that these *human means* were absolutely necessary not merely to the well being but to the existence of Christianity in each church, and consequently to the maintenance of our holy faith itself – that it tended to turn the attention away from the real supports of our religion (the independence and the inherent power of the word of God).[19]

Pusey's respect for the 16th century reformers was to remain part of his make-up for considerably longer than his wariness of Articles, however, and was probably based on his conviction that they had made Scripture the authoritative source of Christian knowledge. When Pusey contemplated the fate of biblical scholarship in Germany in the 17th century, he could not refrain from speaking of the theologians' 16th century predecessors as those 'immortal heroes' and 'mighty agents'.[20] Similarly, Pusey felt obliged to regret that the German Reformation had not developed more than it did.

> Had this been perfected in the spirit in which its great instrument [Luther] might have completed it, if permitted tranquilly to finish his work, or supported by others in his own principles, and surveying the whole system of Revelation with the comprehensive and discriminating view of his master mind, the history of the German Church had probably been altogether different.[21]

In 1830, indeed, there as no doubting Pusey's admiration of Luther. Three years previously he had spoken of Luther as 'the greatest Christian since St Paul'[22], and now he credited him with intuitive insight into the nature of Christianity, enabling him almost unfailingly to differentiate between essentials and non-essentials. This gift 'raised him not only above the assumed authority of the church, and above the might of tradition, but above the influence of hereditary scholastic opinions, the power of prejudices and the dominion of the letter'.[23] Clearly, only as a Tractarian did Pusey come to place great value in Tradition and the authority of the Church. At this time, Pusey preferred to echo a German sermon preached in 1805.

> To the Reformation of the sixteenth century we owe the light in which we live, the freedom which we enjoy, the order which is given to our most important concerns, and a great portion of that progress which our race since that time has in every way made.[24]

3. Pietism

Following his bleak portrayal of the religious state of Germany after the death of Luther, Pusey turned sympathetically to the rise of Pietism; only when this too degenerated did he consider that rationalism gained a firm hold among the Germans:

> It seems as if it were not until other methods had been employed in vain, that the storm of unbelief was allowed to burst over so much of this fair portion of the Christian Church; not until they had refused to return from the light of their self-kindled fire, to the sun of pure Christianity; that that sun was for a time obscured to them.[25]

The section of Pusey's *Enquiry* which is devoted to the Pietist movement at its height is the apex of the whole work, and probably that which he recounts with the greatest fervour. Beginning with a discussion of the ideas and activities of Pietist precursors, Pusey singled out for especial notice such figures as 'the ever memorable and pious Arndt', the author of *True Christianity*, Calixtus, branded as a Syncretist for his ecumenical acts, J. Gerhard, the devotional writer, and J.V. Andrea, the progressive educationalist. It was among such people that Pusey felt that the living spirit of Lutheranism had survived during the darkest days of 'orthodoxism'; a time which Herder described as one in which 'every leaf of the tree of life was so dissected that the dryads wept for mercy'.[26] By the close of the 17th century, however, a variety of constituents – evangelical, mystical and speculative – had combined together and issued in the revivalist movement known as Pietism.

Pusey did not attempt to trace the origins of Pietism; he remained content to describe the aims, achievements and weaknesses of such late 17th and early 18th century Pietist leaders as Spener, Francke, Thomasius and Arnold, and to mention only briefly Zinzendorf and the connections between the Pietists and Moravians. The enthusiastic manner, however, in which he praised and detailed Spener's piety, religious zeal, reform of preaching and catechetical instruction, his founding of *collegia pietatis* and the value of his writings, particularly the *Pia Desideria*, reveal in Pusey an emotion stronger than simple admiration. He was especially anxious to point out the virtues of the University of Halle, founded in 1694, which he likened to 'Geneva of old, the heart from which the impulse of the new principles became felt in every part of the system'. The labours of Francke in founding orphanages and supporting the Canstein Institute's work of distributing Bibles also won Pusey's approval. Nevertheless, he further recognized that Pietist influence extended beyond Germany for a time and reached as far as Denmark, Sweden and even Mount Athos in Greece.

In spite of his obvious regard for Pietism, Pusey did not shirk the sad task of accounting for the movement's decline. Essentially he thought of this as an instance whereby religious forms, especially those expressive of religious feeling, had a tendency to lose their original impetus; the retention of the form without the spirit resulting in conscious hypocrisy. As examples of this in later Pietism, Pusey cited the stress placed upon private and edifying Christian conversation, the exclusion from the movement of persons known to have danced or played at cards, and the frequent rivalry betwen Pietist cells or ecclesiola and the main body of the Church. He also recognized how certain individuals, such as Arnold and Thomasius, who either attacked orthodoxy or advocated more freedom in theological debate, encouraged unwittingly the growth of rationalist principles. In this sense, Pietism had become not only a pervasive influence in education, language and literature and had helped to thaw the glacial atmosphere of Lutheran scholasticism, but, by its insistence on individualism had encouraged free-thinking. In the domain of ethics, both the later Pietists and the Rationalists, with their emphasis on individual conscience, were allies against those whose morality was merely traditional.

Throughout Pusey's account of the rise and fall of Pietism, it is important to remember that he was writing allusively.

> I could not but see things in England [he said later] which corresponded in their degree to that former condition of Germany. I could not help owning to a certain stiffness among some, who maintained what I believed to be the truth; one-sidedness in those who corresponded with the Pietists . . . Neither the strict traditional school of Luther, nor the Pietists who in their first origin had so remarkably resembled our 'Evangelicals', had been able to stand against unbelief.[27]

The recognition of Pietist failings, however, did not prevent Pusey at this time from entering into intimate friendship with many of the theologians of Germany, who claimed to owe a great deal to the movement. It is possible that Pusey himself was unaware of the extent to which his own outlook was influenced by his contact with such as Tholuck, Neander, Sack, Lücke and Nitzch, but the nature of his views in the years 1828 to 1830 suggests that he was affected by his study of Pietism; this also perhaps accounts for his friendly approach to English Evangelicals later on.

The immediate effect on Pusey's thought was two-fold; it deepened his hereditary conviction that 'positive views of Christian doctrine, where there is not a deep practical religion must always be at best superficial'[28] – a statement he supported with particular reference to Spener's qualities – and it accounted for his particular attitude to biblical studies. Imbued with Spener's idea that no real theology can be conceived without piety and religious interest, Pusey insisted on applying the same maxim towards study of the Bible:

> In religious writings it is plain that the spirit required is a religious spirit; that none can truly understand St Paul or St John, whose mind has not been brought into harmony with theirs, has not been elevated and purified by the same spirit with which they were filled: and this, unquestionably was what the pious Spener meant by his much disputed assertion, that none but the regenerate could understand Holy Scripture.[29]

This same principle, so akin to Coleridge's assertion that 'the heart must have fed upon' the truth before it can be possessed[30], was probably also at the root of Pusey's comparative indifference to Episcopacy at this stage.

In his reply to Pusey's *Enquiry*, Rose noted Pusey's total omission of any mention of the absence of Episcopacy as a possible cause of the rise of rationalism in Germany. Rose called this 'most singular' and complained that 'Mr Pusey is a member of an episcopal establishment, and yet he does not appear to consider the abrogation of this apostolical form of church government in Germany a matter even worth notice'.[31] The extent, indeed, to which Pusey stood outside the confines of both the Hackney Phalanx and the High and Dry party, with their belief in certain theological implications appertaining to episcopacy, or in their straightforward acceptance of Bishops as being of the 'bene esse' of the Church, is vividly shown in Pusey's response to Rose's charge. 'As far . . . as past experience or the nature of things could guide me', Pusey wrote in 1830, 'I could see no reason to think that a different form of Church government would have changed the destinies of the German Church'.[32]

When Bishop Blomfield taxed Pusey with the same matter, Pusey remained adamant and indicated his deeper reasons for not having mentioned Episcopacy. He told Blomfield:

> I trust that your Lordship will not think me pertinacious, if I confess that I cannot as yet change my opinion. If indeed the Episcopal body were self-elected, it would then possess a principle of immutability, which might defy any changes in the opinions and principles of the body of the Clergy;

> but when its members are appointed by the state, I own I do not see any reason to suppose that those appointed to this high office would be free from the general infection. Even in this country we have had Prelates, of whom it was little to say that they were very lax (as Hoadley, Law and Watson).[33]

Even when acknowledged as one of the leaders of the Oxford Movement, and when he had abandoned many of the ideas he had acquired in Germany, Pusey retained his independent outlook regarding the Episcopate; his attitude partly accounts for his behaviour later on during such crises as that over the Jerusalem Bishopric. There is no evidence to suggest, for example, that Pusey ever shared Newman's belief that 'A Bishop's lightest work "ex cathedra" is heavy'.[34] On occasion, such as when Wilberforce was appointed to the Bishopric of Oxford, Pusey was even prepared to lecture a member of the Episcopate on his duties.

4. The age of enlightenment

Following his discussion of how 'orthodoxism' and the decline of Pietism had contributed to the rise of rationalism in Germany, Pusey then turned his attention to the attempts which were made to introduce Wolfian philosophical ideas into theology, and to the 'moral faults of the age', particularly during the reign of Frederick II. This latter monarch, by his encouragement of French literature and by his reception of unbelievers at his court – 'some of them (such as the wretched La Mettrie and Voltaire,) the most reckless and unprincipled'[35] – was held by Pusey to be largely responsible for the prevalent 'conceit and absence of moral earnestness', the imprudent enthusiasm for supposed discoveries, and the dazzlement by novelties.[36] Unbelief was further increased by the translation of the works of English Deists, such as those of Lord Herbert of Cherbury, Toland and Hobbes.

Pusey then traced the successive decline of theology and he described how, by colliding with unbelief, it partook of some of its features. Even so, he pointed out firmly that such theologians as Baumgarten, Ernesti and Michaelis, though giving rise to doubts, nevertheless remained faithful to their systems; their disciples, Semler and Morus, had also not altogether abandoned any fundamental article. Pusey's overall picture of theology's decline, indeed, is less antagonistic than Rose's; his treatment of theologians who courted rationalism is less harsh. For such as Nosselt, however, who 'deprived the doctrines of Christianity of their high and efficacious import', or Teller and Spalding, who 'Socinianized them', Pusey had little to say; their activities to him being but 'casting away the shell when the seed of future fruit was already gone'.[37] Pusey's gentle tone did not go unnoticed; Bishop Blomfield was especially provoked by some of the sentiments expressed in the *Enquiry*. He told Pusey:

> You state your opinion that 'earnestness of mind and love for their God remain amongst most of the German rationalists' – I would not certainly affirm, of any body of men, whose lives are moral, and their conduct *honest*, that they are *without* these qualities; but that is a very different thing from saying that they *have* them ... This sort of compliment to men who mutilate and pervert the Word of God and strip Christianity of its characteristic attributes is more than charity requires.[38]

Finally, Pusey praised the poets Klopstock and Claudius for their piety and discussed the work of German writers and philosophers in the late 18th century. It was in this section at least that Pusey relied most heavily on the notes he possessed of Tholuck's 1825 lectures, and where he was at pains to analyse the good as well as the faults in the authors under consideration. In spite of Lessing's failings, for example, Pusey was anxious to indicate how he had 'restored the key to the right understanding of the Old Testament', and how he had drawn a distinction between the activities of the theologian and the Christian who 'felt' his religion to be true. Such value did Pusey place on this remark of Lessing that he pointed out that Coleridge, in his *Aids to Reflection*, had also given 'seasonable advice to those, who think that in the reception of Christianity the intellect alone is concerned'. Clearly in 1827 Pusey felt a kinship with Coleridge, who had visited Germany before him and who was conversant with Lessing's *Tracts*, the *Fragments* of Reimarus and Eichhorn's *Introduction to the Old Testament*; he may even have applauded his attempts to rescue Englishmen from the fastnesses of fundamentalism and their fears of biblical scholarship'.[39] Certainly at this stage, Pusey would probably have endorsed Coleridge's statement –

> Evidences of Christianity! I am weary of the word. 'Make' a man feel the want of it; rouse him, if you can, to the self-knowledge of his 'need' of it; and you may safely trust it to its own Evidences.[40]

He would at least have recognized that Coleridge's outburst closely resembled Lessing's question as to 'what do this man's [the theologian's] hypotheses, and explanations, and proofs, concern the Christian'?[41] Thus it was that Pusey, even though he confessed that he was often perplexed by Lessing, could regard his work as preparation for a 'higher order of Christian apologetic authors'; his rejection of christianity on historical grounds, Pusey considered to be the mere product of superficiality in Lessing's philosophy and the result of living in a controversial age.

Pusey's treatment of Herder and Kant perhaps illustrates most vividly his anxiety to achieve a high degree of objectivity in the *Enquiry*. He explained to Tholuck that he feared he had been too harsh in his judgement of Herder, not having liked the vagueness and indefiniteness of his *Christliche Schriften* and the emphasis he placed on the literary value, to the detriment of the religion of the Prophets, in his *Geist der Herbraischen Poesie*. In the case of Kant, Pusey also had to overcome his own innate distrust of philosophy applied to theology, but the seriousness with which he, nevertheless, examined the defects in Kant's philosophy and the causes of its eventual decline, reveals the extent to which Pusey was prepared to sink his own personal feelings. He went out of his way, indeed, to stress how Kant, by indicating the inadequacy of speculative reason to pronounce on matters outside the scope of the intellect alone, 'led many who were not bound by the fetters of the new philosophy, to listen to the voice of nature, the revelation of God within them, and to seek as the direct result of consciousness, the truths which speculation was unable scientifically to justify'.[42]

The works of Fichte, Schelling and Jacobi were also considered, but so briefly that Pusey was probably either relying almost totally on Tholuck's notes, or else he was becoming increasingly disillusioned by the Age of Enlightenment. Appreciating that the period he was describing may have been one of renaissance in literature and art, Pusey saw that in religion and theology it was a time of grave misfortune for Protestantism in Germany. He was of the opinion, however, that this had been succeeded by a broader and more scientific conception of Christianity; his friends, such as Tholuck, being in the vanguard of this new era.

5. Hostile reactions

When the *Enquiry* was published, Pusey sent copies of it to Keble, Newman and Blanco White among others, of whom in England only the latter gave it his entire approval. His friend Tholuck, at least, greeted the book warmly. He commented:

> It must be very pleasing that England sees at last German Theology represented to her in a liberal (literally: free) spirit and yet really Christian. Even if your countrymen call out: To the Stake! as several will do, later on the recognition is sure to follow.[43]

In the event, Tholuck's prediction of hostility proved accurate, and *The Edinburgh Review* commented acidly on H.J. Rose's haste to attack the *Enquiry*.

> Without loss of time or anger he [Rose] sends forth a reply to Mr Pusey, which for ill-temper and unfairness, – for the prodigal use of what Warburton calls 'hard words and soft arguments' – has few parallels that we know of in the range of theological controversy.[44]

Pusey himself soon became dejected by the unfavourable criticisms made of his work. He told Tholuck that it had become hopeless to expect even a candid hearing from theologians in general; most of them, he said, thought of him as a Rationalist 'because I think that Rationalism was an instrument in the hand of God to awaken Germany out of a dead "orthodoxism"'. Others, he informed Tholuck, regarded him as a 'rash innovator', or considered that 'I deem feeling ... everything in religion, no matter whether the doctrines be right or wrong', and yet more spoke of him as a Methodist.[45]

Perhaps the most serious charge made against Pusey was that he denied Inspiration in the Scriptures. As early as April 1829, Keble had objected to Pusey's language on the subject in relation to the historical books of the Bible, and Rose had raised a similar protest. Pusey told Keble:

> On 'historical inspiration' I own that, if taken in its most extensive and rigid sense, I have felt myself obliged to abandon it: that is, if applied to all the minute facts, not immediately connected with religious truth. The promises of our Saviour seemed to me confined to this: in everything then which bore upon this I believe that the Apostles were assisted; in other things in which I do not myself see this reference I should not presume to define what was or what was not the result of inspiration; yet I am prevented from extending it to all by what appear to me in minute collateral points to be historical contradictions ... It has no effect in diminishing in the least the *practical* value of Scripture, but seems to me to be the truth and to get rid of *theoretical* difficulties. In any matter of practice or of doctrine the authority of Scripture is to me as great as to those who hold the most plenary inspiration.[46]

Pusey, however, was worried by the problem; a few months later he was seeking the assistance of Newman and, as a result, making his first real study of the writings of the Fathers and of the 17th century Divines. At the same time, Pusey was careful to remain in close consultation with

Tholuck and to refer to the problem of Inspiration as a mutual one. He told Tholuck:

> I have been enquiring into the opinions of the early Fathers on the subject of Inspiration. It appears to me that we must retire from the orthodox-Protestant opinions, yet still the gradual retreat which we have been making, and in which I am in this country making a further step, has certainly a disadvantageous appearance; it looks as if we required only to be pressed a little further to make us give up this last post which we had taken, as we had those before. I wish therefore by the bye, to shew that some of the principal of the Fathers had the same views to which we are now coming. The differences of my own view . . . from that usual here is that I think the Bible 'an inspired book' because it is the 'writing of inspired men' i.e. of such whose minds had been supernaturally illumined on religious truth, an illumination higher in degree and differing both in immediateness and certainty, but not in kind, from that bestowed upon subsequent Christians.[47]

Twelve years later, these same views were to precipitate Pusey into controversy with a radical Evangelical periodical *The Record*[48]; they were undoubtedly the product of his visits to Germany and lent weight to Bishop Blomfield's observation, in 1829, that Pusey's ideas in general savoured strongly (Blomfield said 'too strongly') of the channel through which the current of his recent thinking had flowed.[49]

Tholuck, on the other hand, was more concerned about Pusey's decision to investigate the writings of the Fathers. He informed Pusey that, whilst subscribing to the letter of his opinion on inspiration, he could find only little support for it in Patristics. 'With them [the Fathers]', he wrote, 'the idea has become fixed, that form and matter were inseparable. The most decided for our opinion is the School of Antioch and Hieronymus'.[50] His greatest fear, however, was that the deeper Pusey sank his studies into the Fathers, the more he would lose something of the breadth of outlook he had gained in Germany. Pusey's researches certainly did lead to an alteration in his views, and, as late as 1837, Tholuck was still endeavouring to warn his friend.

> Your plan – of reprinting the Fathers of the Church is beautiful yet I consider that of the Reformation more beneficial. We have to confess that at the time when Augustine [and] Chrysostom wrote, much of what is impure had crept in, that by God's direction through the Reformation a real progress, particularly in knowledge, was made . . . Above all take care not to lose the kernel which Luther gained again: the Christian liberty. Hold your eye open even for what is good in your opponents the Dissenters and Evangelicals. Remain aware that on your side there lies as much danger as on that one.[51]

In 1839 Tholuck repeated his advice, but by then Pusey had long since abandoned many of the views he had held on his return from Germany.

When Pusey was preparing to write a second part to his *Enquiry* in 1829, Newman also weighed in with suggestions of another kind. He wrote to Pusey:

> It has since struck me you have nowhere entered a protest against an approval of schism – and since the Bishop of London thinks your censure of a rigid traditionary system *in* a Church casts suspicion on the soundness of your Ecclesiastical views, it might be as well to disclaim any opinions favourable to self-willed separation from the Church – and in so doing I will venture to say, you will be doing as much to the sweetening of your book (especially if you say some sharp things against Dissenters) as by your humanities towards Mr R[ose].[52]

Anxious to heed the advice of a valued friend, Pusey was prepared to accommodate his views, but, as yet, only in a qualified manner. At this stage, the most that Pusey would say along the lines suggested by Newman, was that 'there was nothing harsh in supposing that those who wilfully so separated from the Church excluded themselves from "some" of the benefits intended by God for us, since some can only it appears, be thus conveyed'.[53] He was ready to believe that proof of this was forthcoming from the 'partial manner in which Christianity has generally been embraced by separatist bodies'[54], but, even so, it is doubtful whether Newman would have agreed that this was saying 'sharp things against Dissenters'.[55] What Newman probably did not appreciate was that Pusey was totally dissatisfied with the widespread but narrow conception of schism entertained by many of his contemporaries. He had returned from Germany with Christian sympathies which extended beyond the bounds of the Anglican Church; within the latter, they also enabled him to appreciate the value of the Evangelical party, even at the height of the Oxford Movement. Pusey made at least his early views on schism quite clear to his wife's cousin in 1831:

> Schism would I imagine generally be defined 'a needless separation from the body of Xtians so as to produce division in that body' and it is limited generally to those who originate or perpetuate absolute divisions. Other unloving actions which tend to produce these divisions are condemned generally as contrary to Xtian duty but not under this name. I own that I must myself think that it would be more practical to include them, so that all want of charity, all harshness, unfriendliness, ungentleness, everything opposed to Xtian love, and calculated to disturb the harmony of Xtians, *as a body*, should be included under it . . . It would include also divisions within as well as without the main body; there is I fear much of a schismatical spirit in the two great parties of our church; much contentious division, much violation of Xtian love although the outward bond of unity be not broken. I should then define Schism to be 'needless and contentious division of the body of believers'.[56]

He was certain at this time that physical division did not necessarily imply schism; the different national churches were natural outcomes of a necessary reformation, and the variations in emphasis which they each might place on certain doctrines therefore were inevitable. 'England, Denmark, and Sweden would think that they had formed their Churches' constitution more apostolically than Germany, Holland or Scotland . . . but still it would not be schism'.[57] Pusey also deprecated the notion that anyone should change his membership from one church to another, unless the individual considered it sinful to remain where he was. Above all, he was anxious to promote the idea that 'it is the first duty of an *individual* not to risk disturbing the peace and love of his brother believers'.[58]

It was perhaps this reason that led Pusey to ignore the question that Newman put to him in 1829. 'Have the Germans a Liturgy?' asked Newman. 'If not, may not *this* (at least as much as the Episcopal Form) have kept us steady?'[59]. It was not until the years immediately following his *Tract on Baptism* (1835), that Pusey was led to alter radically whatever views he originally had on the subject.[60] At the time when he wrote his *Enquiry*, Pusey was convinced that the Lutheran church was a valuable instituion.

> It seems neither too sanguine nor presumptuous to hope that the time is not far distant when the religious energy, now widely visible in Germany, shall produce its fruits, and the Evangelical Church, strengthened by the increasing internal unanimity, fortified against error by past experience, and founded on Scriptural faith, shall again, in religious as well as scientific depth, be at least one amongst the fairest portions of the universal Church of the Redeemer.[61]

6. Hints of changing attitude

It was not long before Pusey was having serious second thoughts concerning Germany. At a time when he was experiencing a deep sense of loss through the deaths of his father and Bishop Lloyd, and worried about the unfavourable criticisms made of his *Enquiry*, Pusey also began to express uneasiness about the effect on 'the too susceptible mind of Germany' of the 1830 political revolutions in

Europe. He told Tholuck:

> I fear that this political excitement will again awaken the dreams of human strength and human capabilities from which Germany has suffered so much, and which are the most adverse to all the feelings and the whole frame of mind necessary to embrace the doctrine of the Cross.[62]

Within this context, it is not difficult to estimate Pusey's reactions when, a few years later, Tholuck wrote telling him that in Germany more and more educated people were embracing Hegel's philosophy, and others were declaring themselves Pantheists. The publication by Strauss of his life of Christ, offended Tholuck particularly, who remarked:

> He puts together in a most dazzling sharp-sighted manner all the historical discrepancies which have ever been found – and even increased by new ones – thus this history appears as a building of mere arbitrariness, as a *Myth*. The book has made a deep impression on all minds which are not *entirely* and on the way of experience fortified by faith. A new epoch will be dated from it . . .[63]

He reported to Pusey how the books of other authors, such as Vatke, Bohlen, Lengerke and Hitzig, were frivously designed to carry negative criticism of the Old Testament to extremes. His conclusions were gloomy indeed.

> I see it coming that in Germany a hundred years hence only Pantheists and Faithful will be opposed to each other, Deists and the old Rationalists will entirely disappear; with this, thousands will be lost who are now at least still comforted by the glimpse of Revelation.[64]

When, therefore, in 1839, Newman told Pusey that Strauss's book was said to be doing harm at Cambridge, it is not surprising that Pusey was shocked and feared that his own *Enquiry* might also have caused unrest. In later years Pusey attempted to explain the processes whereby his outlook on Germany had altered. He wrote to Tholuck:

> I watched with deep interest and great hopefulness the early stages of revival of religious earnestness among you; then (I suppose about 1840, perhaps earlier) I became discouraged and unhopeful. I was told, or I saw, that A was unsound on this point, B on another, C on a third, (e.g. Neander appeared to be a Sabellian) and so I turned heart-sick.[65]

Nevertheless, in the late 1820s and early 1830s, and before he experienced a considerable revolution in his outlook, Pusey's own views on such things as Articles, the Reformation and individual reformers, the role of 'feeling' in religion, the value of the Episcopate, the nature of Inspiration in the Bible, the meaning of schism and the future of the Church in Germany, were all evidence of how greatly he had been influenced by his contact with German theology. The overall picture of Pusey in these years is vastly different from that of a later time.

NOTES

Introduction

1. A. Mozley (ed), *Letters and Correspondence of John Henry Newman* (1891) I, p.186.
2. See R.H. Greenfield, 'Such a Friend to the Pope' in P. Butler (ed), *Pusey Rediscovered*, S.P.C.K., 1984.
3. See F.M.L. Thompson, *English Landed Society in the Nineteenth Century*, (1963), pp.15–18.
4. MS Copy of Letter from E.B. Pusey to Maria Barker, 1 Feb 1828.
5. H.P. Liddon, *Life of E.B. Pusey* (1894), I, pp.5–6.
6. See C. Smyth, 'The Study of Church History', *The Priest as Student* (ed H.S. Box 1939), pp.263–264.
7. C. Fletcher, MS Narrative, Pusey House, Oxford, p.17.
8. cf John Keble in G. Battiscombe, *John Keble* (1963), p.165.
9. MS Copy of Letter from E.B. Pusey to R. Jelf, 1820.
10. See Ford K. Brown, *Fathers of the Victorians* (1961). The author is however confused about different members of the Pusey family and mistaken about their religious sympathies.
11. See G.F.A. Best, *Temporal Pillars*, (1964), pp.142–145.
12. MS Copy of Letter from E.B. Pusey to Maria Barker, 16 May 1828.
13. *Ibid*, 19 April 1828.
14. The Edinburgh Review (July–Oct. 1894), Vol. 180, No. 369, p.3.
15. G. Prevost (ed), *The Autobiography of I. Williams* (1892), p.70.
16. See E.C. Mack, *Public Schools & British Opinion, 1780 to 1860*, (1938), pp.73–81.
17. See C. Smyth, *Simeon and Church Order*, (1940), pp.73f.
18. MS Copy of Letter from J. Parker to E.B. Pusey 3 March 1825.
19. H.P. Liddon, *op.cit.*, I, pp.12–13.
20. J.H. Newman, *Apologia Pro Vita Sua*, (Fontana ed 1959), p.142.
21. See N.G. Annan, 'The Intellectual Aristocracy', *Studies in Social History* (ed J.H. Plumb, 1955).
22. D.H. Newsome, *Godliness and Good Learning* (1961), p.16.
23. *Ibid*, pp.16–19.
24. See O. Chadwick, *The Victorian Church* (1966), p.25 n. 2.
25. MS Copy of Letter from E.B. Pusey to Maria Barker, 27 Dec 1827.
26. MS Copy of Letter from R. Jelf to E.B. Pusey, August 1821.
27. See Isaiah Berlin, 'Preface' to H.G. Schenk, *The Mind of the European Romantics* (1966), pp.XIV–XV.
28. See H.P. Liddon, *op.cit.*, 1, p.41.
29. *The Deformed Transformed*, Pt.1, Sc.1, 11, 331–332.
30. See A. Watson, 'Byron at First Hand, A talk with his Doctor' in *Daily Telegraph*, 19 April 1924.

31. See H.G. Schenk, The Mind of the European Romantics (1966), pp.139–140.
32. MS Copy of Letter from E.B. Pusey to Maria Barker, Jan. 1828.
33. *Ibid.*
34. cf Julius Hare's contrast of the influence of Wordsworth and Coleridge with 'the noxious taint of Byron'. See D.H. Newsome, *Godliness and Good Learning* (1961), pp.15–16.
35. MS Copy of Letter from E.B. Pusey to Maria Barker 28 Nov 1827.
36. This document is at Pusey House, Oxford.

1

1. See T. Mozley, *Reminiscences Chiefly of Oriel College and the Oxford Movement* (2 Vols. 1882), 1, ch. 3.
2. See O. Chadwick, *The Victorian Church* (1966), p.43.
3. J.H. Newman, *Apologia Pro Vita Sua* (1864), p.286.
4. J.H. Newman (ed R. Tristram), *Autobiographical Writings* (1956) p.73.
5. See D.H.Newsome, *The Parting of Friends* (1966), pp.62–70.
6. J.H. Thom, (ed) *Life of Joseph Blanco White* (1845), III, p.130.
7. MS Copy of Letter from R. Jelf to E.B. Pusey, August 1821; see H.P. Liddon, *Life of E.B. Pusey* (1894), 1, p.28.
8. MS Letter from 'J' to E.B. Pusey, 1823.
9. MS Copy of Letter from E.B. Pusey to Maria Barker, 16 Nov 1827.
10. *Ibid*, 21 Feb 1828.
11. See W.R. Ward, *Victorian Oxford* (1965), ch.2 & pp.43–44.
12. MS Copy of Letter from E.B. Pusey to J. Parker, 25 May 1825.
13. MS Letter from Sheffield Neave to E.B. Pusey, 1824.
14. See C. Brinton, *English Political Thought in the 19th Century* (1962 ed), pp.130–148.
15. See J.A. Froude, *Short Studies on Great Subjects* (1866), IV, pp.239f.
16. See A.B. Webster, *Joshua Watson* (1954), pp.18f.
17. J.H. Newman, (ed H. Tristram), *Autobiography Writings* (1956) p.191.
18. See S. Neill, *Anglicanism* (1958), p.232.
19. e.g. See A.R. Vidler, *The Church in an Age of Revolution* (1961). pp.35–36.
20. MS Copy of Letter from E.B. Pusey to Maria Barker 4 Oct 1827.
21. *Ibid.*
22. J.H. Newman, *Autobiographical Writings* (ed H. Tristram, 1956) p.194.
23. *Ibid*, pp.195–196.
24. *Ibid*, p.191.
25. *Ibid*, p.203.
26. MS Copy of Letter from E.B. Pusey to Maria Barker, 2 Oct 1827.
27. *Ibid.*
28. See G.F.A. Best, 'The Protestant Constitution and Its Supporters, 1800–1829', *Royal Historical Society Transactions*, 5th Series, Vol.8.
29. MS Copy of Letter from E.B. Pusey to Maria Barker, 8 Jan 1828.
30. Syncretism was the term given to Calixtus' efforts to construct a

theological system to reconcile Lutherans, Calvinists and Catholics. He believed reunion could be effected on a foundation of the Scriptures, the Apostles' Creed and the faith of the first five centuries, interpreted in the light of the Vincentian Canon.

31. See E.B. Pusey, *Theology in Germany* (1828), Pt.1, p.62.
32. MS Copy of Letter from E.B. Pusey to C. Lloyd, 6 Oct 1828.
33. MS Copy of Letter from E.B. Pusey to W.F. Hook, 17 Feb 1838.
34. See R.H. Greenfield, 'The Attitude of the Tractarians to the Roman Catholic Church 1833–1850' (1956), unpublished D. Phil. thesis in the Bodleian Library, Oxford, p.58.
35. See W.J. Reader, *Professional Men. The Rise of the Professional Classes in the Nineteenth Century England* (1966), pp.6–9.
36. *Ibid.* p.15.
37. Cf remarks on the clerical profession in D.H. Newsome, *The Parting of Friends* (1966), pp.69–70.
38. MS Letter from J. Luxmoore to E.B. Pusey, 6 Oct 1823.
39. R.L. Edgeworth, *Essays on Professional Education* (1812), p.64.
40. MS Copy of Letter from E.B. Pusey to R. Wilberforce, 2 Oct 1828.
41. See A.M. Wilberforce (ed), *The Private Papers of W. Wilberforce* (1897), pp.242–243.
42. W.R. Ward, *Victorian Oxford* (1965), p.52.
43. MS Copy of Letter from E.B. Pusey to Dr. W. Ince, 18 Nov 1878.
44. *Ibid.*
45. Hansard, Vol.XXI, New Series, pp.79f.
46. See F. Oakley, *Historical Notes on the Tractarian Movement* (1865 edn) p.13.
47. See A. Mozley (ed), *Letters and Correspondence of John Henry Newman* (2 Vols. 1891), 1, pp.111–112.
48. *Ibid*, 1, pp.109–110.
49. MS Copy of Letter from E.B. Pusey to Dr. C. Lloyd, 23 Nov 1826.
50. E.B. Pusey, *Theology of Germany*, Pt.II, (1830), preface, pp.vii–viii.
51. H.P. Liddon's account of this episode (see H.P. Liddon, *Life of E.B. Pusey* (1894), I, pp.44–49) is inadequate and misleading. Though he recognised the significance of the event, Liddon concealed Hibbert's identity under the letter 'Z', gave the false impression that Hibbert was resident in France, referred to Pusey's brother's loss of faith as having occurred to an 'intimate friend' of Pusey's, and made no mention of Hibbert's radical activities.
52. See G.W.E. Russell, *Dr. Pusey* (1907), pp.15–16.
53. Pusey endeavoured to refute certain of Taylor's writings in 1831. See H.P. Liddon, *op.cit.*, 1, pp.217–219. (Liddon does not mention Hibbert's connection with Taylor).
54. See DNB and W.J. Linton, *James Watson: a Memoir* (Hamden, Connecticut 1879).
55. See G. Wallas, *The Life of Francis Place* (2nd ed. 1918), pp.271–275.
56. MS Letter from J. Hibbert to E.B. Pusey, 22 Oct 1823.
57. H.P. Liddon, *op.cit.*, 1 p.49.
58. MS Copy of Letter from E.B. Pusey to R. Salway, 8 Feb 1824.
59. MS Letter from J. Hibbert to E.B. Pusey, Nov 1823.

60. *Ibid.*
61. MS Letter from J. Hibbert to E.B. Pusey, 11 Dec 1823.
62. MS Copy of Letter from E.B. Pusey to R. Salway, 18 Aug 1824.
63. *Edinburgh Review*, No. 369 (July 1894), Art.1. p.5.

2

1. Gottfried Less, author of *Beweis der Wahrheit der Christlichen Religion* (Bremen, 1768).
2. MS Copy of Letter from E.B. Pusey to J. Parker, 25 May 1825.
3. See O. Chadwick, *The Mind of the Oxford Movement* (1960), pp.16–20.
4. *Ibid*, pp.21–22.
5. See C.C.J. Webb, *Religious Thought in the Oxford Movement* (1928), p.39.
6. 'Article X' in *Edinburgh Review*, Vol. LIV, No.CVII. (Aug–Dec 1831), p.238.
7. *Ibid*; see reference to this in E.B. Pusey, *Cathedral Institutions* (1833) pp.64–65.
8. See H.P. Liddon, *Life of E.B. Pusey*(1894), I, p.147.
9. J.D. Michaelis, *Introduction to the New Testament* (2nd ed 1802). (Translation by H. Marsh), Preface, p.1.
10. 'Article X' in *Edinburgh Review*, *op.cit.*, p.250. Cf situation in America – see R.M. Grant, *A Short History of the Interpretation of the Bible*, (1965), p.129.
11. (Ed) J.J. Stewart Perowne and L. Stokes, *Thirlwall Letters* (1881), p.159.
12. F.D.E. Schleiermacher, *Essay on the Gospels of St. Luke* (trans. C. Thirlwall, 1825), Introduction, p.IX. Cf J.D. Smart, *The Interpretation of Scripture* (1961), p.239.
13. *Edinburgh Review*, *op.cit.*, p.253.
14. *University of Oxford Commission, Pt.I. Minutes of Evidence* (1877) p.295.
15. T. Hodgskin, *Travels in the North of Germany* (Edinburgh, 1820) II, pp.265–269.
16. *Quarterly Review*, XXIII, pp.446–448.
17. See W.R. Ward, *Victorian Oxford* (1965), pp.63–64.
18. In 1825 Newman had accepted a commission from the *Encyclopaedia Metropolitans* to write an article on Apollonius of Tyana and the validity of miracles.
19. MS Copy of Letter from E.B. Pusey to J.H. Newman, 9 Aug 1825.
20. *Ibid.*
21. *Ibid.*
22. See J.H. Newman, *Apologia Pro Vita Sua* (Fontana edn. 1959), p.111.
23. E.B. Pusey, *Theology of Germany* (1828), Pt. 1, p.137, n 1.
24. H.P. Liddon, *op.cit.*, I, p.77.
25. See A.L. Drummond, *German Protestantism since Luther* (1951), p.80.

26. See P. Hazard. *European Thought in the Eighteenth Century* (1954) pp.67–71.
27. *Ibid*, pp.71–73.
28. *Ibid*, pp.426f.
29. MS Copy of Letter from E.B. Pusey to J.H. Newman, 9 Aug 1825.
30. See J.D. Walsh in *New Cambridge Modern History*, Vol.IX, 1793–1830, p.168.
31. MS Copy of Letter from E.B. Pusey to Maria Barker, 4 Oct 1827.
32. *Ibid*, The section of this letter which is quoted in H.P. Liddon, *op.cit.*, I p.124, has been skilfully edited to exclude Pusey's references to doctrine.
33. MS Copy of Letter from E.B. Pusey to Maria Barker, 18 Nov. 1827.
34. *Ibid.*
35. MS Copy of Letter from E.B. Pusey to Maria Barker, 3 Jan 1828. The contrast between Pusey's ideas here and those of 1835 is vividly shown in his Tract *Scriptural Views of Holy Baptism.*
36. MS Copy of Letter from E.B. Pusey to Bishop C. Lloyd, 6 Oct 1828. Though H.P. Liddon quotes the bulk of this letter (see H.P. Liddon, *op.cit.*, I, pp.184–185), this paragraph significantly is omitted.
37. See H.R. Mackintosh, *Types of Modern Theology* (Fontana 1964), p.49.
38. *Ibid*, p.64.
39. *Ibid.*
40. See W. Walker, *A History of the Christian Church* (Edinburgh 1949), p.533.
41. MS Copy of Letter from E.B. Pusey to C. Lloyd, 20 Aug 1826.
42. E.B. Pusey, *Theology of Germany*, (1828), Pt. I, p.115.
43. H.P. Liddon, *Life of E.B. Pusey* (1894), I, p.80.
44. See R. Mehlis, 'Die religiose entwicklung des jungeren E.B. Pusey', (Diss. 1954; Vollst Lit-Vers. Bonn), pp.71–72.
45. E.B. Pusey, *Theology of Germany*, Pt.II (1830), p.399.
46. MS Copy of Letter from E.B. Pusey to F. Tholuck, 29 June 1829.
47. MS Copy of Letter from E.B. Pusey to J.H. Newman, 25 Nov 1826; see H.P. Liddon, *op.cit.*, I, p.101.
48. H.P. Liddon, *op.cit.*, I, p.97.
49. See Letter from E.B. Pusey to J.H. Newman, 9 Jan 1827, quoted in H.P. Liddon, *op.cit.*, I, p.104.
50. E.B. Pusey, *Theology of Germany* (1828), p.115 n 1.
51. MS Copy of Letter from E.B. Pusey to C. Lloyd, 20 Aug 1826.
52. *Ibid.*
53. MS Copy of Letter from E.B. Pusey to Maria Barker, 28 Nov 1827.
54. *Ibid.*
55. MS Copy of Letter from E.B. Pusey to Maria Barker, Jan 1828.
56. 'He (Pusey) only did not burn the volumes which contained it, because they also contained the sacred text, "disfigured", as he said, "by my mistakes"'.(H.P. Liddon, *op.cit.*, I, pp.121–122). Pusey also forbade in his will any publication of the revision.
57. E.B. Pusey, *Theology of Germany*, Pt. II (1830), Preface, p.vii.
58. MS Copy of Letter from E.B. Pusey to Maria Barker, 30 May 1828.

59. E.B. Pusey, *Theology of Germany*, Pt. II (1830), p.14.
60. J.J. Stewart Perowne and L. Stokes (ed), *Thirlwall Letters* (1881), p.261.
61. *Quarterly Review* (July–Oct. 1882), Vol. 154, p.521.
62. See J.D. Smart, *The Interpretation of Scripture* (1961), p.239.
63. See T.M. Parker, 'The Tractarians' Successors: the Influence of the Contemporary Mood', *Ideas & Beliefs of the Victorians* (1949), pp.123–124.

3

1. H.P. Liddon, *Life of E.B. Pusey* (1894), I, p.116.
2. *Ibid*, I, p.23.
3. *Ibid*, pp.83–84.
4. See *Ibid*.
5. R.W. Church, *The Oxford Movement* (1932 edn.), p.131.
6. C. Fletcher, 'Narrative' (undated), p.54.
7. Recorded conversation between H.P. Liddon and J.H. Newman, 5 June 1883, contained in Exercise Book used by Liddon in preparation for his biography of Pusey.
8. O. Chadwick, *The Mind of the Oxford Movement* (1960), p.48.
9. MS Copy of Letter from M. Barker to E.B. Pusey, 18 Nov 1835.
10. *Ibid*, 28 Oct 1827.
11. MS Copy of Letter from E.B. Pusey to M. Barker, 12 Feb 1828.
12. MS Copy of Letter from R.W. Jelf to M. Barker, 21 June 1828.
13. MS Copy of Letter from E.B. Pusey to M. Barker, 15 Jan 1828.
14. MS Copy of Letter from M. Barker to E.B. Pusey, May 1828.
15. *Ibid*, 7 Nov 1827.
16. *Ibid*, 1 March 1828.
17. *Ibid*, 11 Jan 1828.
18. MS Copy of Letter from E.B. Pusey to M. Barker, 3 June 1828.
19. *Ibid*, 14 Feb 1828.
20. See MS Copies of Letters from M. Barker to E.B. Pusey, 14 May 1828 and 15 May 1828 and MS Copies of Letters from E.B. Pusey to M. Barker 11 Dec 1827 and 7 Feb 1828.
21. MS Copy of Letter from M. Barker to E.B. Pusey, 2 Feb 1828.
22. MS Copy of Letter from E.B. Pusey to M. Barker, end of 1827.
23. *Ibid*, 3 Nov 1827.
24. *Ibid*, 7 Feb 1828.
25. *Ibid*, 30 Jan 1828.
26. MS Copy of Letter from E.B. Pusey to M. Barker, 1 Feb 1828.
27. *Ibid*, 8 May 1828.
28. See H.R. Murphy, 'The Ethical Revolt against Christian Orthodoxy in Early Victorian England', *American Historical Review*, July 1955, pp.800–817.
29. MS Copy of Letter from M. Barker to E.B. Pusey, 3 Oct 1827.
30. *Ibid*.
31. MS Copy of Letter from E.B. Pusey to M. Barker, 16 Oct 1827.
32. *Ibid*.

33. MS Copy of Letter from E.B. Pusey to M. Barker, 16 Oct 1827.
34. *Ibid.*
35. MS Copy of Letter from M. Barker to E.B. Pusey, 18 Oct 1827.
36. MS Copy of Letter from M. Barker to E.B. Pusey, 18 Oct 1827.
37. MS Copy of Letter from E.B. Pusey to M. Barker, 16 Oct 1827.
38. MS Copy of Letter from E.B. Pusey to M. Barker, 6 April 1828.
39. MS Copy of Letter from E.B. Pusey to M. Barker, 16 May 1828.
40. MS Copy of Letter from E.B. Pusey to M. Barker, 3 Jan 1828.
41. MS Copy of Letter from E.B. Pusey to M. Barker, 8 Jan 1828.
42. *Ibid*, 16 May 1828.
43. H.P. Liddon, *Life of E.B. Pusey* (1894), I, pp.194–197 and 203–207.
44. MS Copy of Letter from E.B. Pusey to W. Pusey, 1 Oct 1830.
45. H.P. Liddon, *op.cit.*, I, p.211.
46. MS Copy of Letter from E.B. Pusey to M. Pusey, 2 April 1834.
47. See D.H. Newsome, *The Parting of Friends* (1966), p.7.
48. MS Copy of Letter from E.B. Pusey to M. Barker, 12 Feb 1828.
49. See H. Scott Holland, *Personal Studies* (1905), pp. 76–77 and D.H. Newsome, *op.cit.*, p.7.
50. See Letter from F. Von Hugel to F. Wane, Sept 1918, printed in B. Holland (ed), *Selected Letters* 1896–1924 (1927).
51. It was perhaps no accident that in 1878 Pusey chose to translate the Abbé Gaume's *Manual for Confessors*. This document stemmed from the Jansenist tradition in French Catholicism.
52. MS Copy of Letter from E.B. Pusey to M. Pusey, 1 Nov 1835.
53. MS Copy of Letter from M. Pusey to E.B. Pusey, 3 Nov 1835.
54. MS Copy of Letter from E.B. Pusey to M. Pusey, 1 Nov 1835.
55. E.R. Williams, 'Tractarian Moral Theology', unpublished D. Phil. thesis in Bodleian Library, Oxford. (1951). p.106.
56. MS Copy of Letter from M. Pusey to E.B. Pusey, 18 Nov 1835.
57. MS Copy of Letter from E.B. Pusey to M. Pusey, 6 Nov 1835.
58. MS Copy of Letter from E.B. Pusey to M. Pusey, 8 Nov 1835.
59. *Ibid*, 19 Nov 1835.
60. MS Copy of Letter from E.B. Pusey to P. Pusey, 19 Aug 1839.
61. E.B. Pusey, *Parochial Sermons*, Vol. I (1848), p.168.
62. MS Copy of Letter from E.B. Pusey to M. Pusey, 25 Oct 1836.
63. MS Copy of Letter from E.B. Pusey to M. Pusey, 4 Nov 1835.
64. See MS Copy of Letter from E.B. Pusey to M. Pusey, 7 June 1837.
65. MS Copy of Letter from M. Pusey to E.B. Pusey, 23 June 1838.
66. See MS Letter from E.B. Pusey to Lucy and Mary Pusey, 5 June 1839, MS Eng. Letters C 130. Bodleian Library, Oxford, and printed in M. Trench, *The Story of Dr Pusey's Life* (Anon. 1900) pp.146–147. Written soon after the funeral of Maria, it recommends that they should think of their mother's 'dear cold body' lying in the grave.
67. O. Chadwick, *The Victorian Church* (1966), p.198.
68. J.A. Möhler, *Gesammelte Schriften*, II, 166, as quoted by P.A. Günthor, *Möhler und das Mönchtum* (Weingarten, 1942).

4

1. MS Letter from T. Arnold to E.B. Pusey, 18 Feb 1834.
2. M. Ward, *Young Mr Newman* (1948), p.146.

3. Letter from R. Whately to J.S. Mill, 30 April 1836, quoted in M. Ward, *op.cit.*, p.296.
4. MS Copy of Letter from E.B. Pusey to M. Pusey, 4 Nov 1835.
5. J.H. Newman, *Apologia Pro Vita Sua* (Fontana edn. 1959), p.142.
6. J.H. Newman, *Ibid*, p.108.
7. D. Newsome, *Godliness and Good Learning* (1961), p.12.
8. See J.J. Newman, *Autobiographical Memoir* (1891), ch. IV and W.J.A.M. Beek, *John Keble's Literary and Religious Contribution to the Oxford Movement* (Nijmegen 1959), p.6.
9. MS Copy of Letter from E.B. Pusey to J.H. Newman, 21 Oct 1835.
10. See C. Dawson, *The Spirit of the Oxford Movement* (1945), ch.6.
11. See R.W. Church, *The Oxford Movement* (1932 edn.) pp.159–162.
12. J. Keble, *Sermons Academical and Occasional* (1848), Postscript to sermon viii, p.358.
13. W. Lock, *John Keble, a Biography* (1893 edn.) p.230.
14. J.H. Newman, *Apologia Pro Vita Sua* (Fontana (edn.) 1959), p.110.
15. MS Copy of Letter from J. Keble to E.B. Pusey, 19 April 1829.
16. MS Copy of Letter from E.B. Pusey to J. Keble, 13 May 1829.
17. See W.E. Houghton, *The Victorian Frame of Mind* (1957), pp.106–109, and A.O.J. Cockshut, *Anglican Attitudes* (1959), ch.2.
18. Y.T. Brilioth, *The Anglican Revival* (1925), p.124.
19. J. Keble, *op.cit.*, sermon iii, p.54.
20. MS Letter from J. Keble to A.P. Percival, 1 March 1833. See also MS Copy of Letter from J. Keble to J.H. Newman, 8 Aug. 1833.
21. MS Copy of Letter from J.H. Newman to A.P. Percival, 6 Sept 1833.
22. MS Copy of Letter from J.H. Newman to E.B. Pusey, 24 Jan 1836.
23. For a discussion of the influence of Lamennais on Newman and H. Froude in particular and on Tractarians in general, see W.G. Roe, *Lamennais and England* (1966), ch. IV. C. Dawson in his *The Spirit of the Oxford Movement* (1945), p.61, discusses the resemblance between the *Tracts* and the *Avenir* and H. Froude's hope to make the *British Magazine* into a sort of *Avenir*.
24. See O. Chadwick, *The Victorian Church* (1966), p.133.
25. MS Copy of Letters from J. Keble to E.B. Pusey, 4 and 16 Oct 1836.
26. See D.H. Newsome, *Godliness and Good Learning* (1961), p.12.
27. H. Scott Holland, *Personal Studies* (1905), pp.91–92.
28. MS Copy of Letter from E.B. Pusey to J. Keble, 15 Nov 1837.
29. See J.B. Mozley, *Letters of J.B. Mozley* (ed. by his sister 1885), p.70.
30. MS Copy of Letter from E.B. Pusey to J. Keble, 15 Nov 1837.
31. E.B. Pusey, *Parochial Sermons*, Vol.III (1866 edn.), p.189.
32. *Ibid* p.208.
33. MS Copy of Letter from E.B. Pusey to J.H. Newman, 19 Jan 1840.
34. J.H. Newman, *Apologia Pro Vita Sua* (Fontana edn. 1959), p.142.
35. MS Copy of Letter from E.B. Pusey to J.H. Newman, Oct 1829.
36. See also J.H. Newman, *Apologia Pro Vita Sua.* (Fontana edn. 1959), p.147.
37. See F.L. Cross, *The Oxford Movement and the Seventeenth Century* (1933), p.10.
38. MS Copy of Letter from E. B. Pusey to J.H. Newman, 25 Nov 1826.
39. MS Copy of Letter from J.H. Newman to E.B. Pusey, 5 Dec 1832.

40. J.H. Newman, *Apologia Pro Vita Sua* (Fontana edn. 1959), p.115.
41. *Ibid.*
42. *Ibid.*
43. *Ibid*, p.116.
44. MS Copy of Letter from E.B. Pusey to J.H. Newman end of 1833 or beginning of 1834.
45. See H.P. Liddon, *Life of E.B. Pusey* (1894), I, p.112.
46. MS Copy of Letter from E.B. Pusey to J.H. Newman, 1836.
47. *Ibid*, 7 Dec 1836.
48. See J.H. Newman, *Apologia Pro Vita Sua*, (Fontana ed. 1959), pp.132–134.
49. E.B. Pusey, *Scriptural Views on Baptism* (1836 edn.) comprising Tracts 67, 68 and 69 published separately in 1835, p.192.
50. E.B. Pusey, *Letter to the Bishop of Oxford* (1839), p.12.
51. *Ibid*, p.22.
52. MS Copy of Letter from E.B. Pusey to J.H. Newman, 21 Aug 1844.
53. MS Letter from J.H. Newman to Sir J. Stephens, 15 March 1835; see D. Newsome, *The Parting of Friends* (1966), p.74.
54. L.I. Guiney, *Hurrell Froude* (1904), p.164.
55. MS Copy of Letter from E.B. Pusey to J. Keble, 29 Jan 1839.
56. MS Copy of Letter from J. Keble to E.B. Pusey, 18 Jan 1839.
57. E. Churton, Memoir of *Joshua Watson* (1861), II, p.82.
58. MS Copy of Letter from E.B. Pusey to J.H. Newman, Jan 1840.
59. See C. Dawson, *The Spirit of the Oxford Movement* (1945), ch. 4 and 5.
60. R.H. Greenfield, *The Attitude of the Tractarians to the Roman Catholic Church* (1956), unpublished D.Phil. thesis, Bodleian Library, Oxford, p.210.
61. E.B. Pusey, *Letter to the Bishop of Oxford* (1839), p.15.
62. *Ibid*, p.17.
63. J.H. Newman, *op.cit.*, p.266.
64. MS Copy of Letter from E.B. Pusey to M. Pusey, 2 June 1838.
65. O. Chadwick, *The Mind of the Oxford Movement* (1960), p.14.
66. E.B. Pusey, *Sermons During the Season from Advent to Whitsuntide* (1848), Preface, pp.vi–vii.
67. *Ibid*, p.viii.
68. *Ibid*, Sermon, 'The Christian's Life in Christ', pp.232–233.
69. E.B. Pusey, *Parochial Sermons* (1886 edn.) Vol. 3, Sermon, 'Holy Communion – Danger in careless receiving', p.334.
70. *Ibid*, p.345.
71. See E.R. Fairweather, *The Oxford Movement* (New York, 1964), Introduction, p.11.
72. E.B. Pusey, *Sermons during the Season from Advent to Whitsuntide* (1848), Sermon v, 'The Incarnation, A Lesson in Humility', pp.61–64.
73. *Ibid*, p.72.
74. See C.C.J. Webb, *Religious Thought in the Oxford Movement* (1928), p.45 and W.E. Houghton, *The Victorian Frame of Mind* (1957), pp.228–231.

two points were to be observed in 'the Scriptural history of the planting of the Church'; firstly there was 'great observance of order' in sending out missionaries, and secondly there was 'great and instant care in preserving a regular ministerial system in the Churches thus formed'.[34] He maintained that a 'well ordered ministry' was essential to the growth of the body, to its unity, to its connection with its Head, to its internal well-being and the avoidance of error, to the increase of faith, knowledge and grace and to the completion of God's Kingdom.[35]

Thus it was that Pusey attached so much importance to the erection of missionary seminaries. He expressed the wish to Harrison that the special funds occasionally raised for the S.P.C.K. by the publication of Royal Letters might be used for the building of such institutions, especially in Australia.[36] Anxious, however, that the mother country should also foster the training of missionaries, Pusey played no small role in the founding of St Augustine's College, Canterbury; a subject Pusey's biographer H.P. Liddon discusses nowhere.

Edward Coleridge, an Assistant Master at Eton and former classmate of Pusey, was the prime mover of the campaign in the 1840s to open a Missionary College in England, but he leant very heavily on Pusey for advice. He wrote to Pusey in 1842:

> You will be anxious, no doubt to hear about the progress of the Miss. Coll. Scheme. I am happy to tell you that so far my course has been very smooth and successful . . . I now have received about 400 distinct promises of co-operation from some of the noblest, as well as wisest and holiest of the land; and I have little doubt that I can raise the necessary money if the *site* be decided, and the Archbishop bold enough to allow me to begin the work openly with the new year. The *site* is, as I always thought it would be, the real difficulty, because the decision must turn in every case on a nice consideration of pros and cons. This more particularly applies to Oxford, to which *almost everyone seems* to object more or less – not on a Theological ground

> – but from a one-sided view of the dangers, to which such an institution would be exposed by immediate or near vicinity to a great body of students of a somewhat higher grade, and living at a much greater expense.[37]

Pusey clearly wanted the college in Oxford, for Coleridge later told him.

> I am delighted and *strengthened* by the contents of your letter, as regards the Miss. College, and shall fight hard with the Archbishop for Oxford. But I shall require some further demonstration on the part of the University to convince him, that it will not be regarded by half its members as a work of the other half.[38]

In 1845, however, as a result of a gift of property and a promise from Alexander Hope to provide restoration work, the site for the college was settled at Canterbury. The Archbishop had also given Coleridge permission to launch a public appeal the moment his private promises of money amounted to £25,000.[39] Charles Marriott the Tractarian and Fellow of Oriel hinted to Pusey that there was a chance too of a closer connection between the new college and 'the fat chapter of Canterbury'.[40] With the site settled, Coleridge was then anxious to obtain from Pusey his views regarding '*necessary* and *essential* Statutes' for the college.[41] St Augustine's was eventually opened in 1848.

3. A Christian empire

Pusey's friendship with Coleridge and Marriott enabled him to keep in close touch with development overseas, particularly in Australia, New Zealand and Tasmania. In 1841, Coleridge had collected £750 for Bishop Broughton of Australia as a contribution towards the latter's efforts to build forty-two new churches in the colony. Coleridge was not content, however, simply to receive an annual subscription from Pusey and books for the bishop's library, he also regularly sent him letters from Broughton, Selwyn of New Zealand and Nixon of Tasmania.[42] On more than one occasion Coleridge enlisted Pusey's aid in remedying what he termed 'a gross dereliction of Christian duty on the part of the Colonial Government', by the provision of Chaplains for convicts transported overseas.[43] Marriott, whose cousin was the Archdeacon of Tasmania, did the same.[44] In 1842 Coleridge wrote to Pusey –

> The Bp. of Tasmania, a man in all respects worthy of his high calling, is to be sent out without a Chaplain, and *Eighteen Thousand Convicts* (it is a fact) are *concentrated* in Tasman's Peninsula without one Minister of the Church to care for them, but with one Wesleyan Teacher paid by a Church – professing Government.[45]

Less than a year later he was writing –

> The Bishops of New Zealand and Tasmania are both in want of men of constructive minds, and the latter has received authority from Ld. Stanley to select 13 ministers to be distributed among 8,000 convicts with a salary of at least £150 per annum, rations and probably lodgings. Ernest Hawkins and Archdeacon Manning are coming hither tomorrow, and I will consult with them on the subject and you shall hear from me ere long.[46]

Pusey, however, had realized the extent of the convict problem some years before; he had remarked on it in his sermon *The Church the Converter of the Heathen*:

> Year by year 6,000 persons are forced into exiles for crimes, to which it must be said our neglect in providing pastors for our great towns had led many. For our safety, they are transported; that *we* may sleep, walk, at ease; that *our* property may be secure. While confined in this land, they have means of grace; every prison, by law of this land, has its chaplain; we acknowledge the principle, that we have no right to cut them off from the means of restoration; . . . spiritual punishments are with God and His Church; but what else is it than to inflict eternal, when we separate these unhappy persons from all the good and from

> all good, congregate them together, so that the contagion should become tenfold through their exclusive intercourse with one another; sever those not yet hardened from calls to repentance, plunge them in renewed and worse temptations, until the stink of their ill-deeds produce a moral pestilence.[47]

It must be admitted that Pusey was largely concerned only with religious issues raised by transportation; he did not like Benjamin Franklin question whether, if England was justified in sending her convicts to the colonies, the latter were entitled to send their rattlesnakes in exchange.[48] Pusey's views on colonization in general and as shown in another sermon, preached at Bristol in 1840, were based on moral grounds. He remarked of the period from 1831 onwards:

> We have been relieving ourselves of the pressure of our population by a thoughtless system of colonizing, exporting the members of our Church, as though they had been sheep and oxen for the slaughter, not Christian men. We have in Australia alone laid the foundation of what in the course of a century will probably be four mighty empires or, as we are now acting, republics; but if our exertions be only such as they have hitherto been, four Heathen states, whether empires or republics, with a weakly church, keeping by God's mercy a seed of life in her, a light amid the surrounding darkness.[49]

Pusey was occupied not only with the state of affairs in the Antipodes; any thoughts that he was not interested in missionary activity, and that he was not fully aware of the needs of the Church in such places as India, North America and the West Indies, are dissipated by the sermon he preached for the S.P.G. at Clifton in 1841, entitled 'The Preaching of the Gospel a Preparation for our Lord's Coming'.[50] Three years before, he had been desperately anxious to stress the responsibilities which had fallen on England as a result of her imperialist activities, and the moral obligation that she had to employ her wealth to further the Christian cause, 'All you can give', he said, 'is fearfully needed, needed by those who with you have been made members of Christ, or who have been subjected to this Christian Empire'.[51] The idea of a 'Christian empire' provided Pusey with a dilemma when it came to deciding the relations between the State and the Church overseas. On the one hand he deplored the lack of government aid to the Anglican Church in Canada[52], and, after 1834, the cessation of parliamentary grants to the S.P.G.[53]; on the other hand he objected to the government's nomination of bishops for the colonies, and he made known his views to the Bishop of London and his own diocesan bishop.

4. Colonial bishoprics

Perhaps with more than a slight degree of exaggeration, it has been remarked that the erection of colonial bishoprics was not only the most notable achievement of the Church of England in the 19th century, but that this event affected it more than any other movement in history, including the Reformation.[54] Nevertheless, when one considers that whereas in 1800 there were only seven Anglican episcopal sees outside the British Isles (five in the U.S.A. and two in Canada), by 1847 they numbered fifty-one, one can appreciate the pace of change. The person most responsible for this, as far as the colonies were concerned, was Bishop Blomfield of London.[55] What has not been known hitherto, is that during the vital stage of setting up a Colonial Bishoprics Fund, Blomfield was in close consultation with Pusey. Because Liddon failed to mention this, all subsequent writers on colonial bishoprics, especially those dealing with the constitutional problems involved in the erection of sees abroad, have assumed that Pusey had no hand in the matter.

Until 1863, the procedure adopted by the Crown for the establishment of a colonial see and the appointment of a colonial bishop was by the issue of Letters Patent. In law and by the imperial Act 25 Henry VIII c 19, the right of nomination to a bishopric lay in the Crown, and Letters Patent were required to make the nomination effective. (The legal competence of English bishops to consecrate subjects of foreign powers not subject to the Act of Supremacy, had been assured by an Act of Parliament in 1786). It was this procedure which Blomfield debated with Pusey in the early 1840s.

Pusey was never under any illusion that additional bishoprics were not needed.[56] By 1841, sees had been erected in the Empire at Nova Scotia (1787), Quebec (1793), Calcutta (1813). Madras (1835) Australia (1836), Bombay (1837), and Newfoundland and Toronto (1839). The immediate aim of the trustees of the Colonial Bishoprics Fund, once it was in being, was to found others, especially for the English in the Mediterranean region, in New Zealand, New Brunswick, the Cape of Good Hope, Tasmania and Ceylon. When Blomfield was endeavouring to set up this Fund, it was natural that he should send Pusey a copy of his *Letter to His Grace the Lord Archbishop of Canterbury* (1840), in which his ideas were outlined.[57] For many years, Pusey and Blomfield had worked in close association in their efforts to erect more churches in London.

The temper of Pusey's mind in relation to the idea of a bishop to serve the needs of the English in the Mediterranean, can be gauged from a letter he wrote his former student Benjamin Harrison. Pusey considered the plan 'very desirable, but care', he said, 'must be taken that his functions were limited to those speaking English, which is the real ground for sending him, else he would become a sort of Apostolic Legate and a centre of schism'.[58] He was certain that the British in Malta and Gibraltar had every right to a bishop, but he would have preferred that the bishop should be sent to them under the auspices of the S.P.G., 'the accredited channel', rather than the C.M.S.[59]

In acknowledging Blomfield's *Letter*, Pusey had strongly urged that the Mediterranean Bishop's function should be well defined, and he further suggested that colonial bishops should be appointed not by the State, but either by the two Archbishops and the Bishop of London, or by the whole Episcopal body.[60] This in time became a sore point between Pusey and Blomfield, but for the moment they were in broad agreement. At least in June 1840, Blomfield was of the opinion that if the Crown gave the new bishops no endowment for political privileges, 'it can hardly be entitled to claim the nomination, although perhaps the formal appointments may be vested in the Sovereign in virtue of her prerogative, which in the Colonies is plenary'.[61] He also wanted Pusey's opinion on what should be done about appointments, if Colonial Legislatures were prepared to furnish a part of the endowment of a new bishopric.[62]

By the end of the year, however, Blomfield had met with opposition from the government on the question of nomination. He told Pusey:

> They think that it would be an infringement of the Royal Prerogative; and they probably apprehend that it would be drawn into a precedent and applied to the appointment of Bishops at home. *Practically* they would take the recommendation of the Archbishop for these Bishoprics. Whether they are right or wrong in their determination, it is *fixed*, and I have reason to think that it is approved of by the leaders of that party who would succeed the present Ministers in case of any change. What then is to be done?[63]

Blomfield himself was of the opinion that the need for additional bishoprics was so great, that they should proceed for the moment in co-operation with the government. He also considered that 'in the present state of the Church, at least in the Colonies, it is necessary that the Bishops should have coercive jurisdiction which can be derived only from the secular power'.[64] It must be admitted, indeed, that Blomfield's views were probably in line with those held by the existing colonial bishops. Inglis in Nova Scotia, Moutain in Quebec, Middleton and Heber in India, the first West Indian bishops, and certainly Broughton in Australia, had all striven to assure the Church of England a position in the colonies as the officially recognized religion.[65] Pusey, however, though admitting that Blomfield meant well, became thoroughly angry by his latest news and wrote to Keble for advice:

How far is it good, as Churchmen, to go on extending this system of giving Bishops authority from the State?

Supposing this not decisive against the measure, could the difficulty of recognizing this assumption of the State, to nominate to Bishoprics, which it in no degree even endows, be met, if there were certain Bishoprics, in which this State authority and State nomination were both got rid of? If e.g. we had a Bishop of Sierra Leone to whom the State gave no authority and would consent not to nominate, would one or two such cases save the principle, and establish a precedent of sufficient value, to counter-balance the mischief of the others? (These Bishops to be chosen by the Bench or the Archbishop.)

Is the objection of State nomination valid enough, in your mind, to prevent your having anything to do with a scheme, much needed in itself, but which involves this?[66]

In this predicament, and following the line adopted by Keble, Pusey wrote to the Bishop of Oxford stating his objections to the plan of state nomination, but saying that if the bishop, as his diocesan, recommended him to contribute to the Fund, or if the whole body of bishops agreed to the scheme, he would support it nevertheless on their responsibility.[67] He also wrote again to Blomfield, who repeated his own views in even stronger language; by now the bishop was utterly exasperated by Pusey's scrupulous objections.[68]

Pusey's final view of the plan for Colonial Bishoprics was that the conditions attached to it were a disappointment to those 'who long to see our Church somewhere develop herself unshackled', but 'still we may be thankful that it has been put into the minds of our Bishops to devise a plan of such character and magnitude, hoping . . . that the plan is a beginning of better days'.[69] It was against this background that Pusey supported especially the labours of Selwyn in New Zealand and Nixon in Tasmania.

When one considers Pusey's efforts up to 1850 on behalf of the missions, particularly in his preaching, his contact with affairs in America and the Colonies, his interest in the establishment of missionary colleges and his concern for the erection of colonial bishoprics, it is quite clear that his contemporaries at least did not underestimate the importance of his opinions. Of all the Oxford Tractarians, with the possible exception of Charles Marriott, Pusey took Anglican expansion overseas the most seriously and contributed most to its success.

8
THE EVOLUTION OF PUSEY'S THEOLOGY

1. Views on Baptism

In earlier chapters it has been indicated that, before 1835, Pusey's outlook was so variegated that his adhesion to the Oxford Movement came as a surprise to his contemporaries. Though Pusey had hitherto honestly considered himself to be basically High Church, his sympathy for the positive content of Evangelical teaching, his early Liberalism, his views on Religious Articles, his mode of interpreting Scripture, and his attitude to the episcopate, had rendered him suspect to at least H.J. Rose, and probably also to most of the faithful High Church remnant, who, according to Joshua Watson, 'had not bowed their knees to Baal'.[1] Like Henry Manning's indeed, Pusey's early career proves the futility of discussing ecclesiastical and theological matters in the first two decades of the 19th century in terms of party labels.[2] If anything, Pusey's early churchmanship can only be described as comprehensive or as reflecting the deep theological confusion existent in the Church of England before the advent of the Oxford Movement.[3]

Even after Pusey became a Tractarian, and when he consciously disowned many of his former opinions, it has been shown how his outlook remained individual, and to some of his critics, doubtless ambiguous and illogical. Much as Pusey may have acquired his subsequent loathing of Erastianism and Rationalism, together with a deepened understanding of Sacramentalism, from Keble, and though he may have been indebted to Newman for his first real introduction to the Fathers and Caroline divines, he persisted in retaining certain very definite views of his own.[4] Within the internecine quarrels between the old High Church party and the Tractarians, and even in the differences between the members of the Oxford Movement themselves, Pusey cannot be fitted into a closely defined category until the first half of the 19th century was coming to a close. Before that, he had characteristics in common with the old High Church Hackney Phalanx, the followers of Newman's searching intellectual path, and the more sober 'Bisley School' of Isaac Williams and Thomas Keble. Specifically Pusey stood alone amongst all the Tractarians, not only by reason of his greater knowledge of German theology and Old Testament studies, his concern for the industrial towns, his efforts to improve clerical education, his attention to ecclesiastical politics and interest in missionary affairs, but also in his approach to Primitive Christianity, to the Reformation and to Roman Catholics. In his own per sonal and rigorously ascetic life he was unique. It was, however, as a Tractarian and during the years 1835 to 1845 that Pusey matured in his theological outlook, especially in his grasp of doctrine; a process which most effectively began when he wrote his first *Tract on Baptism*.

Soon after he had formally joined the Oxford Movement, Pusey began agitating for such a tract to be written, and he was not slow to make known the reasons for his concern. He told Newman:

> Men need to be taught that it [Baptism] is a Sacrament, and that a Sacrament is not merely an outward badge of a Christian man's profession, and all union must, I think be hollow, which does not involve agreement in principles at least as to the Sacraments. Great good also would be done by shewing the true doctrine of Baptism in its warmth and life, whereas the Low Church think it essentially cold. Could not this be done, avoiding all technical terms? I know nothing or little as to the reception such a Tract would meet with, but you have to decide whether holding back is Christian prudence or compromise.[5]

In the event, Pusey wrote three tracts on Baptism in 1835 (numbers 67, 68 and 69), and, though he later extensively altered all three, only number 67 was ever republished in its revised form.[6] In the Preface to the first edition of this, Pusey elaborated his reasons for dwelling on the subject at length:

> Our general habits of mind are rationalizing; we live in the world of sense; the knowledge which we acquire is a matter of sense; what we call 'science' is the knowledge of things tangible to sense: a truly *common*-sense, or rather a common-place sense, is our rule in all things; and all this we make our boast. This is an unhealthy atmosphere for faith, which has to do entirely with things unseen, not of sense ... One must give way; a more vivid faith must penetrate our social, domestic, intellectual system, or it must itself be stifled ... The Blessed Sacraments are a peculiar obstacle to its [Rationalism's] inroads, for their affects come directly from God, and their mode of operation is as little cognizable to reason as their Author.[7]

Pusey was well aware that he aimed at encouraging what he termed 'far more exalted notions of Holy Baptism, than are in these days current among those who think they appreciate it even highly'.[8] In order to achieve this, he maintained that, until the late 16th century and 'the unhappy innovation of Zwingli', the whole Church had interpreted Christ's words, 'Except a man be born again of water and the Spirit', in the same sense.[9] Pusey also attacked the subsequent 'watering down' of doctrine, and singled out R.D. Hampden's Bampton Lectures as evidence of a divine who suggested that the efficacy of sacraments depends on the mind of the believer.[10] He went on to insist on the extreme gravity of post-baptismal sin and the difficulty for a sinner to obtain any guarantee that he might be forgiven it.

Pusey was firmly opposed to any suggestions that the condition of those fallen from grace was not immensely grave, and that forgiveness was easily obtainable.

> To those who have fallen, God holds out only 'a light in a dark place', sufficient for them to see their path, but not bright or cheering as they would have it: and so, in different ways, man would forestall the sentence of his

> Judge; the Romanist by the *Sacrament* of penance; a modern class of divines by the appropriation of the merits and righteousness of our Blessed Redeemer; the Methodists by sensible experience: our own, with the Ancient Church, preserves a reverent silence, not cutting off hope, and yet not nurturing an untimely confidence, or a presumptuous security.[11]

Considering that within a few years' time Pusey was to become the foremost Anglican advocate of private confession, his harsh tone of 1835, even towards venial sins, is astonishing.[12] Basing himself on a text of St Paul and later on Saints Athanasius, Cyril of Jerusalem and Basil, Pusey was insistent that 'it is impossible for those who have once been enlightened ... and yet have fallen away, to renew them again unto repentance'.[13] He was adamant that 'we have no account in Scripture of any second remission, obliteration, extinction of all sin, such as is bestowed upon us by "the one Baptism for the remission of sins" '.[14] The only consolation that he held out to the sinner was by way of public discipline as practised in the Early Church; by this means Pusey maintained, quoting Tertullian, God had provided against post-baptismal sin, for 'though the door of *full-oblivion* (*ignoscentiae*) is closed, and the bolt of Baptism fastened up, [God] alloweth (it) *somewhat* still to be open'.[15]

It was Pusey's severe language which troubled people much more than his conventional recitation of 'emblems' in scripture, such as the flood and the passage of the Red Sea, whereby Baptism was foreshadowed. H.J. Rose, now a close friend of Pusey, was worried and reminded him of St John's words, 'If any man sin we have an advocate with the Father, Jesus Christ the Righteous'.[16] To F.D. Maurice, Pusey's Tract represented the parting of the ways between him and the Oxford Movement; he 'always spoke of it with a kind of shudder, as it were of an escape from a charmed dungeon'.[17] Three years later, Samuel Wilberforce in his capacity as Select Preacher to the University, bluntly abhorred the undue stress placed on the fearfulness of post-baptismal sin, and preached what he called an 'anti-Pusey' sermon on the theme of the Prodigal Son.[18]

Much of Pusey's severity perhaps derived from the fact that he based his doctrine on the stark statements of Scripture, unsoftened by the mitigating interpretations of tradition, or by the relief to the burdened conscience offered by the absolving powers of the institutional Church. He was emphatic that 'in examining whether any doctrine be a portion of revealed truth, *the one subject of inquiry* must be whether it be contained in Holy Scripture'.[19] At this time, Pusey had also clearly not considered any notion of development in doctrine. Much more, however, Pusey's bleak outlook undoubtedly stemmed from his own temperament and the revolution towards asceticism which occurred in his own personal life in 1835. In addition, he was deeply troubled by what he termed the nation's lethargy in regard to sin.

> What one does mourn, is the loss of that inward sorrow, that overwhelming sense of God's displeasure, that fearfulness of having provoked his wrath, that reverent estimation of His great holiness, that participation of His utter hatred of sin, that loathing of self for having been so unlike to CHRIST, so alien from God; it is that knowledge of the reality and hatefulness of sin, and of self, as a deserter of GOD; that vivid perception of Heaven and Hell, of the essential and eternal contrast between GOD and Satan, sin and holiness, and of the dreadful danger of having fallen into the kingdom of darkness . . . It is this we have lost.[20]

Whatever the effects produced by Pusey's severe outlook and language concerning post-baptismal sin, the three tracts also revivified the seemingly endless debate over the twin issues of Justification and Baptismal Regeneration. Throughout history, Anglican theologians have employed at least two conceptions of Justification. Cranmer, for example, had favoured the Lutheran idea that justification should be viewed as an actually perceived relation to God, and that its realization in good works was simply evidential. Such Caroline divines as Jeremy Taylor had taught that grace came chiefly via the sacraments and that justification should be treated as an object of hope, for which man might prepare himself by leading a moral life.[21] In the 18th century, the question first gained in importance in face of Deist arguments in support of moralism outside the bounds of Christianity, and then it received prominence in the hotly contested debates between the Evangelical Overton and the ultra High Church Daubeny. Much ink was spilt between the contestants on the question of whether there was one justification in the Evangelical sense or two, one at Baptism and the other for which works were the condition on the Day of Judgment.[22] At the beginning of the 19th century, one of the foremost defenders of Baptism as a vehicle of Justification was Alexander Knox; an author whom Pusey read attentively and whose *Remains* he quoted in his *Tract on Baptism*. By 1835, Pusey had long since clarified his own ideas on the subject of justification; now he merely aligned himself with those who taught that justification came at Baptism.

It is probable indeed, that having read Spener and having been compelled to discuss the relationship between faith and good works in his early debates with his fiancée, Pusey reached a conclusion to the problem before Newman. In 1840 Pusey was at least adamant that it was he that had initially prompted his friend to tackle the subject in writing. 'Indeed', he told Newman, 'you did write your *Lectures on Justification* at *my* suggestion: though you, of course, felt the difficulties too, it was at my request that you set yourself to remove them'[23]. How much, therefore, Newman's famous 'umbrella' definition of justification[24] was the result of Pusey's promptings in the first place is open to conjecture. Certainly Pusey, who in earlier years had declared that he considered faith and works to be inseparable, would have approved of Newman's solution.

> Whether we say we are justified by faith or works or by the Sacraments, all these but mean this one doctrine, that we are justified by grace, given through the Sacraments, impetrated by faith, manifested in works.[25]

It was Pusey's early acquaintance with the manifold misconceptions that could arise over the problem of justification, that also enabled him to understand the jealousy of Evangelicals for the claims of Conversion; this remained so, even when he became one of the foremost upholders of baptismal regeneration. Although this latter is upheld in the Book of Common Prayer, in 1850 it was still misunderstood and conceived of as denying the need for conversion, whenever there had been baptism in infancy.[26] The breadth of Pusey's sympathies, however, prevented him from being quite so disturbed as many other High Churchmen eleven years later at the time of the Gorham Judgment. His mature sermon of 1853 on 'Justification' embodied both of the conceptions of justification which had always found some form of expression in the Church of England.

Equally important as far as Pusey's own theological development was concerned, was his discovery as a Tractarian of how closely baptismal regeneration was bound up with the notion of the Christian life as a mysterious incorporation of the individual into the Humanity of God Incarnate. Apart from stressing Baptism as an objectively effective means of grace, it was this aspect that Pusey had emphasized in his *Tract 67*:

> The view, then, here held of Baptism, following the ancient Church and our own is, that we be engrafted into CHRIST, and thereby receive a principle of life, afterwards to be developed and enlarged by the fuller influxes of His grace; so that neither is Baptism looked upon as an infusion of grace distinct from the incorporation into CHRIST, nor is that incorporation conceived of as separate from its attendant blessings.[27]

It was this view of sacraments as a whole that Pusey considered to be an effective means, not only of meeting the inroads of rationalism and of awakening the nation out of lethargy, but of safeguarding against the Protestant notion of imputed outward atonement on the one hand, and against the Roman tendency to suggest a doctrine of merit on the other. In this spirit, and partly to relieve anxiety created by his harsh teaching on post-baptismal sin, Pusey then turned in 1837 to consider the doctrines relating to the Eucharist.

2. Eucharistic doctrine

According to David Newsome, Pusey's understanding of the central position of the Eucharistic Sacrifice and the supreme importance of its mediatory role, was so closely related to his baptismal teaching, that to have challenged the one must have entailed at least a partial repudiation of the other.[28] Until 1843, however, Pusey published little on the Eucharist[29]; his *Tract 81* of 1837 was essentially a catena of passages from past Anglican writers on the subject. Its most notable features were its gentleness with the English Reformers and its approval of certain of the Non-Jurors; he placed the blame for what he considered unfortunate changes in Anglican teaching on Eucharistic doctrine on the influence of continental reformers, and he extolled the liturgy of 1549, distinguishing it from that of 1552 which he believed had been spoilt by foreigners. Unlike other Tractarians in 1837, Pusey as yet saw no contradiction between the work of English Reformers and the teaching of antiquity; he spoke kindly of Cranmer and singled out Ridley for praise.[30] It was not this tract but his sermons, *The Holy Eucharist a Comfort to the Penitent* (1843) and *The Presence of Christ in the Holy Eucharist* (1853), which convey Pusey's studied views on the subject.

His original purpose in preaching the 1843 sermon, (for which he was subsequently condemned by the Vice-Chancellor of the University and six doctors of divinity and suspended from the university pulpit for two years), was to indicate to the penitent the 'comforting character' of the Eucharist in two ways; 'indirectly, because it is the Body and Blood of his Lord, and is the channel of His Blessed Presence to the soul . . . [and] because in Holy Scripture the mention of remission of sins is connected with it'.[31] Throughout the sermon, Pusey was anxious to employ the language of the Fathers rather than his own, and he was careful to insist that he believed the elements remained 'in their natural substances'; he made no attempt to define the mode of the Mystery, and he thereby considered he was echoing the manner of Bishop Andrewes and Archbishop Bramhall, whose outlook was 'the type of the teaching of our Church'.[32] He was at pains to indicate the common features between Baptism and the Eucharist, even though he appreciated that they had not the same end.

In addition, Pusey drew attention to earlier types or prophecies of the Eucharist, such as the Tree of Life being withheld from Adam when he sinned, the bread and wine given by Melchizedek to Abraham, the Manna given to the Jews after crossing the Red Sea, and the bringing of a cake to Elijah by an angel.[33] Throughout, however, Pusey constantly returned to his theme of the Eucharist as 'ulteriorly, the cleansing of our sins'.[34]

Essentially practical in purpose, Pusey's 1843 sermon contained little theological argument. After its condemnation for supposedly teaching error, however, Pusey's friend Henry Manning, submitted it to careful scrutiny; he decided that, though the sermon contained nothing that was not 'capable of good sense', it did embody phrases which might sound dubious.[35] Two of these were based heavily on Chrysostom and related to the doctrine of the eucharistic sacrifice; Manning thought that they might be interpreted as implying that Christ suffered anew in every Eucharist.

1. But that which He suffered not on the Cross this He suffers in the oblation for thy sake, and submits to be broken that He may fill all men.[36]
2. That Precious Blood is still, in continuance and application of His One Oblation once made upon the Cross, poured out for us now, conveying to our souls, . . . the remission of our sin also.[37]

Manning suggested that Pusey should make an explicit distinction between the actual offering on the cross and the act of representation and memorial before God, which is made in the Eucharist.[38] Pusey agreed with him, and said it would be plain 'heresy to affirm, that His [Christ's] humiliation and Passion had not taken place once for all'.[39] It was possibly, therefore, for this reason and in the light of Manning's criticisms, that Pusey later maintained that he had preached a commemorative sacrifice 'in that He enables us therein to plead to the Father that one meritorious Sacrifice on the Cross, which He, our High Priest, unceasingly pleads in His own Divine Person in Heaven'.[40] In 1845, however, Pusey was acutely aware of how little the doctrine was understood among his fellow churchmen. He told Manning:

> The Eucharistic Sacrifice alas! is not a doctrine which it can be assumed that a high churchman holds. Do you think that to above one in a hundred so called, S. Chrysostom's words . . . would represent what they felt, or even conceived or aimed at? Would the idea of it, as a solemn act, distinct from Holy Communion itself, occur to them?[41]

It was to this problem of establishing how and in what sense it is possible to conceive of the eucharistic sacrifice as propitiatory, without lessening the value and place of the sacrifice on the cross, that Pusey later applied himself in his *Letter to the Bishop of London* in 1851[42]; in this way he played an important part in educating members of his own party, let alone Anglicans in general, on this subject.

Concerning what is offered in the Eucharist, Pusey believed that 16th century theologians treated oblation as 'prominently mental', a spiritual act of worshippers, that even to the Non-Jurors it eventually became 'prominently material', an offering of bread and wine, but to the ancient Church it was an offering of Christ.[43] It was this latter view that he had come to share, and in 1843 Pusey had been careful to quote Hooker and connect the Real Presence in the Eucharist with the Incarnation[44]; nevertheless, he repeated his injunction that one should not attempt to explain the Mystery. In 1846, Pusey summarized his thoughts for his pupil, T.E. Morris, 'I believe', said Pusey, 'the true doctrine to be, without defining, that we present to the Father what has by the words of

Consecration become sacramentally, not carnally, the Body and Blood of our Lord'.[45]

Pusey's most fully developed and mature views, however, were contained in his 1853 sermon, *The Presence of Christ in the Holy Eucharist*. Two years later, he expanded the sermon to include 'every passage in every Christian writing' on the subject that he could find, from the time of St John the Evangelist to the Fourth General Council.[46] In his 1859 Preface to the original sermon, Pusey claimed that his purpose in preaching on the topic was to show 'the distinctness and tenableness of the ground held by the English Church'. On the one hand, he wished to exhibit the difference of Anglican teaching from that of the 'Schoolmen' as to the continuance of the visible elements in their natural substances, (he maintained that Roman Catholic teaching, as distinct from that of the 'Schoolmen', had been modified at Trent); on the other, he wanted to prove that as men either accept or reject the doctrine of the Real Objective Presence, so they either retain the outlook of the ancient Church or are 'mere Zwinglians'. Pusey was certain that this doctrine would be found to be the 'point of divergence' in teaching on the Eucharist, just as Baptismal Regeneration was in doctrines of grace. He was equally insistent that 'the gift of grace which those ordinarily believe who deny the real objective Presence, falls far short of the indwelling of God the Holy Ghost'.[47]

In the actual sermon, Pusey advised against 'too much clearness' in seeking to intellectualize Divine Mysteries and he was adamant that such a quest was a temptation. He condemned both the doctrine of Transubstantiation and any notion of Consubstantiation of the elements, but he emphasized that the words 'This is My Body' should be interpreted literally and 'in their plain sense'. Unlike later Anglo-Catholic divines, such as Gore, Pusey stopped short of explanations. Though as firm as Pusey in teaching a Real Objective Presence, Gore, for example, was to go further and suggest that it was the Faith of the church which constituted the Presence of Christ in the Eucharist.[48] Pusey, however, was content without explanations:

> the presence, of which our Lord speaks has been termed Sacramental, supernatural, mystical, ineffable, as opposed *not* to what is real, but to what is natural. The word has been chosen to express, not our knowledge, but our ignorance; or that unknowing knowledge of faith, which we have of things divine, surpassing knowledge. We know not the manner of His Presence.[49]

In his later life, Pusey once declared that he had been taught the doctrine of the Real Presence by his mother, who had learnt it from 'older clergymen'.[50] Whether this was the same as that which he was teaching in the last years of the Oxford Movement concerning the Real Objective Presence is, however, highly unlikely. This outlook Pusey had acquired from his study of the Fathers, though as early as 1839 in his *Letter to the Bishop of Oxford*, he was maintaining that the Articles taught such a doctrine. His concern for this belief in the Presence also probably explains his vehement criticism in his *Letter* to the Bishop of the Church of Rome's refusal of the cup to the laity, his rejection of the doctrine of concomitance, and his dislike of Latin in the Eucharist liturgy.[51] All these, Pusey regarded as deviations from Christ's original and straightforward intentions. By contrast and in respect to the Real Presence, Pusey was anxious to point out that the Fathers had adhered strictly to Christ's teaching, even though several of them had employed such words in connection with the act of consecration as 'transmute, transmake, transform, trans-element, re-order'. Pusey was ever to believe of the elements in the Eucharist that 'Physically they are what they were: sacramentally they are the Body and Blood of Christ'.[52]

3. The Sacrament of Penance

Nothing, however, illustrates to the same extent the change and development in Pusey's theological outlook during the decade beginning in 1835, as his attitude to the Sacrament of Penance. In later life, Pusey regarded his two sermons, entitled *Entire absolution of the Penitent*, as simply part of his previously planned programme to balance his stern teachings on post-baptismal sin by preaching on the sacraments; it is possible, therefore, that Pusey himself was unaware of the enormous revolution that had occurred in his outlook on the subject of Confession. In his *Tract on Baptism*, however, he had taught one thing, and eleven years later he had altered his opinions completely. He wrote in 1835:

> [The Roman Church] held in words as well as we, that the Sacrament of Baptism could not be repeated, and that its efficacy alone would not wash away sins subsequently committed; but by devising the new Sacrament of Penance, they did contrive, without more cost, to restore men, however fallen, to the same state of undisturbed security in which God had by Baptism placed them. Penance became a second Baptism. Man's longing to be once again secure, was complied with: his old sins were effaced, not to rise up again against him: again and again he was told, 'Thy sins are forgiven thee' and so the salutary anxiety about past sin, and its fruit 'a righteous, godly and sober life', were in ordinary minds choked and effaced. Perverting the earnest sayings of the Fathers, they turned the hard and toilsome way of Repentance into the easy and royal road of *Penance*.[53]

By 1846, Pusey was of an utterly different frame of mind:

> Consciences *are* burdened. There is a provision of the part of God, in His Church, to relieve them. They wish to be, and to know that they are in a state of grace. God has provided a means, however deeply any have fallen, to replace them in it.[54]

And Pusey was here speaking of Confession. In the Preface to the first of his two sermons, *Entire Absolution*, which the *Quarterly Review* later described as 'one of the most insidious pieces of special pleading which could well be found in such literature'[55], Pusey went out of his way to suggest that the Church of England explicitly provided private confession for 'cases of heavy sin', 'timorous, scrupulous consciences', 'persons who ... have carried about them the oppressive consciousness of some past secret sin', and 'tender consciences'.[56] He described how those who betook themselves to confession derived comfort and strength from 'the special application of the power of the keys'.[57] At the same time, Pusey stressed the voluntary nature of confession.[58] He was afraid, however, that his sermon might be misunderstood, even though it contained teaching owned by the Church of England; his fears were occasioned by the fact that confession had been so much neglected in the previous century, had been only partially restored, and because the language of past divines and Reformers on the matter was unfamiliar to so many.[59] In the event, Pusey's fears were justified; as a portent of much later controversy, his views were attacked a short time afterwards from the University pulpit, by Dr Jeune, the Master of Pembroke.

Validity for confession in the Anglican Church, Pusey found in four sources; the 1549 Book of Common Prayer, which had permitted 'auricular and secret Confession'[60], the Homily 'Of Common Prayer and Sacraments'[61], the ordination ceremony of priests, and instructions for administering special confession for the sick.[62] Authority for priests in general to remit sins, Pusey found in Scripture and chiefly Matthew XVI: 19 and XVIII: 18. Nevertheless, he also quoted Origen, and Saints Chrysostom, Cyril, Ambrose, Leo and Pacian to support his views.[63]

How does one account for Pusey's altered views? In the first place, it is likely that he himself was ultimately driven to confession by the intensity of his own feelings of guilt. He carried this burden, however, from 1839 when his wife died, to December 1846 when he made his first confession to Keble. It was undoubtedly during these seven years that Pusey radically changed his opinions, and to such an extent that the *Quarterly Review* later suggested that 'as time went on, it seems hardly too much to say that Dr Pusey's concentration of mind on this subject, and on the offensive topics connected with it, became positively morbid'.[64] In his *Letter to the Bishop of Oxford* of 1839, Pusey had retained his earlier views. 'Romanism as well as Ultra-Protestantism', he said, 'would consult readily for man's feverish anxiety to be altogether at ease: . . . What I would urge . . . is to hold out the prospect of peace, but as God's gift through the deepening of repentance; not to cut short His work, whether by the Sacrament of Penance, or inward persuasion'.[65] In private, however, Pusey was having second thoughts and requesting the advice of his friend W.F. Hook. In reply to a letter of Pusey's, Hook expressed his pleasure at this change of mind:

> My other object in writing was [curious enough] to ask *you* what you ask *me*, the name of some book or books on the subject of Absolution. I have had occasion lately to read a second time your admirable *Letter to the Bishop of Oxford*. . . And I was forcibly struck with the fact that in your system, if I may use the expression, without offence, you do not leave room for the grace of Absolution whatever it may be. I feel a great desire to obtain information on this subject and I rejoice that you are taking it into consideration. Perhaps it will lead you to modify your view of sin after Baptism.[66]

From Pusey's frequent reference in his first 1846 sermon on confession to Hooker's *Private Confession and Absolution with us*, it seems probable that this was the book which contributed most to Pusey's altered outlook. It is not unlikely either, that it was Keble who supplied him with much of the information he was seeking. Not only was Keble Pusey's closest friend and, after 1846, his spiritual director, but he was also the authority at the time on Hooker. In addition, not only did Keble experience like many other Tractarians from 1840 onwards the phenomenon of penitents coming forward spontaneously to seek the Sacrament of Penance, but he had been in the custom of receiving Hurrell Froude in this way as early as 1826.[67]

The revival of Confession in the Anglican Church as a whole, probably arose naturally from Tractarian emphasis on a post-baptismal sin, and the new spiritual life engendered by the Oxford Movement. Charles Marriott also suggested that the absence hitherto of the practice in the Church of

England was a factor in influencing people to secede to the Roman Church, where the sacrament was available.[68]

It has recently been argued, however, that the Tractarian restoration of Confession was accompanied by 'a somewhat less healthy view of penance', that often they gave the impression that 'an attempt was being made to *atone* for sin by penance', and that 'Pusey himself carried this to extremes'.[69] No one would deny that the disciplinary rule that Pusey followed himself was mortifying, but, just as he was unique among the Tractarians in that he was probably a Mystic[70], so in ascetic matters he was, therefore, an exceptional person. His constant aim in his spiritual life was to detain Christ's Presence in the soul, and to achieve this he followed not merely the path of moral action, but that of utter self-denial. In the realm of mysticism this is the means whereby one arrives at total passivity or 'self-emptying and suffering quietude'[71]. Pusey was only too well aware of the dangers for others of excessive asceticism; in the preface to his first 1846 sermon on confession, he had specifically warned the young against this, and he had advised them to read Newman's sermon, 'Dangers to the Penitent' on the same subject.

> There is much risk lest in the first fervour of penitence, a person should bind himself with rigid rules, disproportioned to his weakness, which might injure body or mind; or entangle himself with indefinite or too minute, or unbending rules, which under altered circumstances, or in time, might become unfitting of a snare for the conscience.[72]

Just as Pusey himself always heeded the advice of his director, Keble, so he suggested that in general it was better 'not to be one's own physician'.[73] It was precisely in order that priests might be better equipped in their office of administering the power of the keys and offering direction, that Pusey later published an edition of the *Manual for Confessors* by the Abbé Gaume and similar works. Whatever limitations Pusey may have exhibited in his concern for the restoration of the Sacrament of Penance, they were largely due to the fact that, like all Tractarians, he was a pioneer in the revival of moral theology in the Church of England.[74] The measure of the Tractarians' ultimate success can be partly judged from the fact that, in 1873, a petition was presented to Convocation by 483 of the clergy, calling for 'the licensing of duly qualified Confessors in accordance with the provisions of canon law.[75] In the subsequent controversy Pusey was looked to as a natural leader.[76]

4. Tradition and antiquity

In order to understand Pusey's original volte-face concerning Confession, however, it is important to look deeper than to purely personal causes. In his early years, Pusey had sought doctrinal authority solely in scripture, but, as he admitted in 1846, this was no longer enough on its own.[77] Much of Pusey's development as a whole, indeed, during his years as a Tractarian, was due to his changing attitude towards tradition and its function as a source of doctrinal authority. As his outlook altered on the role of tradition, so inevitably did his conception of the Church.

As R.H. Greenfield has effectively shown, opinion among Tractarians became acutely divided in time on the question of doctrinal authority. Conservatives, such as Palmer of Worcester and H.J. Rose, based their outlook on credal definitions and episcopal government, and valued antiquity only when its customs were corroborated in scripture; others, such as Froude, John Keble and Newman regarded the Primitive Church as the norm. The conservatives appealed to antiquity when it was convenient as a method of justifying Anglicanism; on the whole they were satisfied with the Church of England as it had been reformed in the 16th century, and they were only seeking a revival of Laudian theology.[78] To the more radical Tractarians, however, all doctrines and customs found in the Early Church (whether mentioned in scripture or not), were valuable; antiquity for them gradually became the standard by which the Church of England was judged and the model for reform. The conservative appeal to the Primitive Church was, therefore, 'static', whilst that of the others was 'dynamic'[79]. This difference of outlook heightened still further the considerable friction, not only over the contents and style of the Tracts, the policy that should be followed in regard to the State, their opinion of the Reformers, their relations with the *British Critic* and their view of the Non-Jurors, but eventually over their attitude to Roman Catholicism and their basic conceptions of the Church. From 1840 onwards, the younger element among the Tractarians, such as W.G. Ward and Oakley, went even further and refused to confine their investigations simply to the Early Church. They endeavoured to trace a 'dynamic' element or theory of development in succeeding centuries of the Church's history.[80] It was against this background that Pusey's own theologial outlook matured and his views on such things as the sacraments of Baptism, the Eucharist and Penance evolved.

When he first joined the Oxford Movement, it was not clear which section among the Tractarians would most win Pusey's allegiance. His friendships with Newman and Keble led him to work closely with them, and Rose at least may have felt that Pusey in 1836 was allying himself with the radical wing. At that stage Rose felt obliged to warn both Newman and Pusey about certain dangers attached to their scheme of translating the Fathers. He wrote:

> I will honestly confess that I am a little apprehensive of the effects of turning the readers, such as they are out to grass in the spacious pastures of Antiquity without very strict tether. *All* that is in Antiquity is not good; and much that was good for Antiquity would not be good for us.[81]

Specifically for Pusey's benefit, Rose became even stronger in his advice:

> *We* are not like our own Reformers *looking* for Truth and not knowing what will break upon us. We know exactly what the Truth is. We are going on no voyage of discovery. We know exactly the extent of the shore. There is a creek here, and a bay there, – *all laid down in the charts*; but not often entered or re-surveyed . . . One thing more . . . Surely,

a practice not noticed in Scripture, and the interpretation of a doctrine noticed there, do not stand on the same ground![82]

Pusey endeavoured to reassure Rose by pointing out that they took care 'not to build on one or the other Father, but on Catholic Antiquity'.[83] It was not for some time, indeed, that Pusey was prepared to advocate practices not explicitly laid down in the Book of Common Prayer. When the idea of a Library of the Fathers was first mooted, it was for practical purposes. Though Anglican theologians in the 17th century had been conversant with the Patristic Age, during the 18th century it was largely neglected in official Anglican circles. This may have been because the study of the Fathers was associated with the troublesome Non-Jurors, or because the Deist controversy required more immediate attention. The restoration of interesting primitive teaching and principles, however, was a natural corollary of Tractarian activity in the 19th century. At first, Newman also considered that it would have the added value of showing how Roman Catholics were 'wanting in *deference* to the Fathers'.[84] When the Tractarians first began translating and studying the Fathers, it is doubtful whether they appreciated how many results would ensue from a revival of Patristics.

Up to the early 1840s, Pusey seemed anxious only to remain simply an exponent of the *via media*; he seemed incapable of believing that Newman's restless intellectualism would extend further. In his *Letter to the Bishop of Oxford* of 1839, written specifically to indicate that the Tractarians were following the motto *stare super antiquas vias*, Pusey claimed that the Oxford school preached no new doctrines and appealed to formularies of the Church of England only in the manner of former standard divines. He asserted that they were anxious simply 'to recall to men's minds forgotten or depreciated truths, to invite them to enlarge, or correct, or modify their systems by consideration of points upon which they had not hitherto dwelt'.[85] If anything, in the late 1830s,

Pusey had become wary of complete acceptance of tradition and customs found in the Fathers; the exposition of his principles in his *Letter* to Bishop Bagot won the hearty congratulations of the conservative high-churchman, W.F. Hook. It may be that his words of caution in 1838, for example, to those about to study the Fathers, were engendered by fears expressed by older Tractarians concerning the activities of the younger generation.[86] Pusey's advice to students of the Fathers at this stage was very akin to that which Rose had proferred to him in 1836:

> The Fathers are indeed, *absolutely*, no terra incognita which we have to explore, no sea, to which men are committed without a compass; rather its bearings have been laid down, and its depths sounded, by our standard Anglo-Catholic divines; and what remains to be filled up, is in detail only. Still, they are relatively unknown; and it is to be expected that many mistakes might be made by ardent minds, throwing themselves at once into the rich and pleasant fields opened to them, if uncautioned.[87]

In the years immediately following the publication of his *Letter to the Bishop of Oxford*, however, Pusey was compelled to reconsider his views on doctrinal development and the meaning of the Church as he conceived of it. Not only was he forced to face a Romeward trend within the Oxford Movement and to accept the fact that Newman's outlook was not content to remain static, but a succession of controversies in the early 1840s, such as those over *Tract XC*, the refusal of the Bishop of Winchester to ordain Keble's curate, the defeat of Isaac Williams for the Professorship of Poetry, the establishment of the Jerusalem Bishopric and condemnation of his own sermon in 1843, all combined to cause Pusey to sort out his own theological position in the maelstrom. It is not unlikely that his work on translating and adapting foreign devotional manuals in these years, and his founding of women's religious orders, also contributed (albeit unconsciously) to a profound change in his outlook.

5. Pusey moves into final position

Hitherto, Pusey had always clung to the Primitive Church as corroborating Tractarian thought in the Church of England, and he had been unusual among Tractarians by his recognition of the 'blessings' gained by the Reformation; now his views underwent a revolution almost as great as that which in 1835 had marked his original adhesion to the Oxford Movement.[88]

Writing to Manning in the autumn of 1843, Pusey spoke of his pain that Greswell of Worcester College was preparing a Declaration against the doctrine of development as contained in Newman's last university sermon. Although at this stage Pusey had not yet moved from his old standing ground of antiquity, it is clear that he was beginning to reconsider his position:

> Newman's defence of Development in the abstract is perfectly distinct. The question still remains – whether the articles of the Council of Trent, are developments. N's principle only admits a possibility that they may be because there had been such in the Church; but there is ample scope for its application in the early Church without any reference at all to the later. It may be e.g. that this was a part of the fulness of the illumination through the indwelling Spirit, while the Church was one, which was forfeited, when her Unity was impaired.[89]

The question of Church unity was one which had been troubling Keble a short time before, and he had sought Pusey's views on the matter.[90] The line taken by the younger Tractarians and the possible directions of Newman's thoughts, compelled, indeed, both Keble and Pusey to examine how the Church of England stood in relation to other Communions. Pusey told Keble:

> My feeling about unity is I believe, the same as N's; that we have a degree of unity left, although not the highest sort, yet that there is enough to make the Roman, Greek and our own Church parts of the one Church, though with holi-

ness, unity has been impaired, and we altogether suffer for it ... the very language of St Cyprian seems also a comfort, since he insists so much that what is really cut off must die; since then our present state after 300 years shews that, however maimed, we have a vigorous and increasing life, we are not cut off.[91]

Pusey's conception of the Church of England was, therefore, twofold – doctrinal and existential – and within it was the classical Anglo-Catholic idea of the Church as a 'society' existing in three divided fragments; the Anglican Communion, the Eastern Orthodox and the Roman Catholic Church. This became then the basis of Pusey's loyalty to the Anglican Church in 1843; in its turn, it demanded of him that he should revise his thinking concerning the English reformation and the Roman Church.

As early as 1839, Pusey had begun to temper his former high estimate of the work of the Reformers. From a letter he wrote to Benjamin Harrison at this time, it is clear that the more Pusey had become acquainted with antiquity and had deepened his theology of the sacraments, so he began to alter his views. He doubted, for example, whether Cranmer 'held the truth as to the Communion', and he felt no assurance that those who had put Reformers to death had not intended to suppress genuinely erroneous ideas. Although the Anglican Church had been protected by Providence and 'in part restored also from what they [the Reformers] did amiss as in the Service for the Eucharist', he feared that error had been committed on both sides.[92] By 1844, these views had almost hardened into a disavowal of the Reformation; a fact made plain in a letter he then wrote to Manning:

I fear the *mode* of our Reformation was a great mistake; in that we reformed ourselves by ourselves, still more with such allies as the Lutherans and Zwinglians. But apart from this, I fear there was something fundamentally wrong, which manifested itself outward in such a junction. The first hint of this kind which impressed me was in Thorndike, who seems in so many things to have seen

> further than others. Not that I am in any way disturbed in our position. I never had a misgiving about it. But I do fear that there were very serious errors, and especially in our independence, from which we shall not recover except by confession of our fault.[93]

Just as Pusey was now condemning the Reformation, so he was writing of the 1688 Revolution in terms much stronger than he had used hitherto. He had now come to think of the Revolution as a totally 'unmixed evil', to which more than anything external he traced the decay of Church life in the 18th century. 'It seems', he said, 'like some dreadful taint taken into one's system, poisoning all our strength, and working decay and all but death'.[94] Pusey also decided to have done with speaking against the Roman Church and thought that to criticize it 'without explicit confession of our own sins, a great moral mistake and very injurious to our religious temper'.[95] In this, he clearly resembled Keble, who had expressed the wish a few months previously 'to keep up a kind of neutrality as to the points in which we differ from Rome'.[96]

How much Pusey was led to develop his views out of devotion to and dependence on Newman is highly debatable; much as he may have been influenced by his friend's course to advance his own opinions, he never ceased, however, to believe in the validity of Anglican claims. When others, such as Ambrose St John and Charles Marriott, were racked with doubts on account of Newman's approaching conversion and appealed to Pusey for help, he remained steadfast in his loyalty to the Church of England. Development there undoubtedly was in Pusey's outlook; without it the heightening in his views on the sacraments of the Eucharist and of Penance are meaningless. It also enabled him in 1845 to take his place among those in the extreme wing of the Tractarian party, but it was to Henry Manning, not Newman, that Pusey opened his heart about the change in his outlook.

Writing to Manning in August 1845, Pusey said that the only thing which he could see clearly was his duty to remain

75. Their importance was first noticed by A. Härdelin in his *The Tractarian Understanding of the Eucharist* (Uppsala 1965). They also received considerable attention in A.M. Allchin, 'The Theological Vision of the Oxford Movement', in J. Coulson and A.M. Allchin (eds) *The Rediscovery of Newman* (1967), see also D. Jasper's treatment of them in *Pusey Rediscovered* (ed P. Butler), 1983.
76. MS Letter from F.W. Faber to J.B. Morris, 31 Jan 1837 and quoted in A. Hardelin, *op.cit.*, p.17.
77. See V.P. Storr, *Development of English Theology in the Nineteenth Century* (1913), pp.252f, and Y.T. Brilioth, *The Anglican Revival* (1925), ch. 5.
78. A. Lovejoy, 'The Meaning of Romanticism for the Historian of Ideas', *Journal of the History of Ideas*, Vol. II, (1941), No.3, p.267. Cf H.G. Schenk, *The Mind of the European Romantics* (1966).
79. See e.g. J.H. Newman, *op.cit.*, pp.168–169; J. Keble, *De Poeticae vi Medicia* (1844), Dedication to Wordsworth; R. Chapman, *Father Faber* (1961). pp.42–44 and B.S. Smith, *Dean Church* (1958), pp.26–27.
80. See G.S.R. Kitson Clark, 'The Romantic Element, 1830 to 1850', *Studies in Social History* (ed. J.H. Plumb 1955), pp.236–237. For an attempted refutation of the theory that Romanticism and Tractarianism were connected, see H. Fairchild, 'Romanticism and the Religious Revival in England', *Journal of the History of Ideas*, Vol. II (1941) No.3, pp.332 f.
81. See H.P. Liddon, *op.cit.*, p.270.
82. Y.T. Brilioth, *The Anglican Revival* (1925), p.71.
83. E.B. Pusey, 'Lectures on Types and Prophecies of the Old Testament' (1836), (Unpublished), p.16.
84. See A. Hardelin, *The Tractarian Understanding of the Eucharist* (Uppsala 1965), pp.32–33.
85. E.B. Pusey, *op.cit.*, p.6.
86. *Ibid*, p.39.
87. *Ibid*, p.8.
88. *Ibid*, p.14.
89. *Ibid.*
90. *Ibid.*
91. *Ibid.*
92. *Ibid.*
93. *Ibid.*
94. MS Copy of Letter from E.B. Pusey to W.F. Hook, 12 Aug 1838.
95. See D. Newsome, *The Parting of Friends* (1966), pp.179–180.
96. *Ibid*, pp.75–76.
97. E.B. Pusey, 'Lectures on Types and Prophecies of the Old Testament' (1836), Unpublished, p.70.
98. *Ibid*, p.25.
99. *Ibid*, p.37.
100. *Ibid*, p.9.
101. J. Keble, *Tract 89, On the Mysticism attributed to the Early Fathers of the Church* (Undated, but probably 1840–1841), p.135.

102. E.B. Pusey, *op.cit.*, p.107.
103. O. Chadwick, *The Mind of the Oxford Movement* (1960), p.46.
104. A.M. Fairbairn, *Catholicism Roman and Anglican* (1899), p.82.
105. MS Letter from F. Faber to J.B. Morris, 19 June 1837 and quoted in R. Chapman, *Father Faber* (1961), p.43.

5

1. Y.T. Brilioth, *Evangelicalism and the Oxford Movement* (1934), p.36.
2. See D. Voll, *Catholic Evangelicalism* (1963), pp.37–38, 114, and 121, where it is argued that Pusey's teaching at least lent support and sympathy to the later hybrid Conversion School of George Body and George Wilkinson, within the Church of England.
3. MS Copy of Letter from F. Tholuck to E.B. Pusey, 4 April 1837.
4. See L. Pullan, *Religion Since the Reformation* (1923), pp.95–96.
5. MS Copy of Letter from E.B. Pusey to M. Barker, Oct 1827.
6. *Ibid.*
7. *Ibid.*
8. E.B. Pusey *Theology of Germany* (1830), Pt. II, p.318.
9. E.B. Pusey, *Ibid*, Pt. II, p.412.
10. See Y.T. Brilioth, *op.cit.*, pp.11–12, in which the author cites the activities of Wilhelm Löhe as evidence of this new revival.
11. Quoted in Y.T. Brilioth, *op.cit.*, p.22.
12. H.P. Liddon, *Life of E.B. Pusey* (1894), I, p.149, n 1.
13. E.B. Pusey, *op.cit.*, II, pp.317–318.
14. *Ibid*, p.345.
15. F. Oakley, *Historical Notes on the Tractarian Movement* (1865), p.49.
16. MS Copy of Letter from J. Parker to E.B. Pusey, 11 Oct 1824.
17. E.B. Pusey, *Parochial Sermons*, Vol. III (1886 ed), p.160.
18. See A.M. Allchin, *The Silent Rebellion* (1958).
19. See E.B. Pusey, *Parochial Sermons Preached and Printed on Various Occasions* (1865 edn.), Sermon IX and *Lenten Sermons* (1874 edn.) Sermon II.
20. E.B. Pusey, *Sermons during the Season from Advent to Whitsuntide* (1848), pp.59–60.
21. MS Copy of Letter from E.B. Pusey to Earl of Shaftesbury, 17 May 1852.
22. G. Prevost (ed.), *The Autobiography of Isaac Williams* (1892), p.70.
23. See MS Copy of Letter from E.B. Pusey to J. Keble, 7 Nov 1836.
24. J.A.H. Murray (ed.), *New English Dictionary* (1897), III, p.329.
25. J.D. Walsh, 'Origins of the Evangelical Revival', *Essays in Modern English Church History* (ed G.V. Bennett and J.D. Walsh, 1966), p.136.
26. J.D. Walsh, 'The Yorkshire Evangelicals in the Eighteenth Century: with especial reference to Methodism' (1956), unpublished Ph.D. thesis in the Cambridge University Library, p.3.
27. MS Copy of Letter from E.B. Pusey to Earl of Shaftesbury, 17 May 1852.
28. J. Milner, *Practical Sermons*, Vol. 3 (1823), p.71.

29. J.D. Walsh, *op.cit.*, p.25.
30. J.D. Walsh, 'The Theology of the Evangelical Revival' (1967), p.20.
31. Even that bitter critic of the Evangelicals, W.H.B. Proby, had to admit that Simeon and Pusey expressed in similar language the vital truth that salvation was of God and man's destruction of himself. See W.H.B. Proby, *Annals of the Low-Church Party in England down to the death of Archbishop Tait* (2 Vols. 1888), II pp.214–215.
32. See J.D. Walsh, 'The Yorkshire Evangelicals in the Eighteenth century' (1956), p.366.
33. S.C. Carpenter, *Church and People, 1789–1889* (1933), p.29.
34. R.I. and S. Wilberforce, *The Life of W. Wilberforce* (5 Vols. 1838), II, p.216.
35. The increasing rift between the different elements in the Evangelical party after 1820, is described in D. Newsome, *The Parting of Friends* (1966), pp.9–15.
36. See E.B. Pusey, *Sermons during the Season from Advent to Whitsuntide* (1848), Preface, pp.v–ix. Pusey does not seem to have been aware of other possible causes of the birth of Evangelicalism, such as the demand felt for new forms of worship, resulting from the continued existence within the Church of England of High Church spirituality and 17th century Puritanism. He also seemed unconscious of the complex aspects of the movement and the distinctive nature of Anglican Evangelicalism, even before the Methodists became a separate body. For a discussion of these topics, see J.D. Walsh, 'Origins of the Evangelical Revival', *Essays in Modern Church History* (ed G.V. Bennett and J.D. Walsh, 1966).
37. J.O. Johnston and W.C.E. Newbolt (eds), *Spiritual Letters of E.B. Pusey* (1898), p.152.
38. MS Copy of Letter from E.B. Pusey to H.V. Elliott, 25 Sept 1839. Of H. Froude's remarks to Isaac Williams on the eve of the Oxford Movement concerning Evangelical 'half-truths' in G. Prevost, *op.cit.*, pp.63–64.
39. Brilioth was inclined to find significance in Pusey's knowledge that J.B. Sumner (the Evangelical Archbishop of Canterbury) had endeavoured to promote piety at Eton, when Pusey was a schoolboy. See Y.T. Brilioth *op.cit.*, p.33. Liddon was of the opinion that Sumner's religious influence was exercised in the town not school. See H.P. Liddon, *op.cit.*, I, p.17 n 2. C. Smyth's remarks on Sumner at Eton support Liddon's view. See C. Smyth, *Simeon and Church Order* (1940) p.79.
40. See D. Newsome, *The Parting of Friends* (1966), pp.78–79 and 82 where the author makes use of a large album of R. Wilberforce's correspondence, discovered by Miss Irene Wilberforce at Kensington.
41. See J.B. Reynolds, *The Evangelicals at Oxford 1735–1871* (1953), ch. v and vi.
42. See H. Clegg, 'Evangelicals and Tractarians', *Historical Magazine of the Protestant Episcopal Church*, Vol. XXXV, No.2. June 2 and Vol. XXXV, No.3. Sept 1966.
43. MS Letter from A. Tyndale to E.B. Pusey, 11 Nov. 1833.

44. *Ibid*, see also A.O.J. Cockshut, *Religious Controversies of the Nineteenth Century* (1966), p.2 on reaction to the first Tracts.
45. MS Letter from A. Tyndale to E.B. Pusey, 20 Nov 1833.
46. *Ibid.*
47. *Ibid.*
48. *Ibid.*
49. *Ibid.*
50. *Ibid*, 29 Jan 1834.
51. *Ibid*, undated but probably late 1833.
52. MS Letter from A. Tyndale to E.B. Pusey, undated but probably late 1833.
53. E.B. Pusey, *An Eirenicon, In a Letter to the Author of The Christian Year* (1865), pp.4–5.
54. Y.T. Brilioth, *Evangelicalism and the Oxford Movement* (1934), pp.39–46. Cf the views expressed in H. Davies, *Worship and Theology in England. From Watts and Wesley to Maurice, 1690–1850* (1961), pp.247f, and G.W.E. Russell, *The Household of Faith* (1906), pp.313–329.
55. Y.T. Brilioth, *op.cit.*, pp.37–38.
56. C. Simeon, Sermon 256, 'Disbanding of the Troops of Israel', *Horae Homileticae.* See D. Webster, 'Simeon's Pastoral Theology', in *Charles Simeon* (1959) (ed A. Pollard and M. Hennell) p.101.
57. W. Wilberforce, *A Practical View of the Prevailing System of Professed Christians* (1797), p.207.
58. O. Chadwick, *The Mind of the Oxford Movement* (1960), p.11.
59. *Ibid*, p.12.
60. Of Newman's text of an 1826 sermon 'Holiness necessary for future Blessedness'.
61. E.B. Pusey, Sermon 'The Fewness of the Saved', *Sermons during the Season from Advent to Whitsuntide* (1848), pp.128–129. The last sentence of the quoted passage refers the reader to S. Aug. Sermon iii, 61, p.456, Oxf. Tr. on S. Luke XIII.13.
62. E.B. Pusey, Sermon 'Conversion' (preached before 1838), *Parochial Sermons*, Vol. III (1886 edn.), pp.20–21.
63. *Ibid*, p.25.
64. *Ibid.*
65. Of Gladstone's estimate of the Evangelicals' preaching of the Cross in W.E. Gladstone, *Gleanings of Past Years*, Vol. VII (1879), p.207.
66. E.B. Pusey, *Parochial Sermons*, Vol. III (1886 edn.) p.50.
67. C. Simeon, Preface to *Horae Homileticae*, p.xxi. See A. Pollard, 'The Influence and Significance of Simeon's work', in A. Pollard and M. Hennell (ed.), *op.cit.*, p.167.
68. E.B. Pusey, Sermon 'The Day of Judgement', *Parochial Sermons Preached and printed on Various Occasions* (1865 edn.), Preface, p.4.
69. I. Williams, *Tract 87* (1840), p.82.
70. The full text of Pusey's answer is in H.P. Liddon, *op.cit.*, II, pp.140–141.
71. T. Scott, *The Force of Truth* (1779), p.75.
72. J. King, *Memoir of the Rev. T. Dykes* (1849), p.247.

73. G.C. Richards, *Dr Pusey. A Short Study* (1933), Reprint from *Durham University Journal*, June edn, pp.11–12.
74. H.P. Liddon, *op.cit.*, II, p.142.
75. MS Copy of Letter from E.B. Pusey to J. Keble, 18 April 1829.
76. H.P. Liddon, *op.cit.*, II, p.143.
77. MS Copy of Letter from E.B. Pusey to F. Tholuck, 6 March 1837. See also O. Chadwick, *The Mind of the Oxford Movement* (1960) pp.48–49, where the author writes of the 'ecstatic' quality in Pusey's sermons, derived from the Greek Fathers and Christian Platonism, but with roots in the pietism of the Evangelicals.
78. In view of the misleading impression that Ford K. Brown creates in his *Fathers of the Victorians* (1961), that all those who sought to reform England by sponsoring religious and benevolent societies in the early 19th century were Evangelicals, it is necessary to point out that philanthropy was not an Evangelical monopoly. The munificence of Pusey's charities gave him affinity not only with Evangelicals, but with Victorians of all shades of religious opinion. See D. Newsome, 'Fathers and Sons' in *The Historical Journal*, VI, 2 (1963), pp. 295–310 and B. Harrison, 'Philanthropy and the Victorians' in *Victorian Studies* (June 1966).
79. See J.D. Walsh, 'Joseph Milner's Evangelical Church History' in *Journal of Ecclesiastical History* X, (1959), pp.176–177.
80. Letter to his daughter Elizabeth, 12 July 1823, in 'Fragments', pp. 87–8, and quoted in D. Newsome, *op.cit.*, p.307.
81. D. Newsome, 'The Evangelical Sources of Newman's Power', in *The Rediscovery of Newman* (1967) (ed) John Coulson and A.M. Allchin.
82. E.B. Pusey, *Parochial Sermons Preached and Printed on Various Occasions* (1865 edn.) Preface to Sermon 1 (preached 1839), p.4.
83. MS Copy of Letter from W.F. Hook to E.B. Pusey, 9 June 1840.

6

1. No. 369 in vol. 180 (July–Oct 1894), Article 1, p.2.
2. O. Chadwick, *The Victorian Church* (1966), p.198.
3. E.B. Pusey, *University Sermons*, 1859–1872, (1884 ed), Preface, p.v.
4. This is contrary to H.P. Liddon's view as described by the editors of his biography of E.B. Pusey. Liddon regarded Pusey's life chiefly in relation to the Oxford Movement. 'It [Pusey's life] would fall, he used to say, into four parts, to be entitled the Preparation, the Movement, the Struggle, the Victory', See H.P. Liddon, *Life of E.B. Pusey*, IV Preface, p.v.
5. See P.E. Coletta, 'Philip Pusey, English Country Squire', *Agricultural History*, Vol. 18, No. 2. (April 1944). Many of Philip Pusey's ideas on improvements in agriculture were ultimately included in the Agricultural Holdings Act of 1875. Twice he was President of the Royal Agricultural Society of England, and, at the Great Exhibition of 1851, he was a Royal Commissioner.
6. P.E. Coletta, *op.cit.*, p.85, and C. Fletcher, 'Narrative', pp.56–57, 66, and 76.

7. Frances Bunsen, *A Memoir of Baron Bunsen* (2 Vols. 1868), I. p.504.
8. See the MS Copy of Letter which Bunsen sent to P. Pusey on the European situation in 1830, and which Philip Pusey probably passed on to his brother. This is at Pusey House, Oxford.
9. MS Copy of Letter from E.B. Pusey to F. Tholuck, 7 Dec 1829.
10. E. Halévy, *The Triumph of Reform 1830–1841* (1961 edn.), pp.7–8.
11. See O. Chadwick, *op.cit.*, pp.80f.
12. T. Binney, *An Address delivered on laying the first stone of the new King's Weigh House* ... (1833) and quoted in E. Halévy, *op.cit.*, p.150.
13. W.B.D. Heeney, 'The Established Church and the Education of the Victorian Middle Classes: A Study of the Woodard Schools, 1847–1891' (1961), an unpublished D. Phil. thesis in the Bodleian Library, pp.261f.
14. *Ibid*, p.264.
15. See W.R. Ward, *Victorian Oxford* (1965), p.78.
16. E.B. Pusey, 'The Royal and Parliamentary Ecclesiastical Commissions', *The British Critic* (April 1838), p.456.
17. See W.E. Houghton, *The Victorian Frame of Mind* (1957), pp.54–55.
18. E.B. Lytton, *England and the English* (1833), p.281.
19. MS Copy of Letter from J. Keble to E.B. Pusey, 4 Oct 1836.
20. *Ibid*, question written on the letter by Pusey.
21. E.B. Pusey, *Cathedral Institutions* (1833), pp.32–36.
22. MS Copy of Letter from J.H. Newman to E.B. Pusey, 19 March 1833.
23. MS Copy of Letter from E.B. Pusey to W.E. Gladstone, 15 Feb 1833.
24. G.F.A. Best, *Temporal Pillars* (1964), p.287. See also contribution by Roger Jupp in *Pusey Rediscovered*, ed. P. Butler, 1983.
25. E.B. Pusey, *Cathedral Institutions* (1833), Preface, pp.vi–vii.
26. Much of Pusey's political and social outlook of the early 1830s foreshadowed ideas later propounded in the Young England movement, with its Burkean respect for the hierarchical frame of civil society, its wish to infuse new life into the Church and its emphasis on the rights and duties of the landed interest. It is interesting to note that Lord John Manners became acquainted with the Tractarian party in 1838 through his devotion to F. Faber, and that he came to respect Newman and Keble deeply. See C. Whibley, *Lord John Manners and His Friends* (2 Vols. 1925), I, pp.66–70 and 109–111 and 131. See also R. Chapman, *Father Faber* (1961), pp.45–46, and 50–51.
27. E.B. Pusey, *op.cit.*, p.13.
28. See T. Arnold, *Principles of Church Reform*, with an Introductory Essay by M.J. Jackson and J. Rogan (1962).
29. MS Copy of Letter from J.H. Newman to E.B. Pusey, 19 March 1833.
30. W. Palmer, *A Narrative of Events* ... (1833), p.99.
31. See T. Arnold, *Principles of Church Reform*, with an Introduction by M.J. Jackson and J. Rogan (1962), p.19.
32. E.R. Wickham, *Church and People in an Industrial City* (1957), p.70.
33. T. Arnold, *op.cit.*, p.19.

34. MS Copy of Letter from E.B. Pusey to W.E. Gladstone, 15 Feb 1833.
35. *Ibid.*
36. *Ibid.*
37. E. Halévy, *op.cit.*, pp.140–141.
38. *Ibid*, p.130.
39. MS Copy of Letter from E.B. Pusey to W.E. Gladstone, 15 Feb 1833.
40. MS Copy of Letter from E.B. Pusey to P. Pusey, 28 June 1835.
41. See W.R. Ward, *Victorian Oxford* (1965), pp.80f.
42. *Oxford Declaration*, 2 May 1834.
43. MS Letter from E.B. Pusey to Earl of Radnor, 1835.
44. MS Copy of Letter from E.B. Pusey to J.H. Newman, 10 Nov 1834.
45. W.R. Ward, *op.cit.*, p.94.
46. See H.P. Liddon, *op.cit.*, I, p.303.
47. MS Copy of Letter from E.B. Pusey to F. Tholuck, 6 March 1837.
48. MS Copy of Letter from E.B. Pusey to W.E. Gladstone, 1836; cf MS Copy of Letter from E.B. Pusey to H. Manning, 28 April 1837 on the appointment of bishops.
49. MS Copy of Letter from E.B. Pusey to J.H. Newman, 23 Oct 1838.
50. MS Copy of Letter from J.H. Newman to E.B. Pusey, 29 March 1840.
51. See H.P. Liddon, *op.cit.*, II, pp.306–370.
52. W.R. Ward, *op.cit.*, p.118.
53. MS Copy of Letter from E.B. Pusey to W. Pusey, Oct 1844.
54. See A.H. Mead, 'Richard Bagot, Bishop of Oxford, and the Oxford Movement 1833–1845' (1966), unpublished B.Litt. thesis in the Bodleian Library, pp.216f.
55. J.A. Froude, *Short Studies on Great Subjects* (Fontana 1963), p.250.
56. G.F.A. Best, *Temporal Pillars* (1964), p.314.
57. E.B. Pusey, 'The Royal and Parliamentary Ecclesiastical Commissions', *The British Critic* (April 1838), pp.458–459.
58. *Ibid*, p.460.
59. *Ibid*, p.467.
60. *Ibid*, p.464.
61. *Ibid*, p.471.
62. *Ibid*, p.472.
63. *Ibid*, p.501.
64. *Ibid*, p.525.
65. *Ibid*, p.526.
66. See O. Chadwick, *The Victorian Church*, p.139.
67. See O.J. Brose, *Church and Parliament, The Reshaping of the Church of England. 1828–1860* (1959), pp.145–146.
68. See A. Blomfield, *A Memoir of C.J. Blomfield* (1964 edn.), p.170.
69. See R.W. Church, *The Oxford Movement* (1932 edn.), p.127.
70. F.D. Maurice and C. Gore were both later to be influenced in their social teaching by these themes. See F.D. Maurice, *On the Right and Wrong Methods of Supporting Protestantism* (1843), p.10 and W.G. Roe, *Lamennais and England* (1966), pp.188f.
71. For a criticism of the bishops' reluctance to encourage social reform, see S.G. Evans, *The Social Hope of the Christian Church* (1965), pp.156–165.
72. S.C. Carpenter, *Church and People, 1789–1889* (1933), p.18.

73. See K.S. Inglis, *Churches and the Working Classes in Victorian England* (1963), pp.265–266 and G.C. Binyon, *The Christian Socialist Movement in England* (1931), pp.63–64, where the authors show an awareness of Pusey's work but suggest he was only anxious about spiritual and moral matters.
74. See J.W. Dodds, *The Age of Paradox* (1953), pp.160–166.
75. E.B. Pusey, *Cathedral Institutions* (1833), pp.159–160; cf his *Letter to the Bishop of Oxford* (1839), p.215.
76. E.B. Pusey, *Tract on Fasting* (1833), p.14.
77. E.B. Pusey, 'Churches in London', in the *British Magazine* (Nov 1835), Reprint 1837, pp.5–12.
78. See for example E.B. Pusey, *Sermons during the season from Advent To Whitsuntide* (1848), pp.59–60; *Parochial Sermons* (Vol. II, 1853 ed), pp.202–203; *Parochial Sermons* (Vol. III 1886 ed). pp.68 and 160; *Lenten Sermons* (1874 ed.), Sermon 'Why Dives lost his Soul;' *Parochial Sermons Preached and Printed on Various Occasions* (1865 edn.), Sermon, 'The danger of Riches'.
79. E.B. Pusey, *Parochial Sermons* (Vol. III 1836 edn.), pp.142–143.
80. E.B. Pusey, *Parochial Sermons Preached and Printed on Various Occasions* (1865 ed),. pp.20–21. cf a later sermon on 'The Value of Almsgiving in the Sight of God', in *University Sermons 1859–1872*, (1884 edn.), pp.378–379).
81. E.B. Pusey, *Part of an Address to the Free Church Conference at Norwich* (1865).
82. See MS Copy of Letter from E.B. Pusey to B. Harrison, 7 July 1836.
83. For Pusey's advocacy in 1857 of Missions, brotherhoods, guilds, sisterhoods, clergy in the mines, among emigrants and within industry, see his *The Council of the Church* (1857), pp.4–5 and 6.
84. MS Copy of Letter from E.B. Pusey to P. Pusey, 4 March 1845.
85. *Ibid*, 31 July 1845.
86. *Ibid*, 11 June 1846. In this letter Pusey enclosed a draft speech suggesting the line his brother should adopt in the House of Commons to explain his decision to support Peel.
87. W.B.D. Heeney, 'The Established Church and the Education of the Victorian Middle Classes; A Study of the Woodard Schools' (1961) unpublished D. Phil. thesis in the Bodleian Library, p.iii.
88. *Ibid*, p.iv.
89. See J. Cotter, *Nathaniel Woodard, A Memoir of his Life* (1925) p.53.
90. See F.W.B. Bullock, *A History of the Training for the Ministry of the Church of England and Wales from 1800 to 1874* (1955), pp.33–45.
91. E.B. Pusey, *Cathedral Institutions* (1833), pp.24–25.
92. Pusey suggested York and Carlisle (with St Bees) for the Northern Counties; Lincoln, Ely, Lichfield, Worcester, and Oxford (Gloucester too if necessary) for the Midlands; Norwich for the Eastern; Exeter or Wells, Salisbury or Winchester, Canterbury or Rochester for the South and London. See E.B. Pusey, *Cathedral Institutions*, p.79 n.
93. See O. Chadwick, *The Victorian Church* (1966), p.140 and 140 n 1.
94. See MS Letter from Archbishop Howley to E.B. Pusey, 30 Nov 1836.
95. See K.S. Inglis, *Churches and the Working Classes in Victorian England* (1963), p.36.

96. MS Copy of Letter from E.B. Pusey to P. Pusey, 21 July 1845.
97. MS Copy of Letter from E.B. Pusey to P. Pusey, 13 June 1846.
98. *Ibid.*
99. See W. James, *The Christian in Politics* (1962), ch.1, 2 and 3.
100. MS Copy of Letter from E.B. Pusey to P. Pusey, 18 July 1836.
101. *Ibid.*
102. *Ibid.* (For Pusey's denunciation of the Bulgarian atrocities of 1876 and his opposition to a pro-Turkish war, see S.G. Evans, *The Social Hope of the Christian Church* (1965), pp.149–150).
103. *Ibid.*
104. *Ibid.*
105. The Act which Pusey referred to was that of 1736 (9 Geo. II c. 36) which imposed restrictions on the devising of property to ecclesiastical uses. It was not amended until 1888.
106. MS Copy of Letter from E.B. Pusey to J. Keble, 18 Dec 1839.
107. See E. Halévy, *The Triumph of Reform 1830–1841* (1961 edn.), p.205, n 3.
108. MS Copy of Letter from E.B. Pusey to P. Pusey, 18–19 June 1840.
109. *Ibid.*
110. See H.P. Liddon, *op.cit.*, II, pp.249–251.
111. *Ibid*, p.251.
112. *Ibid*, pp.252–253.
113. See R.W. Greaves, 'The Jerusalem Bishopric, 1841', *The English Historical Review* (1949), Vol. LXIV.
114. J.H. Newman, *Apologia Pro Vita Sua* (Fontana edn. 1959), p.206.
115. MS Copy of Letter from E.B. Pusey to P. Pusey, 13 Feb 1841.
116. October 1840.
117. MS Copy of Letter from E.B. Pusey to B. Harrison, 7 Oct 1840.
118. In the Church of England the sphere of affinity is regulated by Archbishop Matthew Parker's *Table of Kindred and Affinity* (1563), authorized by canon 99 of 1603 on the basis of Leviticus 18.
119. E.B. Pusey, *Evidence . . . of the Law of Marriage* (1849), pp. xxx–xxxi.
120. *Ibid*, p.xvi.
121. See MS Copy of Letter from E.B. Pusey to J. Keble, 17 March 1842.
122. See H.P. Liddon, *op.cit.*, III, pp.181–185.
123. E.B. Pusey, *Evidence . . of the Law of Marriage* (1849), p.xxx.
124. MS Copy of Letter from E.B. Pusey to W.E. Gladstone, 13 Dec 1847.
125. *Ibid*; cf the section of this letter which is quoted in H.P. Liddon, *op.cit.*, III, pp.175–176.

7

1. See S. Neill, *A History of Christian Missions* (1964), pp.220–224.
2. The Sole Protestant exceptions were Kings Gustavus Vass and Adolphus, who encouraged missionary work among the pagan Lapps.
3. See S. Neill, *op.cit.*, pp.227–235.
4. E.B. Pusey, *The Church the Converter of the Heathen* (1842 edn.) a sermon first preached in 1838, p.18.

5. For the work of the S.P.G. and S.P.C.K. in the 18th century, see H. Cnattingius, *Bishops and Societies* (1952), ch.1 and 2.
6. For a discussion of the contributory causes of the interest in missionary work, see K.S. Latourette, *A History of the Expansion of Christianity* (1941), Vol. IV, ch.2.
7. See D. Newsome, *The Parting of Friends* (1966), p.216.
8. For the varied motives of missionaries, see M. Warren, *The Missionary Movement from Britain in Modern History* (1965), pp.45–55.
9. MS Copy of Letter from P. Pusey to E.B. Pusey, 15 June 1824.
10. MS Copy of Letter from P. Pusey to E.B. Pusey, 29 June 1824.
11. MS Copy of Letter from W.F. Hook to E.B. Pusey 31 Dec 1823.
12. MS Copy of Letter from E.B. Pusey to W.F. Hook, 1827.
13. *Ibid.*
14. See H.G.G. Herklots, *The Church of England and the American Episcopal Church* (1966), pp.128–139.
15. *Ibid*, pp.119–126.
16. A. Mozley (ed), *Letters and Correspondence of John Henry Newman (1891)*, II, p.377.
17. Oct 1839.
18. E.B. Pusey, 'The Preaching of the Gospel A Preparation for Our Lord's Coming', *Parochial Sermons . . . on Various Occasions* (1865 ed).
19. W.C. Doane, *A Memoir of the life of George Washington Doane* (New York 1860), I, pp.259–260.
20. *Ibid*, p.203.
21. *Ibid*, pp.259–260.
22. See D. Newsome, *op.cit.*, pp.215–218.
23. See H.G.G. Herklots, *op.cit.*, pp.138–139.
24. E.B. Pusey, *The Church the Converter of the Heathen* (1842 edn.) pp.15–16. See also R. Teale, 'Dr Pusey and the Church Overseas' in *Pusey Rediscovered* ed. P. Butler (1983).
25. H.P. Liddon, *Life of E.B. Pusey*, II, pp.93–94.
26. MS Copy of Letter from E.B. Pusey to B. Harrison, 3 Sept 1838.
27. E.B. Pusey, *op.cit.*, p.4.
28. *Ibid*, pp.5–6.
29. *Ibid*, p.10.
30. *Ibid*, p.10.
31. *Ibid*, pp.8–9.
32. MS Copy of Letter from E.B. Pusey to B. Harrison, 3 Sept 1838.
33. MS Copy of Letter from E.B. Pusey to B. Harrison, 18 Oct 1839.
34. E.B. Pusey, *op.cit.*, p.4.
35. *Ibid*. p.8.
36. See MS Copy of Letter from E.B. Pusey to B. Harrison, 20 July 1838.
37. MS Letter from E. Coleridge to E.B. Pusey, 11 Nov 1842.
38. *Ibid*, 16 Nov 1842; see also that of 26 May 1843.
39. *Ibid*, 27 Jan 1845 which contained a MS Letter from Archbishop Howley to E. Coleridge, 1845.
40. MS Letter from C. Marriott to E.B. Pusey, Mon. before Easter 1845.
41. MS Letter from E. Coleridge to E.B. Pusey, 22 Jan 1845.
42. See *Ibid*, Nov or Dec 1842, 11 Nov 1842 and Good Friday 1846.
43. *Ibid*, Nov or Dec 1842.

44. See MS Letter from C. Marriott to E.B. Pusey, 12 Sept 1845.
45. MS Letter from E. Coleridge to E.B. Pusey, Nov or Dec 1842. For a discussion of the numbers and types of convicts being transported at this time, see A.G.L. Shaw, *Convicts and the Colonies* (1966), ch. 7 and 13 and pp.363–368.
46. MS Letter from E. Coleridge to E.B. Pusey, 26 May 1843.
47. E.B. Pusey, *The Church the Converter of the Heathen* (1842 edn.), pp.24–25.
48. See M.W. Jernegan, *Laboring and Dependent Classes in Colonial America*. 1607–1783 (Chicago 1931), p.49.
49. E.B. Pusey, 'Christ, The Source and Rule of Christian Love', *Parochial Sermons . . . on Various Occasions* (1865 edn.), p.12.
50. *Ibid.* pp.18–19.
51. E.B. Pusey, *The Church the Converter of the Heathen* (1842 edn.), p.23.
52. *Ibid.*
53. *Ibid.* p.22.
54. R. Border, *Church and State in Australia 1788–1872* (1962), pp..3–4.
55. See H. Cnattingius, *Bishops and Societies* (1952), pp.197f.
56. See E.B. Pusey, 'The Preaching of the Gospel a Preparation for our Lord's Coming (preached 1841), *Parochial Sermons . . . on Various Occasions* (1865 edn.), pp.17–18.
57. See H. Cnattingius, *op.cit.*, pp.198f.
58. MS Copy of Letter from E.B. Pusey to B. Harrison, 18 Feb 1840.
59. *Ibid.*
60. MS Copy of Letter from E.B. Pusey to J. Keble, 14 May 1840.
61. MS Letter from Bishop Blomfield to E.B. Pusey, 2 June 1840.
62. *Ibid.*
63. *Ibid.* 4 Nov 1840.
64. *Ibid*, 7 Nov 1840.
65. See H. Cnattingius, *op.cit.*, p.108.
66. MS Copy of Letter from E.B. Pusey to J. Keble, 12 Nov 1840.
67. MS Copy of Letter from E.B. Pusey to J.H. Newman, 8 Jan 1841.
68. See MS Letters from Bishop Blomfield to E.B. Pusey, 21 April 1841 and 3 June 1841.
69. E.B. Pusey, 'The Preaching of the Gospel A Preparation for our Lord's Coming', *Parochial Sermons . . . on Various Occasions* (1865 edn.), p.17 n 1.

8

1. MS History of the Oxford Movement by W.J. Copeland at Pusey House, Oxford.
2. See D. Newsome. *The Parting of Friends* (1966), p.200.
3. See A.O.J. Cockshut, *Religious Controversies in the 19th Century: Selected Documents* (1966), pp.1–2.
4. See A.O.J. Cockshut, *op.cit.*, pp.4–6.
5. MS Copy of Letter from E.B. Pusey to J.H. Newman, early 1834. Cf Preface to *Tract 67*.

6. The MS alteration of Pusey to the text of all three tracts can be seen at Pusey House, Oxford.
7. E.B. Pusey, *Tract 67* (1836 edn.), Preface p.IX.
8. *Ibid*, p.VIII.
9. *Ibid*, p.V.
10. *Ibid*, pp.IX–XII.
11. *Ibid*, p.XIV.
12. See *Ibid*, pp.XV, 58 and 70. Cf Newman's strong conviction that Christians too often delude themselves into thinking that the way of salvation was easy. See D. Newsome, *The Parting of Friends* (1966), pp.180–183.
13. E.B. Pusey, *Tract 67* (1836 edn.), p.49.
14. *Ibid*. p.54.
15. *Ibid*, p.60.
16. MS Letter from H.J. Rose to E.B. Pusey, 1836; see H.P. Liddon, *Life of E.B. Pusey*, (1894 edn.), I, pp.351–352.
17. F. Maurice, *Life of F.D. Maurice* (2 Vols. 1884), I, p.186.
18. See D. Newsome, *op.cit.*, pp.190–191.
19. E.B. Pusey, *Tract 67* (1836 edn.), p.1.
20. *Ibid*, p.62.
21. See Y.T. Brilioth, *The Anglican Revival* (1925), pp.174–286.
22. See J.D. Walsh, 'The Yorkshire Evangelicals in the Eighteenth Century: with especial reference to Methodism' (1956), unpublished Ph.D. thesis in Cambridge University Library, pp.43–47.
23. MS Copy of Letter from E.B. Pusey to J.H. Newman, 11 Aug 1840.
24. For a discussion of this, see D. Newsome, 'Justification and Sanctification: Newman and the Evangelicals', *The Journal of Theological Studies* (1946), Vol. XV, Pt. I, p.32.
25. J.H. Newman, *Lectures on Justification* (1840 ed), p.345.
26. See E.B. Pusey, *Letter to the Press* (Dec 1849); see H.P. Liddon, *op.cit.*, III, pp.235–237.
27. E.B. Pusey, *Tract 67* (1836 ed), p.24.
28. D. Newsome, *The Parting of Friends* (1966), pp.179–180.
29. Until recently the place of the Eucharist in Tractarian thought and practice had not been studied in detail. This has now been done by A. Hardelin in his *The Tractarian Understanding of the Eucharist* (Uppsala 1965).
30. E.B. Pusey, *Tract 81* (1837), p.22.
31. E.B. Pusey, 'The Holy Eucharist a Comfort to the Penitent', *University Sermons 1843–1855* (1891 edn.) Preface, pp.III–IV.
32. *Ibid*, p.IV.
33. *Ibid*, p.4–5.
34. *Ibid*, p.27.
35. MS Copy of Letter from H. Manning to E.B. Pusey, 7th Sun. after Trinity 1843.
36. E.B. Pusey, *op.cit.*, p.21.
37. *Ibid*, pp.22–23.
38. MS Copy of Letter from H. Manning to E.B. Pusey, 7th Sun after Trinity 1843.

39. MS Copy of Letter from E.B. Pusey to H. Manning, undated but autumn 1843.
40. E.B. Pusey, *University Sermons 1843–1855* (1891 edn.), General Preface (1859), p.VI.
41. MS Copy of Letter from E.B. Pusey to H. Manning, 20 Oct 1845.
42. See E.B. Pusey, *Letter to the Bishop of London* (1851), p.20, and A. Hardelin, *op.cit.*, pp.214–215, and H.P. Liddon. *op.cit.*, III, ch. 17.
43. MS Copy of Letter from E.B. Pusey to H. Manning, Autumn 1843.
44. E.B. Pusey, 'The Holy Eucharist a Comfort to the Penitent' (1843), *University Sermons 1843–1855* (1891 edn.), p.11.
45. MS Copy of Letter from E.B. Pusey to T.E. Morris, undated but about 1846.
46. E.B. Pusey, *op.cit.*, General Preface, p.VII.
47. *Ibid.*
48. Gore's quasi-Kantian idealism permitted him to say that, just as the common reason of man constitutes reality in the natural order, so the Faith of the Church constitutes the spiritual objective Presence of Christ in the Eucharist. See C. Gore, *The Body of Christ* (1901).
49. E.B. Pusey, *op.cit.*, p.21.
50. H.P. Liddon, *op.cit.*, I, p.7.
51. E.B. Pusey, *Letter to the Bishop of Oxford* (1839), p.138 and p.143.
52. E.B. Pusey, 'The Presence of Christ in the Holy Eucharist' (1853), *University Sermons 1843–1855* (1891 edn.), p.42.
53. E.B. Pusey, *Tract 67* (1836 edn.), pp.58–59.
54. E.B. Pusey, 'Entire Absolution of the Penitent. 1.' (1846), *University Sermons 1843–1855* (1891 edn.), Preface, p.111.
55. *Quarterly Review* (July–Oct 1882), Vol. 154, p.534.
56. E.B. Pusey, *op.cit.*, pp. IV and VII.
57. *Ibid*, p.VIII.
58. *Ibid*, p.XV.
59. *Ibid*, p.3.
60. *Ibid*, Preface p.VIII and Sermon 2, pp.10–2.
61. *Ibid*, Sermon 2, pp.13–14.
62. *Ibid.*
63. E.B. Pusey, *op.cit.*, Preface p.VIII and Sermon 1, pp.7–8 and pp.23–35.
64. *Quarterly Review* (July–Oct 1882), Vol. 154, p.535.
65. E.B. Pusey, *Letter to the Bishop of Oxford* (1839), pp.92–93 and pp.96.
66. MS Copy of Letter from W.F. Hook to E.B. Pusey, 16 Aug 1839.
67. R.H. Greenfield, The Attitude of the Tractarians to the Roman Catholic Church 1833–1850' (1956), unpublished D.Phil. thesis in the Bodleian Library, p.40.
68. MS Letter from C. Marriot to E.B. Pusey, 24 Jan 1846.
69. T. Dearing, *Wesleyan and Tractarian Worship* (1966), p.69.
70. See Y.T. Brilioth, *The Anglican Revival* (1925), pp.296–300.
71. *Ibid*, p.300.
72. E.B. Pusey, 'Entire Absolution of the Penitent', *University Sermons 1843–1855* (1891 edn.), Preface, pp.XIX–XX.
73. *Ibid*, p.XX.

74. See E.R. Williams, 'Tractarian Moral Theology' (1951), unpublished D.Phil. thesis in Bodleian Library, Oxford.
75. *The Times*, 6 Dec 1873.
76. See W.J. Sparrow Simpson, *The Anglo-Catholic Revival after 1845* (1932), ch.6.
77. E.B. Pusey, *op.cit.*, p.18.
78. R.H. Greenfield, *op.cit.*, pp.174–75.
79. *Ibid.*
80. *Ibid*, pp.307 and 348.
81. J.W. Burgon, *Lives of Twelve Good Men* (1881), I, pp.209–213.
82. *Ibid*, pp.219–220.
83. *Ibid*, n 6.
84. MS Copy of Letter from J.H. Newman to E.B. Pusey, 9 Jan 1840.
85. E.B. Pusey, *Letter to the Bishop of Oxford* (1839), p.182.
86. See MS Copy of Letter from J. Keble to E.B. Pusey, 20 Nov 1838.
87. E.B. Pusey, Preface to *Library of the Fathers* (ed E.B. Pusey, J.H. Newman and J. Keble), Vol.1 (1838), pp.XVf.
88. R.H. Greenfield, *op.cit.*, p.491, suggests that this change was occasioned by Newman's Conversion, but Pusey himself tended to view Newman's action 'as determined, like a prophet's mission by reasons peculiar to himself, and thus in no sense an example to be followed by others' (H.P. Liddon, *op.cit.*, II, p.452). See also Pusey's remarks to F. Faber, quoted in R. Chapman, *Father Faber* (1961), p.119.
89. MS Copy of Letter from E.B. Pusey to H. Manning, Autumn 1843.
90. See MS Copy of Letter from J. Keble to E.B. Pusey, 3 Oct 1843.
91. MS Copy of Letter from E.B. Pusey to J. Keble, 23 Sept 1843.
92. MS Copy of Letter from E.B. Pusey to B. Harrison, 15 Jan 1839.
93. MS Copy of Letter from E.B. Pusey to H. Manning, 9 July 1844. Had Liddon been aware of the correspondence that Pusey conducted with Manning in 1844, it is highly probable that he would have had to alter considerably his picture of Pusey in the mid-1840s.
94. *Ibid*, 5 July 1844.
95. *Ibid*, 9 July 1844.
96. MS Copy of Letter from J. Keble to E.B. Pusey, 15 Jan 1844.
97. MS Copy of Letter from E.B. Pusey to H. Manning, 12 Aug 1845.
98. See D. Newsome, *The Parting of Friends* (1966), p.317 and H.P. Liddon, *op.cit.*, III, pp.137–149.

APPENDIX

1. MS Copy of Letter from E.B. Pusey to J.H. Newman, 9 Jan 1827.
2. *Ibid.*
3. J.W. Burgon, *Lives of Twelve Good Men* (1888), I, p.133.
4. *Ibid.*
5. See J. Tulloch, *Movements of Religious Thought in Britain during the Nineteenth Century* (1885), p.89.
6. MS Copy of Letter from E.B. Pusey to Bishop Blomfield, 4 Jan 1830.
7. MS Copy of Letter from E.B. Pusey to F. Tholuck, 18 April 1829.
8. *Ibid.*
9. *Ibid.*

10. In 1829 Rose replied to Pusey in a second and enlarged edition of his *Discourses*. In 1830 Pusey published a second part to his *Enquiry*.
11. E.B. Pusey, *Theology of Germany* (1830), Pt. II, Ch. VI.
12. MS Copy of Letter from E.B. Pusey to F. Tholuck, 18 April 1829.
13. E.B. Pusey, *Theology of Germany* (1828), Pt I, p.15.
14. *Ibid*, p.25.
15. *Ibid*, p.31.
16. *Ibid*, p.35.
17. E.B. Pusey, *Theology of Germany* (1830), Pt. II, p.22.
18. MS Copy of Letter from Bp. Blomfield to E.B. Pusey, 4 Jan 1830.
19. E.B. Pusey, *op.cit.*, p.6.
20. *Ibid.*, p.367.
21. E.B. Pusey, *Theology of Germany* (1828), Pt. I, p.7.
22. MS Copy of Letter from E.B. Pusey to M. Barker, 19–21 Oct 1827.
23. E.B. Pusey, *Theology of Germany* (1828), Pt I, p.8.
24. *Theology of Germany* (1830), Pt. II, p.408.
25. E.B. Pusey, *Theology of Germany* (1828), Pt I, p.53.
26. See A.L. Drummond, *German Protestantism since Luther* (1951), p.52.
27. E.B. Pusey, *Collegiate and Professorial Teaching and Discipline in answer to Professor Vaughan's Strictures* (1854), p.54.
28. E.B. Pusey, *Theology of Germany* (1830), Pt. II, p.371.
29. E.B. Pusey, *Ibid*, p.27.
30. See B. Willey, *Nineteenth Century Studies* (Peregrine edn. 1964), p.40.
31. H.J. Rose, *Letter to the Bishop of London in Reply to Mr. Pusey's work on the Causes of German Rationalism* (1829), p.99 and footnote p.425.
32. E.B. Pusey, *op.cit.* Pt. II, p.15.
33. MS Copy of Letter from E.B. Pusey to Bp. Blomfield, 4–6 Jan 1830.
34. J.H. Newman, *Apologia Pro vita Sua*, (Fontana edn. 1959), p.154.
35. E.B. Pusey, *Theology of Germany* (1828), Pt. I, p.123.
36. *Ibid*, p.122.
37. *Ibid*, p.151.
38. MS Copy of Letter from Bp. Blomfield to E.B. Pusey 4 Jan 1830.
39. See B. Willey, *Nineteenth Century Studies* (Peregrine edn. 1964). pp.46–52 and M. Roberts, 'Coleridge as a background to the Oxford Movement' in *Pusey Rediscovered*, ed. P. Butler (1983).
40. S.T. Coleridge, *Aids to Reflection* (Bohn edn.), p.272.
41. E.B. Pusey, *op.cit.* Pt. I, p.51, n 3.
42. *Ibid*, Pt. I, p.164.
43. MS Copy of Letter from F. Tholuck to E.B. Pusey, 23 March 1829.
44. *The Edinburgh Review*, p.253. (Aug–Dec 1831), Vol. 54, No. 108, Article 10.
45. MS Copy of Letter from E.B. Pusey to F. Tholuck, 7 Dec 1829.
46. MS Copy of Letter from E.B. Pusey to J. Keble, April 1829.
47. MS Copy of Letter from E.B. Pusey to F. Tholuck, 13 Aug 1829.
48. See *The Record* for 18 March 1841, 5 April 1841, 19 April 1841 & 26 April 1841, especially the printed letters of E.B. Pusey & the Editorial of 19 April 1841.
49. MS Copy of Letter from Bp. Blomfield to E.B. Pusey, 4 Jan 1830.

50. MS Copy of Letter from F. Tholuck to E.B. Pusey, 23 Aug 1829.
51. MS Copy of Letter fro F. Tholuck to E.B. Pusey, 4 April 1837.
52. MS Copy of Letter from J.H. Newman to E.B. Pusey, 31 Aug 1829.
53. MS Copy of Letter from E.B. Pusey to J.H. Newman, Sept 1829.
54. *Ibid.*
55. For the charitable manner in which Pusey regarded Dissenters even in 1838, see MS Copy of Letter from him to W.F. Hook, 12 Aug 1838.
56. MS Copy of Letter from E.B. Pusey to G. Boddington, Jan 1831.
57. *Ibid.*
58. *Ibid.*
59. MS Copy of Letter from J.H. Newman to E.B. Pusey, 4 Oct 1829.
60. See E.B. Pusey's personal copy of the 1836 edition of the *Tract on Baptism* (Tracts 67, 68 and 69 combined), now at Pusey House, Oxford. From p.89 onwards, Pusey has deliberately crossed-out or revised all references to Lutheran or Calvinist 'churches', altering the description to 'bodies'. He also erased all suggestions that they were branches of the Church and that they possessed 'liturgies'; Pusey changed the latter word to 'services'.
61. E.B. Pusey, *Theology of Germany* (1828), pp.177–178.
62. MS Copy of Letter from E.B. Pusey to F. Tholuck, 8 Nov 1830.
63. MS Copy of Letter from F. Tholuck to E.B. Pusey, 21 Feb 1836.
64. *Ibid.*
65. MS Copy of Letter from E.B. Pusey to F. Tholuck, 24 March 1865.

BIBLIOGRAPHY

A. Manuscript Sources

1. Pusey MSS. Pusey House, Oxford

a 1 Letter from H.J. Rose to E.B. Pusey, 16 March 1836.
b 11 Letters from J. Parker to E.B. Pusey, 1820–1837.
c Letters of J. Hibbert to E.B. Pusey, 1823–1824.
d 13 transcripts of Letters from E.B. Pusey to G. Boddington, 1828–1867.
e 18 Letters and transcripts from E.B. Pusey to R. Salway, 1821–1839.
f 35 Letters from R. Jelf to E.B. Pusey, 1821–1865
g 4 Letters from Blanco White to E.B. Pusey, 1828–1835.
h 9 Letters from A. Tyndale to E.B. Pusey, 1833–1835.
i 2 Transcripts of Letters from E.B. Pusey to H.V. Elliott, 1839.
j 3 Letters from Archbishop Howley to E.B. Pusey, 1836–1844.
k 1 Letter from Archbishop Howley to E. Coleridge, 1845.
l Large envelope containing early family letters, 1820–1828.
m 1 Letter from T. Arnold to E.B. Pusey, 18 Feb 1834.
n 1 Letter from Ambrose St. John to E.B. Pusey, 2 Sept 1843.
o Transcripts of Letters from E.B. Pusey to W. Ince, 1878.
p Transcripts of Letter from E.B. Pusey to E. Davis, 10 Oct 1837.
q The transcribed correspondence of J.F. Russell, 1828–1843.

2. Liddon Bound Volumes, Pusey House, Oxford

a Copies of 57 Letters from J. Keble, and 24 Letters from J.H. Newman to A.P. Perceval, 1821–1844.
b Copies of 38 Letters of M. Barker to E.B. Pusey, 1827–1828.
c Copies of 43 Letters of Mrs. M. Pusey to E.B. Pusey, 1832–1838.
d Copies of 25 Letters of E.B. Pusey to M. Barker, 1827–1828.
e Copies of 31 Letters of E.B. Pusey to M. Barker, 1828.
f Copies of 57 Letters of E.B. Pusey to M. Pusey, 1828–1839.
g 14 Letters from H.I. Wilberforce to E.B. Pusey, 1833–1854.
h 61 Copies of Letters from various correspondents to T.E. Morris, 1841–1856.
i Copies of 11 Letters from F. Tholuck to E.B. Pusey, and 11 Letters from E.B. Pusey to F. Tholuck, 1829–1865.
j Copies of 40 Letters from various German correspondents to E.B. Pusey, chiefly 1826–1842.
k 23 Letters from E. Coleridge to E.B. Pusey, 1839–1848.
l Copies of 27 Letters from E.B. Pusey to C. Lloyd, 1826–1829.

m Letters of J. Keble to E.B. Pusey, 1823–1850; copies of 97 Letters 1823–1845 and copies of 102 Letters, 1846–1850.
n Copies and originals of 74 Letters from W.F. Hook to E.B. Pusey, 1822–1847.
o Copies of 102 Letters of E.B. Pusey to W.F. Hook, 1827–1848.
p Copies of 54 Letters of E.B. Pusey to B. Harrison, 1831–1837, and 28 Letters 1839–1850 (Some originals).
q 15 Letters from Earl of Shaftesbury to E.B. Pusey, and 6 Letters from E.B. Pusey to Shaftesbury, 1836–1879.
r Copies of 97 Letters from E.B. Pusey to H. Manning (13 obtained 1956), 1837–1850.
s Copy of correspondence between W.E. Gladstone and E.B. Pusey, 1833–1856 (including a volume of Gladstone letters).
t Letters of J.H. Newman to E.B. Pusey, 1829–1846; copies of 89 Letters 1823–1840 and 137 Letters 1841–1846.
u Copies of 73 Letters from E.B. Pusey to J.H. Newman, 1823–1836. 85 copies, 1837–1840; 79 copies 1841–1843 and 45 copies 1844–1846.
v Copies of 113 Letters from E.B. Pusey to J. Keble, 1823–1845.
w Copies of 91 Letters from J. Keble to J.H. Newman, 1829–1840 and copies of 57 letters, 1841–1846.
x Copy of correspondence between P. Pusey and E.B. Pusey, 1821–1854.
y Letters and copies of correspondence between W. Pusey and E.B. Pusey, 1827–1860.
z 23 Letters from C. Blomfield to E.B. Pusey, 1830–1855.

3. *Marriott Papers. Pusey House, Oxford*

128 Letters and transcripts of Letters from C. Marriott to E.B. Pusey, 1840–1851.

4. *Radnor Papers. Pusey House, Oxford*

30 Letters (3 from E.B. Pusey), Printed circulars and outlines of parliamentary bills, all relating to the issue of Subscription, 1834–1835.

5. *Bodleian Library, Oxford*

MS Eng. Letters c.130, pl. 31. Epitome of Settlement of E.B. Pusey's marriage and Letter of E.B. Pusey to his children, 1839.

6. *Additional MSS at Pusey House, Oxford*

a C. Fletcher, 'Narrative' (undated).
b Exercise Book used by H.P. Liddon in preparation for writing his biography of E.B. Pusey.
c Mrs Maria Pusey's Diaries. 3 vols. 1828–1838.
d E.B. Pusey's 'Journal' of his Swiss tour 1822.
e E.B. Pusey's MS Early Sermons.
f E.B. Pusey's 'Lectures on Types and Prophecies', 1836.
g 2 Vols. of MS history of the Oxford Movement by W.J. Copeland (ed. W.C. Borlase)

B. Unpublished Theses or Papers

Greenfield, R.H. 'The Attitude of the Tractarians to the Roman Catholic Church 1833–1850' (1956), unpublished D. Phil. thesis in the Bodleian Library, Oxford.

Heeney, W.B.D. 'The Established Church and the Education of the Victorian Middle Classes: A Study of the Woodward Schools, 1847–1891' (1961), unpublished D. Phil. thesis in the Bodleian Library, Oxford.

Mead, A.H. 'Richard Bagot, Bishop of Oxford, and the Oxford Movement 1833–1845' (1966), unpublished B. Litt. thesis in the Bodleian Library, Oxford.

Mehlis, R. 'Die religiose entwicklung des jungeren E.B. Pusey' (Diss. 1954; Vollst Lit-Verz. Bonn).

Walsh, J.D. 'The Yorkshire Evangelicals in the Eighteenth Century: with especial reference to Methodism' (1956), unpublished Ph.D. thesis in the Cambridge University Library.

'The Theology of the Evangelical Revival' (1967), kindly loaned to the author.

Williams, E.R. 'Tractarian Moral Theology' (1951), unpublished D.Phil. thesis in the Bodleian Library, Oxford.

C. Published Works

This list includes only those books to which references are made in the text or in the notes and those which have been of actual assistance in the writing of this book. The place of publication is London unless otherwise stated.

a Primary sources

Pusey, E. B. *An Historical Enquiry into the Causes of the Rationalist Character lately predominant in the Theology of Germany*. Pt.1, 1828. Pt.2, 1830.

Remarks on the Prospective and Past Benefits of Cathedral Institutions, in the Promotion of Sound Religious Knowledge. Occasioned by Lord Henley's Plan for their Abolition. 1833.

Thought on the Benefits of the System of Fasting enjoined by our Church. (Tract No.18). Oxford 1834.

Tracts for the Times. Nos 67. 68. 69. Scriptural Views of Holy Baptism, with an Appendix. 1836.

Churches in London. Oxford 1837.

'The Royal and Parliamentary Ecclesiastical Commissions', the *British Critic*, No. XLVI, April 1838.

The Confessions of St. Augustine. Oxford 1838. Preface.

A Letter to the Right Rev Father in God Richard Lord Bishop of Oxford, on the Tendency to Romanism imputed to Doctrines held of old, as now, in the English Church. 1839.

A Letter to His Grace the Archbishop of Canterbury, on some circumstances connected with the Present Crisis in the English Church. Oxford 1842.

The Church the Converter of the Heathen. Two sermons originally preached 1838. Oxford 1842.
The Foundation of the Spiritual Life by J. Surin, translated by E.B. Pusey. Preface. Oxford 1874 edn.
Sermons during the Season from Advent to Whitsuntide. Oxford 1848. (This is 'Parochial Sermons' vol. 1).
Marriage with a Deceased Wife's Sister prohibited by Holy Scripture, as Understood by the Church for 1500 years. 1849.
A Letter to the . . . Bishop of London, in Explanation of some statements contained in a Letter by the Rev W. Dodsworth. 1851.
Catena Patrum No. IV. No. 81 of 'Tracts for the Times'. 1837.
Collegiate and Professorial Teaching and Discipline, in Answer to Professor Vaughan's Strictures, chiefly as to the Charges against the Colleges of France and Germany. Oxford 1854.
The Councils of the Church from the Council of Jerusalem, A.D. 51, to the Council of Constantinople, A.D. 381, chiefly as to their Constitution but also as to their Objects and History. Oxford 1857.
Parochial Sermons. Vol.2. Oxford 1853.
Parochial Sermons Preached and Printed on Various Occasions. Oxford 1865.
Nine Sermons Preached before the University of Oxford and Printed chiefly between A.D. 1843–1855. 1891.
Lenten Sermons. 1874.
Parochial Sermons. Vol.3. 1886.
Sermons Preached before the University of Oxford between A.D. 1859 and 1872. 1884.
Ten Sermons Preached before the University of Oxford between 1864–1879. 1894.
Advice for those who exercise the Ministry of Reconciliation through Confession and Absolution, being the Abbe Gaume's Manual for Confessors. 1878.
The Church of England a Portion of Christ's One Holy Catholic Church, and a Means of Restoring Visible Unity. An Eirenicon, in a Letter to the Author of 'The Christian Year'. 1865.
Spiritual Letters of E.B. Pusey (ed. J.O. Johnstone and W.C.E. Newbolt), 1898.

b Secondary Sources

Allchin, A.M. *The Silent Rebellion*. 1958.
Annan, N.G. 'The Intellectual Aristocracy' in *Studies in Social History. A Tribute To G.M. Trevelan* (ed. J.H. Plumb). 1955.
Arnold, T. *Principles of Church Reform*, with an Introductory Essay by M.J. Jackson and J.Rogan, 1962.
Battiscombe, G. *John Keble. A Study in Limitations*. 1963.
Beck, W.J.A.M. *John Keble's Literary and Religious Contribution to the Oxford Movement*. Nijmegen. 1959.
Best, G.F.A. *Temporal Pillars. Queen Anne's Bounty, the Ecclesiastical Commissioners and the Church of England*. Cambridge 1964.
Shaftesbury. 1964.

'The Protestant Constitution and Its Supporters 1800–1829' in *Royal Historical Transactions*, 5th Series, Vol. 8.
Biemer, G. *Newman on Tradition*. Freiburg and London. 1967.
Binyon, G.C. *The Christian Socialist Movement in England*. 1931.
Blomfield, A. *A Memoir of C.J. Blomfield*. 1864 edn.
Brilioth, Y.T. *The Anglican Revival. Studies in the Oxford Movement*. 1925.
Evangelicalism and the Oxford Movement. 1934.
Brinton, C. *English Political Thought in the Nineteenth Century*. 1962 edn.
Brose, C.J. *Church and Parliament. The Reshaping of the Church of England. 1828–1860*. 1959.
Brown, Ford K. *Fathers of the Victorians. The Age of Wilberforce*. Cambridge. 1961.
Bullock, F.W.B. *A History of the Training for the Ministry of the Church of England and Wales from 1800 to 1874*. St. Leonards-on-Sea. 1955.
Bunsen, F. *A Memoir of Baron Bunsen*. 2 Vols. 1868.
Burgon, J.W. *Lives of Twelve Good Men*. 2 Vols. 1888.
Butler, B.C. *The Idea of the Church*. 1962.
Byron, G.G. Lord *The Deformed Transformed. A Drama*. 1824.
Carpenter, S.C. *Church and People 1789–1889*. 1933.
Chadwick, O. *The Mind of the Oxford Movement*. 1960.
The Victorian Church. 1966.
Chapman, R. *Father Faber*. 1961.
Church, R.W. *The Oxford Movement. Twelve Years 1833–1845*. 1932 edn.
Churton, E. *Memoir of Joshua Watson*. 2 Vols. 1861.
Clegg, H. 'Evangelicals and Tractarians' in the *Historical Magazine of the Protestant Episcopal Church*, Vol. XXXV, No.2. June 1966 and Vol. XXXV, No.3. Sept. 1966.
Cnattingius, H. Bishops and Societies. *A Study of the Anglican Colonial and Missionary Expansion 1698–1850*. 1952.
Cockshut, A.O.J. *Anglican Attitudes*. 1959.
Religious Controversies of the Nineteenth Century; Selected Documents. 1966.
Coleridge, S.T. *Aids to Reflection*. Bohn edn.
Coletta, P.E. 'Philip Pusey, English Country Squire' in the *Agricultural History*. Vol. 18, No. 2. April 1944.
Cotter, J. *Nathaniel Woodard. A Memoir of his Life*. 1925.
Cross, F.L. *The Oxford Movement and the Seventeenth Century*. 1933.
Davies, Horton. *Worship and Theology in England. From Watts and Wesley to Maurice, 1690–1850*. 1961.
Dawson, C. *The Spirit of the Oxford Movement*. 1945.
Dearing, T. *Wesleyan and Tractarian Worship*. 1966.
Doane, W.C. *A Memoir of the Life of George Washington Doane, D.D., LL.D. Bishop of New Jersey*. New York, 1860.
Dodds, J.W. *The Age of Paradox*. 1953.
Drummond, A.L. *German Protestantism since Luther*. 1951.
Edgeworth, R.L. *Essays on Professional Education*. 1812.
Evans, S.G. *The Social Hope of the Christian Church*. 1965.

Faber, G. *Oxford Apostles. A Character Study of the Oxford Movement.* 1933 edn.

Fairbairn, A.M. *Catholicism Roman and Anglican.* 1899.

Fairchild, H. 'Romanticism and the Religious Revival in England' in the *Journal of the History of Ideas.* Vol. 2. No.3. 1941.

Fairweather, E.R. *The Oxford Movement.* New York, 1964.

Froude, J.A. *Short Studies on Great Subjects.* 4 Vols. 1886.

Gladstone, W.E. *Gleanings of Past Years.* Vol. VII, 1879.

Gore, C. *The Body of Christ.* 1901.

Grant, R.W. *A Short History of the Interpretation of the Bible.* 1965.

Greaves, R.W. 'The Jerusalem Bishopric 1841' in *The Historical Review*, Vol. LXIV, 1949.

Guiney, L.I. *Hurrell Froude.* 1904.

Halévy, E. *The Triumph of Reform 1830–1841.* 1961 edn.

Hardölin, A. *The Tractarian Understanding of the Eucharist.* Uppsala, 1965.

Harrison, B. 'Philanthropy and the Victorians' in *Victorian Studies.* June 1966.

Hazard, P. *European Thought in the Eighteenth Century.* 1954.

Herklots, H.G.G. *The Church of England and the American Episcopal Church.* 1966.

Hodgskin, T. *Travels in the North of Germany.* Edinburgh, 1820.

Holland, B. (ed) *Elected Letters 1896–1924 of F. Von Hugel.* 1927.

Houghton, W.E. *The Victorian Frame of Mind.* 1957.

Inglis, K.S. *Churches and the Working Classes in Victorian England.* 1963.

James, W. *The Christian in Politics.* 1962.

Jernegen, M.W. *Laboring and Dependent Classes in Colonial America, 1607–1783.* Chicago, 1931.

Keble, J. Tract 89. *On the Mysticism attributed to the Early Fathers of the Church.* Undated. Contained in 1840 Series.
Sermons Academical and Occasional. 1848.
Lectures on Poetry 1832–1841. Trans. E.K. Francis 1912.

King, J. *Memoir of the Rev. T. Dykes.* 1849.

Kitson-Clark, G.S.R. 'The Romantic Element 1830 to 1850' in *Studies in Social History. A Tribute to G.M. Trevelan* (ed. J.H. Plumb). 1955.

Latourette, K.S. *A History of the Expansion of Christianity.* Vol. IV, 1941.

Liddon, H.P. *The Life of E.B. Pusey. D.D.* 4 Vols. 1894 ed.

Linton, W.J. *James Watson: a Memoir.* Hamden, Connecticut. 1879.

Lock, W. *John Keble, a Biography.* 1893 edn.

Lovejoy, A. 'The Meaning of Romanticism for the Historian of Ideas' in the *Journal of the History of Ideas.* Vol. 2. No.3. 1941.

Lytton, E.B. *England and the English.* 1833.

Mack, E.C. *Public Schools and British Opinion 1780–1860.* 1938.

Mackintosh, H.R. *Types of Modern Theology.* Fontana edn. 1964.

Mathieson, W.L. *English Church Reform 1815–1840.* 1923.

Maurice, F.D. *On the Right and Wrong Methods of Supporting Protestantism.* 1843.
Life of F.D. Maurice. 2 Vols. 1884.

Milner, J. *Practical Sermons.* Vol.3. 1823.

Mozley, A. (ed), *Letters and Correspondence of John Henry Newman During His Life in the English Church*. 2 Vols. 1891.
Mozley, J.B. *Letters of J.B. Mozley* (ed. by his sister). 1854.
Mozley, T. *Reminiscences Chiefly of Oriel College and the Oxford Movement*. 2 Vols. 1882.
Reminiscences Chiefly of Towns, Villages and Schools. 2 Vols. 1885.
Murphy, H.R. 'The Ethical Revolt against Christian Orthodoxy in Early Victorian England' in the *American Historical Review*. July 1955.
Murray, J.A.H. (ed), *New English Dictionary*. 1879.
Neill, S. *Anglicanism*. 1958.
A History of Christian Missions. 1964.
Newman, J.H. *Lectures on the Prophetical Office of the Church, viewed relatively to Romanism and popular Protestantism*. 1837.
Lectures on Justification. 1840 edn.
Autobiographical Writings (ed. H. Tristram, 1956).
Apologia Pro Vita Sua. Fontana edn. 1959.
Newsome, D. *Godliness and Good Learning: Four Studies on a Victorian Ideal*. 1961.
'Reviews 2. "Fathers and Sons"' in *The Historical Journal*. VI, 2, 1963.
'Justification and Sanctification: Newman and the Evangelicals' in *The Journal of Theological Studies*. Vol. XV, Pt. 1, 1964.
The Parting of Friends. 1966.
Oakley, F. *Historical Notes on the Tractarian Movement*. 1865 edn.
Palmer, W. *A Narrative of Events connected with the publication of the Tracts for the Times*. 1883.
Parker, T. M. 'The Tractarians' Successors: the Influence of the Contemporary Mood' in *Ideas and Beliefs of the Victorians*. 1949.
Pike, E. Royston, *Pioneers of Social Change*. 1963.
Pollard, A. and Hennell, M. (ed), *Charles Simeon 1759–1836*. 1959.
Port, M.H. *Six Hundred New Churches*. 1961.
Prestige, L. *Pusey*. 1933.
Prevost, G. (ed), *The Autobiography of Isaac Williams*. 1892.
Proby, W.H.B. *Annals of the Low-Church Party in England down to the death of Archbishop Tait*. 2 Vols. 1888.
Pullan, L. *Religion since the Reformation*. 1923.
Pusey, E. Lady. *Waldegrave*. A novel in 3 Vols. Published anon. 1829.
Reader, W.J. *Professional Men. The Rise of the Professional Classes in the Nineteenth Century*. 1966.
Reynolds, J.S. *The Evangelicals at Oxford 1735–1871*. 1953.
Richards, G.C. *Dr Pusey. A Short Study*. Reprint from *Durham University Journal*. June 1933.
Richardson, A. *Christian Apologetics*. 1947.
Roe, W.G. *Lamennais and England. The Reception of Lamennais' Religious Ideas in England in the Nineteenth Century*. 1966.
Rose, H.J. *Discourses on the State of the Protestant Religion in Germany*. 1825.
A Letter to the Bishop of London in reply to Mr. Pusey's work on the Causes of German Rationalism. 1829.
Russell, G.W.E. *The Household of Faith*. 1906.

Dr Pusey. 1907.

A Short History of the Evangelical Movement. 1915.

Schenk, H.G. *The Mind of European Romantics*. 1966.

Schleiermacher, F.D.E. *Religion, Speeches to its Cultured Despisers*. 1799. English trans. 1893.

Essays on the Gospels of St. Luke (trans. C. Thirwall 1825).

The Christian Faith, systematically set forth according to the principles of the Evangelical Church. 1821. English trans. 1928.

Scott, T. *The Force of Truth*. 1779.

Scott Holland, H. *Personal Studies*. 1905.

Shaw, A.G.L. *Convicts and the Colonies. A Study of Penal Transportation from Great Britain and Ireland to Australia and other parts of the British Empire*. 1966.

Smart, J.D. *The Interpretation of Scripture*. 1961.

Smith, B.A. *Dean Church. The Anglican Response to Newman*. 1958.

Smyth, C. 'The Study of Church History' in *The Priest as Student*, (ed H.S. Box), 1939.

Simeon and Church Order. 1940.

'The Evangelical Discipline' in *Ideas and Beliefs of the Victorians*. 1949.

Sparrow Simpson, W.J. *The Anglo-Catholic Revival after 1845*. 1932.

Storr, V.F. *The Development of English Theology in the Nineteenth Century*. 1913.

The Oxford Dictionary of the Christian Church. Ed. F.L. Cross, Oxford. 1958 edn.

Thirlwall, C. *Letters, Literary and Theological* (ed. J.J.S. Perowne and L. Stokes). 1881.

Thom, J.H. (ed) *The Life of Joseph Blanco White*. 3 Vols. 1845.

Thompson, F.M.L. *English Landed Society in the Nineteenth Century*. 1963.

Tracts for the Times. Vols. I–V. 1834–1840.

Trench, M. *The Story of Dr Pusey's Life*. Published anon. 1900.

Trevor, M. *Newman. The Pillar of the Cloud*. 1962.

Tulloch, J. *Movements of Religious Thought in Britain during the Nineteenth Century*. 1885.

University of Oxford Commission. Part I Minutes of Evidence taken (1877) by the Commissioners, together with an Appendix and Index. 1881.

Vidler, A.R. *The Church in an Age of Revolution*. 1961.

Voll, D. *Catholic Evangelicalism*. 1963.

Walker, C. *A History of the Christian Church*. Edinburgh, 1949.

Wallas, G. *The Life of Francis Place*. 1918 ed.

Walsh, J.D. 'Joseph Milner's Evangelical Church History' in the *Journal of Ecclesiastical History*, X, 1959.

'Church and State in Europe and the Americas' in *New Cambridge Modern History*, Vol. IX, 1793–1830. Cambridge, 1965.

'Origins of the Evangelical Revival' in *Essays in Modern English Church History* (ed G.V. Bennett and J.D. Walsh). 1966.

Ward, M. *Young Mr Newman*. 1948.

Ward, W.R. *Victorian Oxford*. 1965.

Ware, T. *The Orthodox Church*. 1963.

Warren, M. *The Missionary Movement from Britain in Modern History.* 1965.
Webb, C.C.J. *Religious Thought in the Oxford Movement.* 1928.
Webster, A.B. *Joshua Watson.* 1954.
Whibley, C. *Lord John Manners and His Friends.* 2 Vols. 1925.
Wickham, E.R. *Church and People in an Industrial City.* 1957.
Wilberforce, A.M. (ed), *The Private Papers of William Wilberforce.* 1897.
Wilberforce, W. *A Practical View of the Prevailing Religious System of Professed Christians.* 1797.
Willey, B. *Nineteenth Century Studies.* Peregrine edn. 1964.

c Periodicals and Newspapers

Agricultural History.
American Historical Review.
British Critic.
British Magazine.
Edinburgh Review.
English Historical Review.
Historical Journal.
John Bull.
Journal of Ecclesiastical History.
Journal of the History of Ideas.
Journal of Theological Studies.
Magazine of the Protestant Episcopal Church.
Quarterly Review.
Revue des Sciences Religieuses.
Royal Historical Society Transactions.
The Record.
The Times.
Victorian Studies.

Additional Bibliography

Bailey, P., *Leisure and Class in Victorian England: rational recreation and the contest for control, 1830–1885*, Routledge & Kegan Paul, 1978.
Baugh, D.A., *Aristocratic Government and Society in Eighteenth Century England*, New Viewpoints, 1976.
Best, G., *Mid-Victorian Britain 1851–1870*, Fontana, 1979.
Bradley, I., *The Call to Seriousness: the Evangelical impact on the Victorians*, Cape, 1976.
Branca, P., *Silent Sisterhood: middle class women in the Victorian home*, Croom Helm, 1978.
Brander, M., *The Victorian Gentleman*, Gordon Cremonesi, 1975.
Briggs, A., *Victorian People*, Odhams, 1954.
Briggs, A., *The Age of Improvement*, Longman, 1979.
Briggs, J.H.Y. & Sellers, I., *Victorian Non-conformity*, Arnold, 1973.
Butler, P. (ed), *Pusey Rediscovered*, 1983.
Clarke, J., *The Price of Progress: Cobbett's England, 1780–1835*, Hart-Davis MacGibbon, 1977.

Colloms, B., *Victorian Country Parsons*, Constable, 1977.
Cookson, J.E., *Lord Liverpool's Administration: the crucial years, 1815–1822*, Scottish Academic Pr., 1974.
Finlayson, G.B.A.M., *England in the Eighteen Thirties*, Arnold, 1969.
Fraser, D., ed., *The New Poor Law in the Nineteenth Century*, Macmillan, 1976.
Fraser, D., *Power and Authority in the Victorian City*, Blackwell, 1979.
Furneaux, R.S., *William Wilberforce*, Hamilton, 1974.
Gash, N., *The Age of Peel*, Arnold, 1968.
Gash, N., *Politics in the Age of Peel*, Harvester, 1977.
Gash, N., *Aristocracy and People*, Arnold, 1979.
Griffin, J.R., *The Oxford Movement: A Revision*, Christendom Pbs., 1981.
Harrison, F.C., *Early Victorian Britain*, Fontana, 1979.
Harvey, A.D., *Britain in the Early Nineteenth Century*, Batsford, 1978.
Hayes, P.M., *The Nineteenth Century, 1814–80*, A. & C. Black, 1975.
Hollis, P. ed., *Class & Conflict in Nineteenth Century England, 1815–1850*, Routledge & Kegan Paul, 1973.
Kitson-Clark, G., *The Making of Victorian England*, Methuen, 1962.
Marsh, P., ed., *The Conscience of the Victorian State*, Harvester Pr., 1979.
Mingay, G.E., *The Gentry: the rise and fall of a ruling class*, Longman, 1976.
Mingay, G.E., *Rural Life in Victorian England*, Heinemann, 1977.
Norman, E.R., *Church and Society in England, 1770–1970: a historical study*, Clarendon Press, 1976.
Olsen, D.J., *The Growth of Victorian London*, Batsford, 1976.
Owen, J.B., *The Eighteenth Century, 1714–1815*, Nelson, 1975.
Petrie, C., *The Victorians*, White Lion, 1976.
Roberts, D., *Paternalism in Early Victorian England*, Croom Helm, 1979.
Royle, E., ed., *The Infidel Tradition: from Paine to Bradlaugh*, Macmillan, 1976.
Royle, E., *Radical Politics, 1790–1900: religion and unbelief*, Longman, 1971.
Royle, E., *Victorian Infidels: the origins of the British Secularist Movement, 1791–1866*, Manchester U.P., 1974.
Sellers, I., *Nineteenth-Century Nonconformity*, Arnold, 1977.
Snodin, D., *A Mighty Ferment: Britain in the age of revolution, 1750–1850*, Deutsch, 1978.
Walvin, J., *Leisure and Society, 1830–1950*, Longman, 1978.
Ward, J., *The Age of Change, 1770–1870: documents in social history*, A. & C. Black, 1975.
Watson, J.S., *The Reign of George III*, O.U.P., 1960.
Willey, B., *More Nineteenth Century Studies*, Cambridge, 1980.
Woodward, E.L., *The Age of Reform*, 2nd ed, O.U.P., 1962.
Wohl, A.S., ed., *The Victorian Family: structure and stresses*, Croom Helm, 1978.
Young, G.M., *Portrait of an Age: Victorian England*, 2nd ed, O.U.P., 1971.

INDEX